Gathering and Writing the News

Books by John Paul Jones

EFFECTIVE NEWS REPORTING (with L.R.Campbell)
NEWS BEAT (with L.R.Campbell)
THE MODERN REPORTER'S HANDBOOK
RADIO AND TELEVISION NEWS (with Donald E.Brown)

John Paul Jones

Gathering
and Writing
the News

a reporter's complete guide to
techniques and ethics of
news reporting

Nelson-Hall nh Chicago

Library of Congress Cataloging in Publication Data
Jones, John Paul, 1912–
    Gathering and writing the news.

    Includes index.
    1. Reporters and reporting.   I. Title.
PN4781.J78   1976   070.4'3   75-33642
ISBN 0-88229-243-9 (cloth)
ISBN 0-88229-583-7 (paper)

Manufactured in the United States of America

10 9 8 7 6 5 4 3 2 1

contents

preface

This book is mainly about the techniques and ethics of gathering and writing news.

It is difficult, if not impossible, to separate the two—techniques and ethics—during the newsgathering and writing process. The reporter is confronted with the need to be fair and accurate at every point along the way—and fairness and accuracy are ethical considerations.

News reporting is changing because the world is changing and people are changing, but in this book I appeal to the reporter not to turn the journalism clock back by becoming so personally involved in the news that he indulges in opinions rather than facts, in editorializing rather than in interpretation based upon fact piled upon fact. "Personal involvement" is not bad for the reporter who is personally dedicated to digging out information that will provide new insight into the news situation, that will stimulate public officials and readers and viewers to seek answers to problems, and that will deliver a fair and accurate report to the news consumer.

Personal involvement becomes bad when the reporter uses his news stories to grind an ax for himself or for a cause he has adopted. In such circumstances he sets himself up as both judge and jury and writes the news in a slanted way. He assumes that he alone is right.

Time has a way of proving most of us wrong over the long haul, and the only way to safeguard the reader is to provide him with fair, honest, and accurate reports.

"Objectivity" in news has come upon hard times these days. While most newsmen would admit, as they always have, that mere human beings are incapable of pure objectivity, the cold fact is that once the newsman ceases to strive for objectivity, his report is likely to become unfairly opinionated.

Objectivity is still the goal of the dedicated, professional writer.

This study deals with the so-called "new journalism," but not in the sense of personal involvement, activist journalism, muckraking journalism, or crusading journalism. It calls for involvement in making the news report, the feature story, and the television report more interesting, more believable, better prepared, and better researched and documented.

It calls upon the newsman in a changing world to pay more attention to his reader, to seek the significant and not the trivial, to be more selective and less confusing, and to take a good hard look at the fundamentals of reporting that have been the standby of reporters for many generations.

The reporting profession is one of the most important in today's world because in many cases the reporter "makes" the news. News is what he presents to his editor, and the extent to which he approaches his job in a responsible and trustworthy manner determines in large measure how people will think and react.

My viewpoint concerning what constitutes good reporting has been shaped by the opinions of many, many other newsmen throughout the nation who care about their profession. I urge the student of journalism to rededicate himself to the old newspaper adage, "Get the news first, but first get it right."

so you want to be a reporter

People live by news. They become angry or sad or troubled or glad according to the way they interpret the news that comes to them daily by way of newspapers and the electronic media. They make decisions based upon facts read in news columns, or heard over the radio, or viewed on television. If they are misled in any way, they feel frustrated and cheated.

There is a kind of magic in news because it frequently works wonders. Sometimes it reunites families separated for years, causes citizens to rally to the aid of a little boy who needs an operation, or stimulates the state legislature to pass a law to correct an evil in our society.

News is magic because it causes everyone, private citizen or high government official, to act. The citizen develops opinions and then votes as a result of what he has read, seen, and heard. The governor of a state flies to the scene of a disaster to see what needs to be done to help those injured or made homeless by a flood or a storm.

The magic of news has been evident for a long time. Even before many men and women learned to read and write, they gathered together to learn from one another what had happened or was going to happen. In Colonial America, citizens gathered in coffee houses to gossip about the events of the

1

day or to hear news read from news sheets by the literate. News was all the more important to them because many lived in a world of darkness created by their own inability to read or write or thoroughly understand issues and events. They were often victims of rumors, lies, and propaganda.

In today's complex society the magic quality of news should be most thoroughly understood by the newsgatherer and writer because he is the first line of defense against untruth. Often the ingredients that go into the making of a report cause the story to be volatile and explosive. The reporter quickly discovers that he has whipped up a veritable witch's brew—and his facts had better be accurate or the magic of news will be turned against him and his newspaper.

Any reporter who thinks that this is an exaggeration or high-flown picture of the responsibility of the news profession today should think seriously about changing his occupation.

The Professionals Know Better

The professionals do know better. They know there is an implied contract between the consumer and vendor that the news must be true and unadulterated. O.K. Bovard of the *St. Louis Post-Dispatch* stated it this way many years ago:

> Between the reporter and the reader a direct and independent relationship exists. Your responsibility to the reader cannot be shifted. If, through his reliance on you, the reader is misinformed or inadequately informed, you have failed in your professional duty.

Forrest W. Seymour, while he was editor of the *Worcester* (Mass.) *Telegram and Evening Gazette,* once said:

> The primary business of the newspaper is NEWS. The press should be judged first of all on its performance as a chronicle of the important events of the day. If it does this badly, it is certainly subject to criticism. If it does this well, it is a good paper, and we are interested only secondarily in the politics of its editorial column.

Speaking at a convention of journalism teachers in 1956, Wallace Carroll, a Washington correspondent for the *New York Times,* urged his audience to teach their students to respect their readers. He went on to say:

I once knew a reporter who kept the picture of the "idiot boy" in the Hall-Mills murder case pasted on his portable. "That," he used to say as he prepared to write a story, "is my average reader." There is too much of that kind of cheap cynicism in the newspaper business. Don't let it infect your students. Teach them this simple axiom: "Respect the reader or he will not respect you."

Another great editor, Malcolm Bauer of the *Portland Oregonian,* told another convention of journalism teachers in 1959 that he wished they would send the newspapers, men and women who could understand depth in the news—and could report it.

The time is long past when a newspaper could preoccupy itself with the surface of events. Today's newspapers could be giving readers some understanding—

—That there is more to education than football.
—That there is more to science than shooting the moon.
—That there is more to law than a murder case.
—That there is more to government than partisan politics.
—That there is more—much more—to life than appears on the surface of the television tube. And this something more is what should be reported in your newspaper.

Lester Markel, when he was editor of the *New York Times* Sunday edition, spoke of the importance of newspaper journalism in these words:

In these times, there rests a grave obligation on those who are responsible for the writing and the presentation of the printed word. . . . We must renew our dedication to the coverage of the news. We must find our circulation in reporting and explaining the great events of the day rather than seeking it frantically in comics and contests and circuses. Our basic job, our very reason for being, is the news. It is a huge and challenging assignment.

Frank Ahlgren, of the *Memphis* (Tenn.) *Commercial Appeal,* surely must have been referring to an implied contract between readers and their newspapers when he said in a speech in Texas, "In a sense, the newspaper is not the editor's but the property of the community."

John H. Colburn, editor and publisher of the *Wichita* (Kans.) *Eagle* and the *Beacon,* was really talking about this same kind of responsibility in a speech in Kansas in 1968. He said, in part:

> The sins of the press generally are in the ignorance and stupidity of reporters, writers and editors whose interests and imaginations have not been stimulated sufficiently to roam the gamut of society. Far too often they feed on their own emotional preconceptions and prejuduces. They ignore the fact that the exploration of contemporary society is never-ending, a professional process of sorting out the contradictions as well as the confirmations of the truths they are seeking to interpret and record.

J. R. Wiggins, former editor of the *Washington Post,* writing in the *Bulletin* of the American Society of Newspaper Editors in 1973, asked the questions, "Who will watch the watchman? Who will censor the censor? Who will police the press?" He answered these questions by saying, "The founding fathers, of course, were confident that the people would provide the only safe check on newspapers." He then went on to explain what he called "The law of credibility." "With every publication," he said, "there is created with Volume 1 and Number 1, its credibility bank account. The newspaper begins to draw upon it with its first issue. By its day-to-day performance it adds to it and subtracts from it. And the final accounting is as inescapable as death and taxes."

What Mr. Wiggins was saying is that the newspaper is published for the reader and that reader keeps the credibility bank account.

Throughout the history of American journalism, dedicated editors, reporters, and publishers have been saying, with conviction, these same things. Throughout their lives in journalism their interests were intertwined with those of their readers.

What About the Changes in the Profession?

On March 7, 1888, in Key West, Florida, some fifty members attended the tenth annual meeting of the Florida Press Association. They heard L. C. Vaughn, editor of the *Orlando* (Fla.) *Sentinel,* read an "essay" on the great progress made by journalism in Florida and the rest of the world. He reported:

> Since the introduction of the press in Florida, journalism

has undergone several revolutions and is likely to undergo many more. The invention of the cylinder press did as much for the profession, which now rules the world, as the discoverer of gun powder did for the savage profession that ruled it before.

The enormous extension of electric wires and ocean cables have superseded the old correspondent, and now the Washington letter, with lightning speed, comes by telegraph. The account of a great battle fought yesterday in the Old World is read today in our columns with as much accuracy as it is in the community in which it occurred. In the newspaper you purchase this afternoon you may read the words, "Queen Victoria spoke to her Parliament this morning," or what a Congress of European representatives said and did on the banks of the Bosophorus the evening before.

The journalist now at one leap takes the world for his province. The question arises, what will be the next revolution? Our newspaper of today presents as many topics of human interest as the average mind cares to consider. Therefore, the probability is, that we will not have a greater variety, but a superior quality of matter from the press. The news should be presented in such a compass, that the reader may master it without interfering with his regular business. One does not desire to have great "masses of undigested news" thrust upon him [but] expects the editor to select the salient points and present them in readily comprehensible form. In the past, the greatest expenditure in conducting a newspaper was the white paper; now it is the news; in the future let us hope it will be the brains.

Vaughn was talking about the newspaper technology of his day and wondering what the next "revolution" would bring. He seemed to feel that the newspaper profession had about reached its zenith, for it was already presenting daily "about as many topics of human interest as the average mind cares to consider."

Eighty years later, in 1968, Editor Colburn of the *Eagle* and *Beacon* recounted even greater advances in the communications industry, as he addressed journalism teachers at Lawrence, Kansas.

On the technological front, the *St. Louis Post-Dispatch* hopes by the end of this year to be publishing, in part, on offset. When the Apollo astronauts make their preliminary test for a lunar excursion, live pictures will be transmitted for the first time from their spacecraft. These are some of the new dimensions for printing of large papers and for broadcasting.

More new developments are just over the horizon. At the ANPA production conference in Washington in June, a high-speed electronic system for displaying and editing computer-stored wire service news stories was demonstrated. An operator, using a cathode ray tube system retrieved news stories from a computer, displayed them on a television-like screen, edited the copy and sent it back to the computer for immediate printout on a hard copy machine—all in a matter of seconds.

Among other advanced techniques that will be used in the near future is transmission of copy via a portable teletype-writer. Reporters will "call in" their stories to a central computer and the information will go to a storage bank for later retrieval by the editor on his display screen. Then he will decide how much to print out for production. There may even come a day with dictation converted from a tape sound track to printer copy.

Many developments that have revolutionized newspaper and television—radio output soon will be outmoded by new technology. More newspapers will get into the electronics field through cable television. In a few years they will be able to pipe hard copy into the home on a virtually noiseless printer that prints up to 1,200 words a minute—or the equivalent of a column and a half of type in 60 seconds. The type characters are formed by particles of ink fired in rapid fashion at ordinary paper. This is a far more efficient—and faster—system of transmitting information than facsimile. It also will sidestep the problem of chemical treatment of facsimile paper.

In your twenty-first century living room, what you are likely to see is something like this: Instead of a stereo-television combination there will be a computer television-stereo console. The computer will enable the householder to pay his bills, order merchandise and call for information in the Inktronic printer. This could be a news digest, current weather information, the baseball scores or information retrieved from a regional library center for the student in the house.

From the television screen, will come three-dimensional pictures, programs transmitted from foreign capitals and picked up from communication satellites with signal scan converters; or, by using the computer, you can show documentaries on the 1968 political convention or the world series, retrieved from video tape libraries. You will have your own video tape recorder to copy programs for later replays.

Many of the improvements Colburn talked about "for tomorrow" are in use today, and more will become realities within this decade. Newspapers are beginning to use cathode-ray tube editing systems, and computers are finding ever-wider use on more and more newspapers as the decade of the eighties approaches. Computers were first used mainly for the justification of lines of type; from there they took on the bookkeeping tasks of the newspaper and then the regulation of newspaper routes and circulation. Today they are invading the newsroom—coupled with video tubes to do the editing work—and assisting news editors and reporters in the analysis of raw data for news and feature stories. Cold type and the offset method of printing have gained such momentum that most community and suburban newspapers are now printed by this process. Approximately 75 percent of the daily newspapers have turned to cold type for all or part of their production.

All of this has happened less than nine decades after L. C. Vaughn declared that the newspaper was printing about all the news that the human mind cared to consider.

Today communication technology is rapidly shifting the news selection process from the newsroom to the living room of the consumer. In the future the job of the communications industry may be simply to serve up a "glut of occurrences" in cafeteria style. By twirling knobs or punching buttons the news consumer will make his selection. Such a system might encourage him to be less informed than he is today. He would be free to choose only one category of news, such as sports, day in and day out, and to ignore all other types of news.

On the other hand, competition for the news consumer's interest, time, and money may force the purveyors of news to such high standards, to such a degree of excellence, that the news consumer may find himself partaking of the "cafeteria delicacies" to a greater extent than ever before.

What About the Reporter?

First, a person must learn to walk. A baby, learning to walk, carefully pulls itself upright and slowly tries its unsteady legs, all the while clinging for dear life to its play pen or the legs of a chair or a backyard fence. As soon as the growing child has learned to use his legs for walking he finds that he can use them for running, and his life seems complete as he darts here and there in childish glee.

Reporting must be learned in much the same way. The reporter who really wants to be a master of his craft must serve a long apprenticeship with words, sentences, paragraphs, and facts. These are the days of his "first steps," learning to be accurate, fair, truthful, and fearless. It is a time when he learns to use words correctly, to write cautiously, to be clear and concise.

Unfortunately, there are reporters holding down jobs on newspapers today who never really learned how to write. Somewhere in their experience they learned to use a typewriter, picked up a few ideas about the "Five Ws" and the inverted pyramid style of newswriting, and—presto—they were reporters. Somebody once named them "typewriter mechanics" or "typewriter jockeys." These fellows can grab a handful of facts and dash off in every direction at once. The readers alone suffer, never the reporters.

Words can be weapons. A reporter needs to handle them like a loaded revolver. Sometimes it is as easy to hurt people with words as with a firearm. That is why the reporter needs first to learn to walk with words before he runs, to run with words before he tries to fly.

That's all very fine, you say, but where do I begin? What must I do first? What do I need to know?

What Is a Reporter?

Reporters on a newspaper gather the news. Sometimes they both gather news and write it up for the paper; other times they merely do the legwork of gathering facts and telephoning them to the newspaper where *rewrite men* put them in news story form for the paper. In large cities, reporters work on *beats* or *runs;* that is, they cover a certain area, just like a policeman. In small towns or cities the reporter's beat may be the entire city. On large newspapers several reporters may be placed on *general assignment.* They are free to dig up their own stories or they may be assigned special events.

Newspapers select beats covering "critical areas" in the community where news is likely to surface. The police station is such a focal point. Newspapers cannot possibly anticipate accidents and disasters and have a reporter already on hand to witness the event. Sooner or later this kind of news reaches the police station, the sheriff's office, the highway patrol, the fire station, or the hospital, where it becomes a matter of record. Newspaper coverage of these critical areas provides the reader with most of the facts he needs concerning such events.

The real, dyed-in-the-wool reporter is always the first to know the news. The "gold" he brings in is not tangible like that gathered by the advertising salesman, but his product sells the newspaper. When he is "on a story," it becomes a part of him, something of his own. Mealtime, or the end of a forty-hour week, means nothing to him. He may grumble about his job, he may tell a college journalism student to shoot himself rather than become a reporter, but try to get him to change his own work!

The good reporter today is well educated. He is a professional in every sense of the word. To a four-year college degree that includes a broad, liberal background and professional courses in journalism, he quickly adds experience in the fields of government, politics, economics, social welfare, and international relations. Many other subjects come as grist to his reporter's mill. In a sense, his education really begins the day he joins the staff of a newspaper or broadcasting station. He must keep up with the news of the day by reading several newspapers and news magazines and listening as much as possible to news on radio and television. Over the years, he often becomes more of an expert in any given field than the people he writes about.

Whether a reporter finds life exciting or dull depends on the kind of person he is. The story is told that once an old man was resting on his cane just below the top of a hill and a young man came bustling along the road.

"Say, old man," he said, "I'm going to work in that town just over the hill. Can you tell me what kind of people live there?"

"What kind of people lived in the town you just left?" asked the old man.

"Oh, I didn't get along with those people," said the young fellow. "They were mean and unfriendly. I was glad to get out of that town."

The old man slowly shook his head. "I'm afraid you'll find the people in the town over the hill the same kind of people you just left," he said.

A little later in the day, while the old man still rested before continuing his journey, another young man came along. With a broad smile, he said, "Kind sir, I'd like to inquire about the town over the hill. My company has transferred me to that town and I'd like to know what kind of people live there."

"What kind of people lived in the town you just left?" asked the old man.

"Now those people were real fine people," answered the young man. "I certainly did hate to leave that town. I had a lot of friends there and I'm sure going to miss them."

This time the old man smiled and said, "You'll find the people in the town over the hill the same kind of people you just left."

If a reporter likes his work, he will approach each day with a feeling of expectancy. He never knows what the day will bring. Some reporters will tell you that ninety-nine percent of each day's work is filled with dull, routine stories, but the reporter who enjoys his work can find something exciting and challenging in every story he writes.

He communicates that pleasure and excitement in the writing of his story. At the end of the day he finds pleasure in looking over the paper and seeing what he has contributed to that day's edition. There are no dull news stories, only dull writers and dull reporters.

A reporter must be dependable. He must be able to turn out good copy in quantity. He must be able to work under pressure as well as he does in ordinary circumstances—perhaps even better. He must be able to plan his work and organize his time. In many situations he must try to write a better story than one being written by competing reporters.

Even more, he needs to be a self-starter, a person who does things on his own, who comes up with ideas for stories without being prodded by a superior.

The good reporter must have a keen sense of the responsibilities that go with the job. He should never allow himself to feel that his community is a giant playing field and that his news sources are mere players in a game, to be pushed around or pinched to see how they react. Reporting can be fun, stimulating, exciting, and rewarding, but it is never a game. It is a serious, exacting business for professionals only.

Questions for Discussion

1. Will technological advances in the newspaper business create a greater or less demand for good reporters?
2. Does the reporter have some kind of fundamental right to write anything he pleases and expect his newspaper or broadcasting station to use it?
3. From what you now know about the news profession, do you feel that anyone who wants to be a reporter should be allowed to be one or should he be required to pass an examination to practice the profession, as in law and medicine?
4. In the news profession is the customer always right? In other words, should the news media seek to present only the news they feel the consumer wants?
5. Do you frankly think you are suited for the news profession? If so, why, or why not?

2 what is news?

Ask a hundred persons to define news and you will probably get a hundred different answers. Throughout a newsman's career he is continuously refining and crystallizing his definition of news. He learns that what is news to one person won't get even a look from another. He learns that what is news in one city is not news in another, what is news to a man may not be news to a woman, what is news to a teenager may not be news to an adult. Throughout this book you will constantly be enriching your own definition of news. But since you must begin somewhere, for the time being let us say only that news is made up of those events that interest people.

One day a reporter was talking to a friend who had just returned from an ocean voyage with his family. After chatting for a few minutes about the things he had seen and done abroad, the friend said, "The most exciting moment of the entire trip for my youngest daughter came the last night aboard ship when she was surprised with a birthday cake, complete with lighted candles, while the ship's orchestra played and sang 'Happy Birthday.'"

The reporter's eyes began to brighten. He had the basis for a feature story. His questions came rapidly and his pencil began to move. What was the little girl's name? How old was she? What was the name of the ship? How did the dining steward know she had a birthday?

The questions continued. The reporter's friend had no idea when he stopped to chat that he would have a feature story for the town paper that day. Only the reporter's own definition of news told him that people would be interested in this unusual birthday party. The unusual will always interest people; therefore, anything unusual is news.

One summer morning in a small Florida Gulf Coast town workmen were busily applying a coating of grey-black material to the town's tallest building. The ugly coating added nothing to the appearance of the structure. Hundreds of persons passing the building that morning wondered what was going on. Finally, a reporter came along. He heard two citizens discussing the situation.

"What in the world are they doing to the Hart Building?" one asked.

"You got me," replied the other, "but whatever it is, it sure looks a mess."

That was enough for the reporter. Off he went to contact the manager of the Hart Building. He learned that the building was being waterproofed in preparation for the approaching hurricane season. That same day the local paper carried a story telling all those who had wondered about the "mystery" coating how much the waterproofing cost, what color paint would be used to hide the ugly coating, how old the building was, why it had not been waterproofed before, and many other interesting facts. Mysteries, no matter how small, interest people; therefore mysteries are news.

The things people talk about are news. You would end up with a red face if you left an accident story out of the paper because "everybody knows about it." The more people have talked about it, the more they "know about it," the more they want to read the details in your newspaper. They want to check what they have heard against what you have written. The chances are that a high percentage of what they have heard is incorrect. They go to the newspaper seeking the truth.

Names make news. A small plane crash in the frozen wastes of Alaska would get only a few lines in most newspapers unless one of the victims was Will Rogers. Then the story with all its grim details and thousands of words of biographical data is flashed around the world.

An acquaintance might remark to a reporter, "Say, I hear we're getting a new airport here," but the reporter would not consider the information *news*. He knows that he cannot rush into print on the word of any John Doe. He must check the statement with a city official whose word would be authoritative. If the mayor of the city or the city manager says the city will get a new airport, then the reporter has a news story.

Don't get the impression that an event must be discussed and talked about all over town before it becomes news. People do like to read about things they have already heard about, but they also like to read about something new. A basic part of the news is whatever is new. Readers pick up the paper for an answer to that age-old question heard all day long, "What's new?" Recency, therefore, has a lot to do with how an event stacks up as news.

In a Midwestern city one summer a rapist was using the vacant houses of vacationing residents for attacks on unsuspecting women. He would first call an employment bureau for a female worker. When she arrived he pretended to be the owner of the house. Once she was inside, he locked the door behind her. A story covering his method of operation was news, particularly to young women on the employment agency lists. The printing of that story throughout the Midwest probably saved one or more lives.

News also includes those events that affect people's lives. The more people affected, the bigger the news. The story that a 50 million dollar manufacturing plant is going to locate in your city is big news to almost everyone because practically everyone will be affected in one way or another by the changes in the economy of the community.

Often news is a developing story, and then a reporter needs to keep his ear to the ground. He must be sensitive enough to reader interest in an event that he knows when to go all out on the story and when to quit. Sometimes it takes a smart reporter to know when a story is washed up. A few examples of continuing news are governmental investigations, strikes, an election campaign, rescue efforts on a sunken submarine, or a trial. Of course, people also have continuing interests that develop into news when the interests are tampered with or affected in any way, or even analyzed or discussed. For example, people are always interested in their health, their way of life, their children, their freedom, food, clothing, and shelter. You will read more about this later on in this chapter.

News Is Relative

Possibly by this time you have arrived at the happy, and correct, theory that news is a relative thing. When one man says something it's not necessarily news, but the same statement by a person in authority is news. When unknown people do something, it may not be news, but the same act by a celebrity is news. The burning of a warehouse in a large city might not get even a paragraph in a big city daily, but the burning of the same size warehouse with the same financial loss in a small town might get banner headlines.

A simple rule-of-thumb definition to use in your day-to-day reporting is that news comes from the things people or groups of people have done, are doing, or plan to do. That covers about everything except natural phenomena, and you can be sure that Mother Nature will make big news all year.

One of your first tasks as a beginning reporter is to learn about the many and varied interests of the people in the area covered by your newspaper. If you learn, for example, that a great deal of wheat is grown in your area you will soon find out that people living in the area are interested in any kind of information dealing with wheat. They will be interested in weather conditions affecting the growing of wheat, government regulations affecting wheat growers, the market value of wheat, and so forth. When you have learned about all the interests of the people of your community you will have a good start toward a definition of news in that area.

Another "first" for the beginning reporter is to learn the

names and jobs of people who make news in the community. A high percentage of any community news comes from a handful of people in authority. A certain young reporter couldn't understand why his newspaper made such a fuss over an old man on the staff who had been reporting the news of the city for more than thirty years. In the eyes of the cub, the old man was a has-been. Then, one day the cub was sent to cover a meeting of the city zoning board. He turned in a few paragraphs of routine copy the next morning and prepared to go out on his beat.

"Hey, kid, this all you got on that zoning board meeting?" called the city editor.

"Yeah," said the cub, "just routine stuff down there last night. Meeting was late starting. Fellow by the name of Carlton Dikes spent half an hour in the hall with Chairman Brown. Thought they'd never get underway."

The Old Time Reporter, the has-been, was reading a morning newspaper in one corner of the newsroom. He lowered his newspaper. "Carlton Dikes, eh?" he said. Without another word he got up and left the office. Within an hour he was back with one of the biggest stories of the year, a story concerning a $40 million plant that was going to locate in the city. Why did he get the story the cub missed?

In the first place the Old Timer knew that Dikes owned a large share of the real estate in the county. He knew that Dikes had been involved in many large real estate deals in the past, and that something was brewing when Dikes took the trouble to attend a meeting of any official city body. The name Dikes meant nothing to the cub. To the Old Timer it meant "news."

People Disagree About What Is News

Possibly the greatest source of controversy today between news media and news consumers is a lack of agreement on what constitutes news. Let's look at a few examples of "controversial" news.

Three teenagers steal a car and lead police on a 100-mile-an-hour chase through city streets before being caught. News media people believe the event is news because:

(a) The youngsters broke the law and endangered lives; and

(b) The public has a "need to know" about such events if its members are going to protect themselves and their property, and help in the passage of laws needed by society.

The parents, relatives, and friends of the youngsters probably do not feel that the event is news. They may feel that the whole thing was an innocent lark and that the newspaper should not concern itself with such things. They may feel that the youngsters made a mistake and that they should not be punished by the full light of publicity. A newspaper, they may believe, should not concern itself with stories about kids who make mistakes but should concentrate instead on the activities of hardened criminals.

The wife of a prominent city commissioner tells her husband that she is going to a neighboring city with friends to attend a club convention. Instead, she goes with a male companion to a vacation hideaway in another part of the state. Her husband, suspicious of his wife, follows her with a loaded shotgun. The journey ends in tragedy for all: the wife and her lover are dead, and the husband is unconscious and dying from a heart attack brought on by his killing of the pair.

To the newspaper and other news media, the event is news, because:

(a) Prominent persons were involved.

(b) Laws were broken and the normal conduct of people was altered.

(c) The entire event should serve as an object lesson to the rest of the population.

(d) The love triangle aspect of the story ties in with people's interest in sex, one of the strongest of all reader interests.

Many in the community might say that if the story had to be printed it should have been buried on an inside page and limited to one or two paragraphs. They may reason that the event was sordid and disgusting and that a newspaper should not concern itself with "this kind of trash." They would say that such an event is not news; newspapers should publish only events that serve to uplift mankind and not publish information that tends to degrade people.

A large factory in a community closes down leaving more than one thousand persons without jobs. The local newspaper headlines the story on page one, believing the story is important because:

(a) The payroll loss will affect the economy of the community.

(b) The jobless eventually may create all kinds of special problems for local government, welfare organizations, and so on.

(c) The closing of the plant is a kind of disaster for the community; readers and listeners need to be alerted so they can help.

Members of the local chamber of commerce would like to see the factory closing story killed or played down because they say it is "bad news" and people don't like to read bad news. The story could cause other businessmen, planning to locate in this same community, to change their minds and the community would suffer. A newspaper should not publish items that will cause people to suffer or a town to decline. Its mission should be to tell the "good news" and help build the community toward greatness, the officials maintain.

In all of these examples, private citizens and government officials disagree with the news media about the definition of news. All are honest in their convictions. The news media, by going against what is considered news by these well-meaning people, are considered to be "trouble-makers," interested only in stirring people up or increasing their circulation by publishing sensational stories.

Who Must Define the News?

This brings up the question, Who must define the news? Should the newswriters go to the chamber of commerce to ask its officials if the factory closing story is news—and abide by the officials' decision? Should newswriters consult a judge about the news value of the arrest of the teenagers? Should the newspaper ask ten persons, or fifty persons, in the community if they think the love triangle story is news before a decision regarding publication is made?

Obviously, no newspaper or broadcasting station could survive for long if it had to consult people in the community before publishing a story. Little news would come out of such a practice. Anyone involved in a news story that reflected the least bit against him would not want it published. "Not news," he would say.

Thus, news must be defined only by working professional newsmen. This practice is not designed to prevent the average citizen, or the mayor of a town, from making news judgments. Plainly and simply it insures that the news media will get a chance to be news media—and remain in business.

Are the newspapers and their readers always to disagree over this question of what is news?

The answer would seem to be both yes and no.

Newspapers and readers will probably never agree entirely on a definition of news. People tend to define news in terms of their own biases, interests, contacts, acquaintances, and general state of mind. Newspapers cannot afford such luxuries if they expect to remain in business and retain their own self-respect.

The only hope for some kind of understanding between the media and the public they serve is for the media to earn the respect of the news consumer by being consistent in the application of their definition of news. If, for example, a newspaper published the auto theft story but failed a month later to publish a similar incident, readers might nod their heads and say, "Uh huh, see what I mean? They were paid off this time!"

Power of the News Definer

Whoever defines the news wields a lot of power, because he is determining in large part what his readers and viewers will know about. Such power carries with it tremendous responsibility.

Once, a reporter was sent to cover a bingo game being conducted by a senior citizens group for charitable purposes.

Such games were illegal in the state under a statute prohibiting lotteries. The reporter attended the event and then refused to write the story on the grounds that there was no real harm in what the old folks were doing, that surely the state statute was not meant to cover such activities, and he "just couldn't pull the rug out from under these people."

Thus, the reporter had decided that the event was not news and should not be published.

On another occasion, a reporter was sent to get a story on abortion counseling activities in her community. Performing an abortion and counseling abortion were illegal in the state, although the state statute was under fire and being tested in the courts.

The reporter pretended to be pregnant and received counsel concerning an abortion. She returned to her editor, told him what had happened, and then said she could not write the story because she felt that the law was wrong and that the abortion counselors were serving the best interests of society. She was saying, in essence, this is not news and we should not stir up the matter by running the story.

In both cases the reporter made a personal judgment that the state law was improper and refused to write a story that would have put the spotlight of publicity on individuals who were breaking the law.

It was pointed out earlier that newspapers would not remain in business for long if individuals in the community ultimately decided what is news. Readers of the newspaper, public officials, and others are of course invited, even urged, to contribute articles and news tips to the media. However, the final judgment concerning what is news and what gets published must remain in the hands of professionals.

The same holds for the reporters in the above examples. Reporters *alone* should not be allowed to decide what is news. The newspaper, as represented by its editors, must make such decisions. The reporter who feels that he has a "conflict of interest," and cannot write a story assigned to him, may find himself out of a job or at least relieved from the assignment.

In actual practice reporters make judgments concerning

what is news and what is not news every working day of their
lives. Basically, however, the reporter is a truth seeker; he
should not seek facts, or neglect them, strictly on the basis of
personal convictions or preconceived notions about society,
or the rightness or wrongness of laws. As a professional, in a
highly responsible and important job, he must gather all the
facts and let the chips fall where they may.

The News Iceberg

The news is often like an iceberg, with only a small crag
or pinnacle revealed to the public gaze. The professional
newsman is constantly searching below the water level of
community consciousness in an effort to bring all of the
iceberg into view. In this search he uses his own and the
newspaper's definition of news. Because the public in
general has no definition of news that would suit the needs of
all readers, it is unaware, for the most part, of much of the
news in its own community, state, or nation. It is the direct
responsibility of the news media to find the news, develop it,
interpret it, and present it to the news consumer.

The better the newsman knows his community
organization, his news sources, and reader interests, the
better and more professional job he can do in probing the
under surface news.

The News and Reader Interest

Any definition of news must take into account the many
and varied interests of the public. Today's news consumer is
better educated and more knowledgeable about local,
national, and world affairs; has traveled more; is more
critical of his news fare; and, in general, is harder to please
than earlier generations. The news medium that makes the
mistake of thinking that the reader's only interests are
"babies, beauties, and beasts" may not survive today's
competition in the news field.

You can make a list of reader interests by analyzing your
own interests. In this chapter you have been told that the
following are newsworthy:

1. Unusual events.
2. Mysteries and the unknown.
3. Prominent people, places, and things.
4. Whatever people are talking about.
5. Statements by persons in authority.
6. New ideas—anything that is likely to be new to the general reader.
7. All events that affect readers' lives.
8. Trends or continuing events that grasp the imagination of readers over a period of time.

To this list you can add the following:

1. Conflict. Readers like to read about conflicts between man and man, between man and nature, between man and himself.
2. Natural phenomena, violence, and disaster.
3. Tragedies and comedies that appeal to the emotions.
4. Topics of health. More than ever, readers today are interested in the health of their families and friends and the fight against disease. (This is really another form of conflict.)
5. Change. Readers want to know all about social, technological, economic, and political change.
6. The environment. (This is yet another form of conflict as man seeks to win the battle of survival.)
7. The why of news. Readers have become more and more interested in knowing why things happen, what makes them happen, who pulls the strings?

This list is by no means exclusive or exhaustive. A reporter on a specific newspaper in a specific community will most often be reporting for news consumers in his own area, and he will need to thoroughly know their self-interests as well as the interests of people generally.

Questions for Discussion

1. How would you define news? Write out your own definition of news and be prepared to defend it.
2. Should a newspaper, or any news medium, respect a "conflict of interest" situation involving one of its

reporters and relieve the reporter of the assignment?
3. In connection with a definition of news, how would you explain the phrase, "All the News Fit to Print"? The phrase, "All the News that Fits into Print"?
4. Do you think that news media tend to emphasize the trivial and unimportant as opposed to the important and significant?
5. Do you believe it is possible for any news medium to please all of its news consumers all the time? Why or why not?
6. Do you believe the so-called underground press is a reaction against the way older "establishment" newspapers have been defining the news? Why or why not?

3 newsgathering techniques

Reporters find much of the routine news at certain key spots where events become public records. In a certain city of 40,000 inhabitants, for example, the Yellow Pages of the local telephone directory lists sixteen news sources under the heading "Government Offices—City," twenty-six sources under state government—a total of 103 news sources. Some of the news from these sources is gathered by reporters, some is volunteered over the telephone by office people, and some is sent in as news releases. During those beginning weeks and months, as the good reporter learns *what* is news, he also learns *where* news can be found. When he finds out, for example, that many of his readers want news about wheat, he must then find out where such news can be found.

Some of the best news stories result from the reporter "being there." Once, a top news photographer, addressing a women's club, was asked how he got so many prize-winning shots. His tongue-in-cheek reply, "f/11, and be there," contained more truth than poetry.

The best news sources will produce little in the way of news if the reporter fails to visit them. News can be, and is, gathered by telephone, but the more frequently the reporter can visit with his news sources face-to-face, and the more time he has for direct observation and conversation, the more good news stories he is likely to produce.

The crying need in this second half of the twentieth century is for more reporters who will conscientiously and consistently work their old news sources, at the same time developing new ones with all the zeal of a prospector panning for gold, in order that more and more local news will be available for their newspaper.

Who are sources of news? Any person who can provide authentic, official information, such as the mayor, the police chief, the school superintendent; persons who have participated in news events, such as a miner rescued from a cave-in; persons who have observed news events, such as an eyewitness to a crime; persons who are affected by events, such as the mother or father of a soldier who defects; or persons who remember, such as the old-timer who recalls details of the city's worst fire.

What are sources of news? Public records and reports of all kinds that reveal trends in government, business, crime, and the weather, to name just a few; the public library, where facts can be checked and historical background found to help enrich current events; the scene of a news event, which a reporter can describe for his readers, who are unable to be present.

The routine sources of news are those the reporter visits regularly on his daily rounds. The nonroutine sources are developed through imagination, experience, and a reporter's growing knowledge of the community and the people in it.

The Reporter at Work

Good newsgathering involves, among other things, a knowledge of how to handle people effectively, alertness and good judgment in sizing up a situation, and dogged determination to get at the facts.

dealing with people

When a reporter goes out on assignment, he should not forget that he represents the newspaper or broadcasting station, that the image he creates for his employer may be a lasting image. In many cases he is the only contact a public official, a witness of a news event, or the general public has with the news media. His attitude should not be that of a person holding a big stick, demanding news. Most people refuse to be forced, but can be led, to cooperate in newsgathering.

The reporter should be friendly, but confident. He should identify himself at the scene of a news event or to his news contact. He should not try to get news by posing as an official, or pass himself off as a bystander, casually making conversation with those around him in order to get them to say things he can use in his story. Persons who are going to be quoted should be told that they are speaking for publication.

Gaining the confidence of news sources is not a sometime thing. The reporter works at it every day by being polite but persistent, by being accurate and fair.

What are you going to do about the person who wants to speak "off the record" with you? First, you need to clarify what he means by "off the record." Does he mean that he will merely give you background information, not to be used? Does he mean that you may use the material as long as you don't attribute it to him? First and foremost, if it is possible for you to get the same information elsewhere, you should not bind yourself or your newspaper not to use the material. If the information is available only from this one source, you should attempt to get it released by him, attributed to him directly, or in some indirect way, such as "a source close to the governor." If the source refuses to release the news at all, attempt to find out when it will be released; that is, try to get a firm date.

What about the person who refuses to comment on a news matter? Let's say, for example, that the mayor of the city is a key figure in an investigation of conditions at the city jail. He refuses to comment on the matter. You should tell him that you must report the fact that he refused to comment. On second thought, he might decide that such a statement would reflect less favorably on him than a statement giving his views on jail conditions.

How do you handle a person who requests that you omit his name from a news story? He may call you on the telephone, or confront you at the police station or at the scene of a news event. He may ask you to "forget" the story, "because it is not important anyway." You must honestly tell him that these are decisions you cannot make. You are there to cover the news. He will have to talk to your editor.

Occasionally a news source will ask you to bring him a copy of your story before it goes into print. What do you tell him? Explain to him that this procedure is impossible because of your deadline. If all reporters agreed to do this for all stories, the newspaper would never come out. You can tell him that you are quite willing to go over your notes with him, then and there, in order to satisfy him that he will be quoted accurately and that all the facts are correct.

Readers frequently bring to the newspaper office items they want published, or they give them to a reporter as he makes his rounds. What do you tell these people, especially if they want the item on page one, or in some other preferred position? The best rule is not to make any promises about preferred treatment. You must explain that all news is relative and that the material will have to be judged along with other news of the day and handled accordingly. Such an incident provides a good opportunity to educate the person bringing in the item about the way in which a newspaper must operate in handling news. You should smile, accept the material, but make no promises.

One day, a news source complains that your story about him the day before was not accurate, or that he was mis-quoted. He demands that you print a correction. What do you say? You should assure him that the policy of the newspaper is to print only that which is true and that if a mistake has been made, a correction will be published; but the facts in the situation will have to be checked by the newspaper. Reporters should retain all notes for at least a twenty-four hour period after the story involving those notes has been published. This policy protects both the reporter and the newspaper.

As indicated earlier, newsgathering is a kind of educational process between the reporter and the news source. Most people do not realize the importance of a free flow of information in a democratic society. They fail to realize that the newsgathering rights of the reporter, legally and ethically, are no different from those of an ordinary citizen. But from a practical standpoint, his job is all-important because he is acting for all of the citizens of the community. Not all citizens can attend every meeting of the school board, or the city commission, or a court trial. Reporters attend in place of those citizens who are unable to be present, uninterested, or too lazy to find out for themselves how their government is functioning. This is the kind of argument the reporter can present to the government official who says, "This matter is none of the newspaper's business."

He may be right, if you think of the newspaper as just another business in the community. But in the traditional, true sense of a newspaper's responsibility, the paper represents the public, and the public does have a right to know what goes on in government.

This educational process is a two-way street. The reporter is educated through information from every news source he encounters.

alertness and good judgment

Alertness does not suddenly occur, nor is it a trait with which a person is born. The good reporter develops alertness by hard work. For one thing, he reads his own newspaper thoroughly. If this sounds self-evident, don't laugh. Many news editors will tell you that their reporters do not read their own newspaper, let alone other newspapers that are available to them.

The good reporter, especially if he is fresh on the newspaper and unfamiliar with the community, sets out to learn his news area. He talks to other reporters on the paper, and uses his newspaper library and the public library to learn about the people who make news and how local government is organized. He cannot expect this knowledge to come to him through experience alone; he must work just as hard to learn the background for his job as he does doing the job itself.

Alertness also comes from being a good listener. Few

people know how to listen. Most hear only what they want to hear and tune out the rest. Others are lazy listeners, hearing only a portion of what is said, while their minds wander aimlessly. The reporter must *train* himself to hear and remember what he hears. He trains himself to listen for key points that tie together an argument or an explanation. He trains himself to get the complete and full meaning of what a person is saying, discarding the irrelevant. If he does not understand, he asks questions.

Good judgment involves fairness above all. It is not the job of the reporter to antagonize a news source, but rather to get his cooperation, and respect. The reporter should remember that he often has the advantage, especially if he calls a news source late at night to get a comment on a breaking story. You may ask the person to comment on something he knows nothing about. If he is wise, he will refuse to comment until he has had an opportunity to acquaint himself with all the facts. Even if you give him the facts, he may not want to comment unless he has great respect for you and your integrity.

Suppose you do succeed in getting a statement under these circumstances. What do you do if the news source later says that after thinking the matter over he realizes that he answered hastily and wishes to correct his statement? If the story has not gone to press, you should allow the news source to correct his statement. There are those who will argue with this point of view, but you should remember that the news source did not have to give you a statement at all. If his second statement is more cautious and evasive, you can probably clear up the entire matter from other sources.

Reporting is not some kind of game in which one news source is pitted against another to stir up controversy. However, the good reporter will consult more than one source in order to get all sides of a question. But the controversy, if there is one, should be legitimate, and not one produced by the reporter.

determination to get the news
All reporters should be determined to get the news when there is legitimate news to get, but they should not trump up a

situation in order to get a story. The days of faking news are
long past.

The first lesson a reporter learns is that he does not give
up because his initial attempt at getting a story fails to yield
anything. He tries another news source, and then another,
and still another, until the story is complete, or until he is
satisfied that the story does not exist or is not ready for
publication.

He will run into many blind alleys, some of his own
making. For example, if he confronts a news source with the
question, "Any news today?" he is likely to get a negative
answer. As noted earlier, most news sources do not know
what news is. The reporter must be prepared with positive
questions.

Effectiveness in getting the news involves many of the
following points:

Beats. If you have a regular area to cover, the first thing
to do is learn the area and the people in it. Get to know who
has the news, who is the news, where to get the facts. Cover
your beat on a regular basis. The first day you fail to see your
news sources will be the day your biggest news story will
break—and you won't get it. Don't miss a particular news
source just because the source has not turned up any news
lately. Try to visit news sources in person. If that is impossible, use the telephone. Have specific questions in mind when
you visit a news source. You get them by keeping up with the
news on a beat and planning new stories ahead. A story on a
new city hall building may lead you to develop a feature on
the old building. You get them by observing people and
conditions on the beat. For example, your observation of
what appears to be a dangerous traffic situation will lead to
one or more stories on that traffic situation, and perhaps
others in the community. You get them by talking to as many
persons as possible on the beat every day. For example, one
person might mention that his daughter reported low attendance in her third grade classroom on a particular day. The
cause? "Some kind of flu, I believe." That sends you off to
check on the possibility of a flu epidemic. You'll have many
specific questions for school officials, health officers, and
private physicians.

Taking Notes. Newsgathering should be an orderly procedure. The reporter who dashes from the office with a sheaf of copy paper stuffed in his hip pocket is unprofessional. Just because the method is simple, and works, is not reason enough to gather news that way forever. You can always improve on any system. Notes should be taken in some kind of notebook, preferably a looseleaf type. In this way you can number the pages and keep material in a neat and orderly manner; or you can tear out the pages and reassemble them in the order the facts will appear in your news story or feature. This process speeds up the movement of your story from notes to typed copy for the copy desk. Get in the habit of taking notes in complete sentences. If you jot down only a few key words, two hours later they may mean nothing to you. Develop a speed writing technique of your own if you are not proficient in standard shorthand. You can do this with abbreviations and use of symbols for frequently used words.

Asking Questions. The key to all newsgathering is to ask questions. It is impossible for a reporter to ask too many questions. Today he must pursue the "why" of everything that happens. The late-night hanging of a young jail prisoner by two fellow prisoners led one reporter to a long investigation into why this kind of thing could happen. His efforts resulted in several stories that set in motion a series of reforms in the local prisons. As a conscientious reporter you must keep asking questions until you are satisfied that you have all the answers it is possible to get at a particular time. Don't hesitate to ask a "crazy" question. Sometimes such a question will bring forth a surprising and interesting bit of news for your story, or an entirely new lead. For example, a reporter researching a feature story on a summer swimming program asked the instructor if he felt the youngsters in the class were taught anything besides swimming. This seemed like a crazy question—what else besides swimming would be taught in a swimming class? The instructor, puzzled at first, admitted finally that he and the other instructors did teach something at poolside in addition to swimming techniques. He said they taught a special kind of democracy, and then launched into a discussion of how the youngsters learned to work together, to respect one another, and many other things beneficial to an orderly society. This extra "bit" gave the reporter an entirely new slant for his story. Try the "crazy" question. It might work for you.

Working an Assignment. Working an assignment such as a fire or accident can be exciting, but you can't do much of a reporting job if you become excited. Good reporting under such conditions calls for a calm, reasoned approach.

(a) Do not rush into the middle of the activity, getting in the way so that you are a hindrance to the operation and in danger yourself.

(b) Do not try to question an official who is in the midst of a tense, critical operation and needs to concentrate all of his energies at the moment on the operation.

(c) Do not make wild guesses in estimating numbers. At the proper time, get authoritative information from officials who have had experience in estimating crowd size or extent of damage.

(d) Do not let "crackpots" take up all of your time. Around every fire, accident, or disaster there are always those who want to get in the newspaper or on the air with their views. You will want some quotes, of course, from eyewitnesses. Try to select those persons who seem rational and can give some real substance to the story rather than those who are already partly out of their minds from excitement or are obviously seeking publicity.

You should remember to:

(a) on arrival, find a telephone you can use to get word to the newspaper. This might not be easy, especially if the news event (plane crash, auto pile-up on an expressway, forest fire, mine cave-in) is in an isolated area. Your nearest telephone may be miles away.

(b) find out who is in charge and stay as close to that person as possible, without interfering in the operation. Reports will come to him. He will give orders to workers at the scene. He should have the facts.

(c) look for facts. Don't take anything for granted.

(d)   take an ample amount of loose change with you for telephone calls. You might not be able to get change in the area.

(e)   observe everything that goes on around you. Look for details. Look for "color" and the unusual.

(f)   identify yourself as a member of the working press.

Access to News

Does a newspaper or broadcast reporter have any legal right to get the news? It has been argued that unless the answer is affirmative, the First Amendment to the Constitution of the United States is meaningless. How can a private citizen speak against government policy, for example, if he cannot find out the facts to use in his complaint? How can a newspaper get the facts about misuse of public funds if it is denied access to fiscal records?

Newspapers and news reporters, and all journalists, have no constitutional rights different from those of ordinary citizens, nor does the Constitution or the Bill of Rights include an explicit right of access to governmental records, legal documents, or other instruments that might be considered newsworthy.

Newswriters do have certain rights of access to news, however. Such rights are granted in federal and state statutes, administrative rules and regulations, and by local ordinance. For the most part, these rights are observed as a matter of tradition where no statute exists. In other words, in the absence of laws specifically barring reporters or private citizens from viewing records, government officials are likely to recognize the special interest of reporters and allow them to examine official records.

If he is new on the job, a reporter must know where he stands with respect to the following questions about access to news:

Does the reporter have a right to attend and report any kind of meeting?

If it is a public meeting, the answer is yes; if it is a private meeting, the answer is no. How does one tell the difference? A public meeting is any meeting open to the general public. A private meeting is one open only to members of the organization having the meeting, guests of the organization, and persons asked to appear on the program. There are exceptions and variations, of course, and therein lies the problem. What about an official school board meeting that is held at the home of the chairman? In many states this would be a public meeting, according to law, and the chairman would have to allow anyone to attend. Florida is such a state. Its so-called government-in-the-sunshine law would force the school board, or any other public body, to meet openly in public. The law reads:

> All meetings of any board or commission of any state agency or authority or of any agency or authority of any county, municipal corporation or any political subdivision, except as otherwise provided in the constitution, at which official acts are to be taken are declared to be public meetings open to the public at all times, and no resolution, rule, regulation, or formal action shall be considered binding except as taken or made in such meeting.
>
> The minutes of a meeting of any such board or commission or any such state agency or authority shall be promptly recorded and such records shall be open to public inspection. The circuit courts of this state shall have jurisdiction to issue injunction to enforce the purposes of this section upon application by any citizen of this state.
>
> Any person who is a member of a board or commission or of any state agency or authority of any county, municipal corporation or any political subdivision who violates the provisions of this act by attending a meeting not held in accordance with the provisions hereof is guilty of a misdemeanor and upon conviction thereof shall be punished by a fine of not more than five hundred dollars ($500.00) or by imprisonment in the county jail for not more than six (6) months, or by both such fine and imprisonment.

A public meeting, therefore, can also be defined as one required by law to be public. This means that in states having such laws even a meeting held in secret in a private place must be open to the public, or public officers holding such a meeting must suffer the consequences of their act. Obviously, a private group that attempts to hold a private meeting in a public place may encounter difficulty, such as the renting of a city-owned auditorium by a religious sect for a private meeting. (The legality of such deals has been challenged from time to time.)

Specifically, what kinds of meetings may be closed to the press?

Certain kinds of court proceedings are often closed to the press, and in any court trial the judge may clear the courtroom at any time. Many states require closed juvenile court trials, trials or hearings involving family matters, or hearings involving sex offenses. State constitutions often provide for executive, or closed, sessions of one or both branches of the state legislature when the legislators so desire. In states that do not have strong open meeting laws, public bodies, such as school boards and city and county commissions, often meet in closed session. In such cases, reporters, along with all private citizens, are excluded from the meeting. The only recourse at that point is to report that the body met in secret to transact public business.

Does the reporter have the right of access to all public records?

The first thing you need to know is the nature of a public record. Generally, public records have been defined in various state statutes as any record which the law requires an officer of the government to keep. Some state statutes have extended the definition to also include any records kept by an official, and not required by law, but kept for his own convenience. If a record is defined as a public record, it shall be open for public inspection, including inspection by reporters, unless specifically closed to the public by special statute. Most state statutes, or interpretations of the law through court decisions, place some constraints on the actual handling of public records. Records must be examined under reasonable conditions, in accordance with regulations designed to protect them or protect employees who have custody of them. This means that you cannot demand records at unreasonable hours. But it also means that records custodians cannot impose unreasonable restrictions on the use of records, such that they would be difficult, even impossible, to use. Records that have been declared "public" by various states include: judicial records, except special cases, such as juvenile courts; city and county records; records of state government; tax records; legislative records; census records; records of marriage licenses; election records; bills and vouchers on file in an auditor's office; minutes and other records of public bodies; police records that have nothing to do with law enforcement (this includes city, county, and state); records kept by such officers as mayors, auditors, treasurers, attorneys for public bodies.

Records that have been declared by law not open to the public include: juvenile court records; family and domestic court records; welfare rolls; diplomatic correspondence; records having to do with the apprehension and prosecution of criminals; records of public institutions that are charged with care and treatment of the mentally ill or those institutionalized for criminal activity; proceedings before a grand jury; and health department records.

How far may a reporter go in copying material from books, pamphlets, or public records?

The answer to this question involves the laws governing copyright and the matter of plagiarism. Obviously, it would be unethical, and often illegal, for a reporter to copy verbatim any written or published material and pass it off as his own. This would include material protected by copyright as well as material not so protected. Most public records, pamphlets, brochures, and documents are not protected by copyright and are intended for public use. Reporters may quote from such material as much as they need, but they should be careful to give the source of the quotes. Copyrighted material is another matter. Such material should not be quoted to any great extent without the permission of the copyright owner. It should be noted that news facts, as well as other facts, generally cannot be copyrighted. The story or article itself can be copyrighted. Thus, the copyright process generally protects the way in which a writer has put together material, his style, his manner of presentation. The facts may have come from noncopyrighted sources that are available to any other reporter or writer. The best rule, however, is not to use copyrighted material without permission.

How far may a reporter go in protecting the identity of a news source or tipster?

News tradition calls for all reporters to protect their news sources, even to the point of going to jail. In only a relatively small number of states are reporters protected by "shield laws" that make communications between a reporter and his news source a matter of privilege. In these states, even if called upon by a judge to reveal the name of a news source, the reporter does not have to comply. In states having no shield laws, refusal by a newsman to reveal the identity of a news source when so ordered by a judge may result in the newsman being cited for contempt of court and possible punishment by fine and/or imprisonment. In general, except in a handful of states a reporter has no legal protection if he refuses to identify his news source when ordered by a court to do so. Until 1972, this was not a situation that came up very often. Only rarely did a court seek to have the identity of a news source revealed. During the second half of 1972 cases occurred rather frequently throughout the nation. A half dozen or more reporters were jailed or threatened with detention.

The United States Supreme Court in a 5-to-4 decision in 1972 ruled that newsmen, like all citizens, have an obligation to answer grand jury subpoenas and supply information in criminal investigations. Five of the judges rejected the contention that the First Amendment grants reporters a special immunity to protect them from disclosing material they obtained from confidential sources.

Concerning the 5-to-4 decision the *Los Angeles Times* said in an editorial on July 2, 1972:

> The Supreme Court of the United States has struck a heavy blow at the independence of the press of this nation. And, striking at the press, the court has diminished the right of the American people to a free flow of information about their government and about all other significant events that affect our lives.

In a 5-to-4 decision, the court ruled that newsmen can be called before grand juries and compelled to divulge the names of their news sources and to answer any and all other questions that a jury decides is relevant to matters under investigation. To refuse means the risk of going to jail.

While much of the public's—and the court's—attention has been focused on the protection of a criminal news source, the truth is that the bulk of sources needing protection are honest businessmen and public officials who could lose their jobs or their livelihoods if they were publicly identified.

The *Times* editorial writer went on to point out, "The decision, in a most fundamental way, will have a crippling effect upon newsgathering. The right to publish is dependent upon access to news. One, without the other, is rendered useless. Compelled testimony by newsmen will impair their access to news sources."

Some newsmen feel that a national shield law is one answer that should be sought in the Congress. Other newsmen oppose such a law. At a Law Day program at the University of Florida in May 1973, Robert R. Feagin, president of the company which publishes the *Florida Times-Union* and the *Jacksonville* (Fla.) *Journal,* said a national shield law for reporters is "unnecessary and undesirable. It would tend to undermine the freedom of the press rather than protect that freedom." He further said, "There seems to be coming a clearer understanding of the hidden pitfalls in laws to protect the press." He said a shield law means going to the government for protection, possibly leading to a closer alliance with government and to a licensed press. He called a shield law a step backward in press responsibility and said it would encourage irresponsibility, encourage a reporter to "shoot from the hip."

What about a news character's right of privacy?

The legal concept of "right of privacy" is simply a person's right to be left alone to live his own life, outside the spotlight of any kind of publicity, if he so chooses. However, a person forfeits this right of privacy in many ways:

(a)   He can sign away the right if, for example, he agrees to the use of his photograph in an advertisement.

(b)   He gives up the right by running for or being elected to public office.

(c)   He involuntarily gives up the right if he is involved in a news story of general public interest. This is not an absolute rule, however, since a jury in a right of privacy suit may decide that the news was not a matter of general public interest.

(d)   He usually gives up the right if he becomes a person who makes his living in some kind of public way, such as an actor, professional football player, minister, or teacher.

Suppose, for example, that a person is involved in an automobile accident and pleads the right of privacy to keep his name and involvement in the accident out of the news. Here he has no right of privacy. His part in the accident becomes a matter of public record, and while he might protest the use of his name and the details of the accident that involve him, his protests will be in vain. What happens if this same person does not want the newspaper to use details of his life that have nothing whatsoever to do with the automobile accident? Does the reporter have to abide by the person's wishes? Generally speaking, the fact that the automobile accident brought this person into the public spotlight would make it possible for the newspaper to use facts about the person that do not relate directly to the auto accident, with or without his consent. How far the newspaper may go in this direction, however, depends upon the particular circumstances and might even have to be decided by a court. This is a kind of twilight zone of reporting. The reporter would be well advised to deal strictly with the facts at hand and not deal with other aspects of the news character's life not directly related to the particular news event.

Questions for Discussion
1.   List all of the sources of news in your immediate community. Discuss the list to see if other sources can be added.
2.   How would you characterize the news coverage of your immediate community? Do you have good coverage or poor coverage? Explain.

3. Discuss the advantages and disadvantages of beats or runs as a way of organizing news coverage of a community. Would you suggest another method of organizing coverage? If so, how would it work?

4. You are sent to cover a political barbecue held at one of the city parks. The main speaker is a United States Senator. In the middle of his speech he says, "If there are any reporters in the audience, I would like to request that the next few minutes of my talk be 'off-the-record.'" Would you respect his request? Why, or why not?

5. At a meeting of the city commission in your college community, the presiding officer announces in the middle of the meeting that the group will go into executive session and that spectators must leave. If you were a reporter assigned to cover the meeting, what would you do? Would the situation change if the speaker said that reporters would be allowed to remain at the meeting but that they would not be allowed to report what took place, that they would remain for "background" only?

4 newswriting techniques

The experienced reporter writes with the reader over his shoulder. He thinks constantly of what the unseen reader wants to know about an event and he puts that into his story, in the order of its importance. He soon learns that the reader wants to know *what* happened, *who* was involved, *why* the event took place, *when* it happened, *where* it happened, and *how* it happened. These are the Five Ws and the How of news. Sometimes a sixth W is added, the WOW, or human interest factor.

Suppose one spring morning you are walking down the main street of your town. The time is ten minutes past eight. Visibility is reduced to almost zero by a heavy fog that the sun has failed to disperse. Suddenly, at an intersection a block away there is the sound of tires screeching, and then the horrible smack of metal against metal and the shattering of glass. Afterwards, for a moment there is absolute quiet. You run to the corner and see two automobiles, one upside down and the other, its front end bashed in, resting on its wheels but facing the curb. The crumpled body of a young man is lying about twenty-five feet from the upside-down car. Still behind the wheel of the other car sits a young woman, apparently dazed. You notice that the traffic light is not working at the intersection.

A crowd quickly gathers, appearing from the fog-covered houses up and down the street, and later an ambulance arrives, followed by a police car. The boy and girl are taken to the county hospital where the boy is pronounced dead on arrival. The girl is found to have a slight concussion, a broken right arm, and possible internal injuries. The boy is identified as Oscar Lee Greene, son of Mr. and Mrs. Edgar Lee Greene. Two nights before the accident he was named captain of the local high school football team for the next season. The girl is his cousin. Her name is Marilyn Dobson, daughter of Mr. and Mrs. Glenn C. Dobson.

Assuming that you knew all these facts, how would you tell a friend about what had happened? Would you begin at the beginning and say, "This morning at 8:10 I was walking along Main Street on my way to school. It was so foggy I couldn't see a block away. Suddenly, I heard a loud crash at the intersection of Main Street and Oak Avenue. I ran to the corner and there I saw one car upside down and another crossways in the street. Both were all banged up. In the street there was a young man, and in one of the cars was a girl. Policemen came up and then an ambulance and they took the boy and girl to the hospital. I learned later the boy was dead when they got him to the hospital. The girl had a concussion, a broken right arm and she may have internal injuries. Do you know who the boy is? He's Oscar Greene, our football captain for next year."

You would never tell the news that way. No one would. In your excitement, and even if you weren't excited, you'd go straight to the news. What is the news? The news is that the captain of the high school football team has been killed, and that is what you would tell first. You'd probably say, "Did you hear about the accident? The high school football captain was killed about a half hour ago. Yeah, Oscar Greene. You know where Oak Avenue crosses Main Street? That's where it happened. His car and one driven by his own cousin crashed. Sure, Marilyn Dobson. No, she's not dead, but she's pretty bad off."

In a newspaper you also begin with the news. You won't tell your story as informally as the above account, but you do

go directly to the news in your first paragraph. That's called
the *lead* of your story (pronounced "leed").

A local newspaper reporter might begin his story as
follows:

> Oscar Lee Greene, captain-elect of the Blanktown
> Bulldogs, was killed in an automobile collision at
> Main Street and Oak Avenue shortly after 8 A.M.
> today.

The headline writer might shorten this news even more
by writing:

> B.H.S. Football Captain Killed in Auto Crash

The paragraphs that come after the lead would tell about
Miss Dobson's injuries, identify her as the cousin of the dead
man, fill in details of the accident, and give any eyewitness
accounts of what happened. This is known as the "inverted
pyramid" style of news writing because the most important
thing is told first and then details follow in order of
diminishing importance.

The lead shown above is a WHO lead because it begins
with the name of the principal character in this news event.
Another reporter might begin this same story in the
following manner:

> Power failure in a traffic light and dense fog
> probably caused the death of Blanktown's football
> captain in an automobile collision at Main Street and
> Oak Avenue shortly after 8 A.M. today.

Still a third reporter might write it:

> Blanktown's football captain, Oscar Lee Greene,
> was killed and his cousin, Miss Marilyn Dobson, was
> critically injured when their automobiles collided at
> Main St. and Oak Ave. this morning.

Other reporters might find still different ways for
beginning this tragic story, but all would have one thing in
common. They all would begin with the same news, the death
of the football star. The lead that begins with the power
failure is called a WHY lead because it starts off by telling the
reader why the accident happened.

In every case, the reporter must sift through his notes to
find the news of his story before he begins to write. In order to

find the news he must first know what makes news. That is why, as pointed out in Chapter Two, it is so important for a beginning reporter to develop a keen sense of what is and what is not news.

In the preceding story, if the reporter had begun, "Shortly after 8 A.M. today, Oscar Lee Greene, Blanktown High School's football captain was killed in an automobile accident," you would call it a WHEN lead because the time element came first. But in this case, as in most news events, the time element is relatively unimportant. The reader wants to know what happened and who was involved.

If the reporter had begun with the location of the accident, such as, "At Main St. and Oak Ave. today two automobiles collided and resulted in the death of Blanktown's football captain and serious injury to his cousin," the lead would be a WHERE lead. However, the location, like the time, is relatively unimportant in this story. The place where the accident occurred is of interest to the reader, of course, but first he wants to know what happened and who was involved.

In addition to deciding what is the news, the reporter must also decide how he is going to present it most effectively for his reader. He must decide whether to begin with the WHO or one of the other Ws. Earlier a sixth W was mentioned: the WOW, or human interest element. In the sample story used here, the WOW is the fact that fate brought together two relatives and the resulting death of one of them. This factor might have been more poignant had the principals been a father and a son. This is the sort of thing that people will discuss over and over; therefore, it has wide human interest.

Someone once called the first few words of a lead the "show window" of the lead. He was simply trying to get across the idea that those first eight or ten words are extremely important. In the "show window" you do a lot of things. You tell the news, you catch the reader's attention, and you make it easy for the desk man who must write the headline for your story.

In a story for his own local newspaper the reporter most

often uses WHO or WHAT as the principal item of attraction in his "show window." If he were writing the same story for a nearby large city daily, or for one of the wire services, he would have to think in terms of a larger readership than just the people in his own community. In the local paper the local name is important because the person in the news is known by many persons. In a metropolitan newspaper, or a wire story that goes throughout the state or nation, the name may mean little. People outside of the area will read the story because of its unusualness, or its human interest appeal, or some other factor, if the story does not affect them directly.

Suppose an automobile accident near your city took the lives of three persons, caused serious injury to two more, and left two unhurt. A blowout caused the car to crash into a concrete culvert. The two uninjured persons were a great-grandfather, age ninety-two, and his great-granddaughter, age three. They were the youngest and the oldest persons in the car.

For a nearby metropolitan newspaper with a "state" page (news occurring in a portion of or throughout the state), or for a wire service, the reporter might write:

A 92-year-old man and a 3-year-old girl were the only persons unhurt early today in a freak auto accident that took three lives and caused injuries to two others near Blanktown.

In order to avoid the weak beginning, "A man . . .," the reporter might have written:

Fate spared only the youngest and the oldest in a freak auto accident that caused three deaths and injuries to two persons near Blanktown early today.

For the local paper, the reporter might have written this same story as follows:

Three local persons were killed, two injured and two escaped unhurt when a blowout caused a car to crash into a concrete culvert four miles north of here today.
The dead are:

The word "local" has special significance in this "show window" of the lead since it immediately tells local readers that their own townsmen have been killed. The next thing the reader wants to know is WHO was killed. The names will be given next in the story and may even be used in the headline.

All of this illustrates that "you write with the reader over your shoulder." Thus, good newswriting becomes an art or science, and not just the business of throwing words together.

Don't Be a Slave to the Five Ws

Now that you know about the Five Ws and the inverted pyramid style of writing, don't let them rule every news story you write.

News facts, even though they are extremely important to the reader, can sometimes be dull and dreary. To cast this kind of material into the routine formula of Who, What, When, Where and Why may make it even more dull. Imagination is called for. Take this example:

Two Blanktown men escaped injury early today in a train-car crash that reduced their small sedan to a twisted mass of steel.

George W. Smith and Ralph A. Saunders, employees of the Tower Baking Co., were struck shortly after daylight as they were crossing the Eastern and Western R. R. tracks at State Road 52. The pair was headed for Lake Tocca for a morning of fishing.

The E. & W. freight train was said to be doing 50 miles an hour as it approached the crossing, its whistle blowing and its headlight flashing.

The Blanktown men had their windows closed because of the chilly morning and failed to hear the train coming, they said.

The train struck their car near the back door and carried the wreckage more than 200 yards before coming to a stop. Both men crawled out of the wreckage without a scratch.

"It was some kind of a miracle," said engineer Carl R. Seil.

This story is fairly typical of the Five W approach, but because it has drama built into it, this approach really does not hurt the story. Suppose, however, the writer had decided to use a surprise-ending technique to give the story even more impact. He might have written the story this way:

This morning was a good day to go fishing.

You'll remember how quiet it was around sunrise. Not a breath of air was stirring and a light fog hung over the warm earth, but there was enough of a chill to make a coat feel comfortable.

George W. Smith and Ralph A. Saunders, employees of the Tower Baking Co., Blanktown, were thinking only of the leaping bass at Lake Tocca as they headed north from the city shortly after sunrise. They cranked up the windows on their sedan and settled down to listen to the news on radio.

Farther to the north an Eastern and Western R. R. freight with a load of empty sand cars was approaching its top speed on a long stretch of straight track. The engineer was looking forward to a hot breakfast at Ellenton, where the crew would change.

Smith and Saunders were joking about the "big one that got away" on their last trip to Lake Tocca as they approached the E. & W. crossing at State Road 52.

"Next time you'll use a net," Saunders kidded his friend.

Engineer Carl R. Seil saw the car coming up to the crossing. He gave his whistle all it had and at the same time began applying his brakes. The two men looked up just as they were dead on the center of the crossing and there was the huge locomotive, swathed in fog, its headlight darting back and forth like an angry dragon.

In a few seconds it was all over.

The train struck the sedan near the rear door and swept the twisted steel that remained of the car in a swirling ball of sparks for 200 yards before coming to a screeching stop.

Engineer Seil jumped from his cab and dropped his pipe in the excitement. As he neared the slightly smoking wreckage, he thought, "Poor devils."

And then the miracle happened.

Out of the crumpled metal Saunders and Smith emerged, shaken but unscratched.

You say you can't write the story that way? Why not? You say it's too long, too fancy, takes too much time to get to the news?

Maybe so, but the point is that you should not be a slave to a dull, formalized recital of facts. You've got an obligation to your readers to be interesting and exciting. There will be more on this topic in a later chapter.

The News Peg

A student once wrote on an examination that a *news peg* was a place where the editor hung his hat. While many editors and reporters don't wear hats anymore, the news peg is still important: it is what the reporter hangs his story on.

A journalism professor once told his class that the word *today* is a stumbling block to many stories. Much news can be written without waiting for a time peg, or the "today" angle, he said.

Which is right? Is the time peg important or is it a stumbling block to good reporting and writing? Certainly the professor was right in saying that too many reporters wait for someone to say something or do something before they print a story that was there all the time. The good reporter will go in and get the story. His news peg is not necessarily "today" but possibly the news itself—the thing that has happened or is going to happen, or the situation that exists.

Editors need a reason to print a news story. They must have something to justify placing material in the news pages or in feature columns. This excuse is the news peg on which the story is hung. This can be a ragged, amateurish hanging or an expert job of "stringing up" the facts.

The news peg is almost as hard to define as news itself. Let's take an example:

A bright young reporter came into the newspaper office one day with a story on the history of the county courthouse. He began by saying, "The Blanktown courthouse will be seventy-three years old, come July 27." Then he told how many bricks were in it, how it had grown from a one-room building to its present size, and so forth.

Immediately the editor wanted to know why in the middle of a hot summer he should run a story on the history of the courthouse. The story wasn't tied to an anniversary date. It wasn't tied in with an interview with an Old Timer

who had been reminiscing that day. The plaster wasn't
beginning to crack and fall, endangering lives of courthouse
workers. There was no reason for running the story that
particular day, or any day, for that matter.

If the material about the courthouse is interesting,
however, the good reporter will find a news peg on which to
hang the story. He returns to the most important part of a
reporter's job—asking questions. A question revealed that
the clock in the courthouse steeple, more than fifty years old,
had developed a weakness in its springs. The clock attendant
called it "heart trouble." The reporter now had a news peg for
his story about the courthouse.

With his lead he can now stop people in the middle of a
hot summer and turn their attention briefly to the old county
courthouse and its clock with "heart trouble." He has made
news out of the courthouse. The news peg for a feature story
is easy to develop, since it becomes the angle for the story. In
the case of a *hard news* story the news peg might be more
difficult to develop.

Suppose the city transportation system in your city is out
of date. There are too few buses, the buses are old, and they
run day after day crowded beyond the limits of safety. No
one, however, has publicly complained. No city official has
tried to explain the situation. No one has made a speech
about the need for more and better transportation. There is a
news story here, but your city editor will want a news peg on
which to hang the story. If you wait for some kind of official
action or official word to use as the news peg, you may wait a
long time. By simply observing conditions, the reporter
might come up with this lead:

> Approximately 200 office workers were stranded
> on four downtown street corners Monday as over-
> loaded buses of the City Transportation System
> pulled away without them.
> This happens every day at 5 o'clock when the
> homeward rush begins.

Again, as in the courthouse story, the reporter has called
attention to a news situation that existed all along. He has
given his editor a "today" angle on which to hang the story
by writing about a situation observed that day. It might also

have been possible to turn the story on a series of interviews with local government officials, assuming, of course, they would have been willing to comment on the bus situation.

The Whole Story

Carl E. Lindstrom, former managing editor of the Hartford (Conn.) *Times,* has eloquently discussed news-writing. In an inspiring and beautiful way he has said something that needs to be said on this topic. His remarks, "The Whole Story," first appeared in *Editorially Speaking,* Vol. 10, a publication of the Gannett Group of Newspapers.

It is one of the secrets of craftsmanship that the craftsman is able, before he begins, to see his job in its entirety; the gift of visualizing the end product in its completeness and perfection.

It is one of the faults of our business that we have looked at our product only in its details, mainly in its beginning. The lead of a story, its human appeal perhaps, its interpretative force—these have concerned us—the parts of a story, but not its sum.

Our techniques grew out of competitive pressure, production and distribution problems and mechanical short cuts which we thought were necessary. In the days when these things were invented, reporters learned to tell the story in the first paragraph because the reader was on the run for the 5:15; they gave him a bulletin in 10-point type in order to beat the opposition to the street; they wrote it so that the printer could be an editor and cut the story from the bottom to make it fit.

This technique was established before television, before radio, before films. Times have changed. Horace Greeley is dead and so is personal journalism; Richard Harding Davis would find his style cramped in Korea; the Yellow Kid is buried along with all the other apparatus of the penny press, but your reporters and mine are still writing the kinds of leads that comply with all the rules and regulations of the year 1900.

Just about everything that is wrong with news writing today can be traced to the pyramid lead. In itself it is bad enough with its primitive, out-of-breath, hit-'em-in-the-eye approach. But to its crudity can be traced many other sins: incoherence, inaccuracy, loss of the unities of time and place, poverty of expression and, finally, the story's death through sheer exhaustion and general debility. Most newspaper stories come to an end like a guttering candle finally blown out.

I don't particularly like the term "pyramid lead" because, even though it is standing on its apex, the word pyramid carries the connotation of solidity which the device does not have.

Consider instead, please, the term "jackpot lead." Let me explain: Your reporter hurries back from the scene of an accident, the fire, the carnival or the caucus, and on his way mentally churns up his facts in the business of finding a beginning. Usually he has it by the time he reaches his typewriter, but sometimes, especially if the deadline isn't breathing on his neck, he will sit and ponder, chew a pencil end or chain-smoke. He may make a try or two, ripping out the copy paper and giving it a crumpling toss in the general direction of the waste basket.

Suddenly he has it! The lead—it's done!

The rest is easy. The typewriter pours out a cascade of clattering, clanking facts in a fearful disorder which continues until the last feeble fraction of a datum has been accounted for.

What is this marvelous device? You have pulled some sort of trigger; you have tripped an escapement; you have hit the jackpot and the payoff is at your feet in a glut of disorder; a plethora of confusion followed by a vacuum.

That is the jackpot lead.

To get his lead, your reporter has seized upon the most dramatic detail in a sequence of events which make THE WHOLE STORY. It was not the first incident in the chain, but probably the climax.

By putting it first he immediately dislocates the time element. Sooner or later—usually half way through the story—he begins to tell things chronologically. That makes it necessary for him to repeat the incident which he told first. The reader is confused. He begins to ask what happened first, and what next?

Unity of time and place is frequently disturbed by the requirement that what happens last must be told first. All the sins of the conventional lead are multiplied by the haste with which we pile new lead upon new lead. We feel mistakenly that a fast-breaking story calls for a new top with every edition. The result is often complete incoherence.

If your man is reporting a speech, he selects the most striking statement and leads off with it. He cannot do this without quoting it out of context. This is the most frequent complaint of public speakers; and usually they are right. The reporter looks at you blankly and declares that every word he put in quotation marks was what the man actually said. True enough. But that is being merely accurate. To be merely accurate is not enough. You've got to be correct as to balance, timing and emphasis. A man has a right to have his crucial statement considered against the background which he has prepared for it. If that dramatic statement is hurled at the reader for immediate and headline effect, an injustice has been done the speaker because he has been quoted out of context.

This is the way in which the pyramid lead risks inaccuracy.

Accuracy is not enough. Accuracy is only a poor beginning. What we want is the truth.

Robert Louis Stevenson wrote: "It's possible to avoid falsehood and yet not to tell the truth. . . . Truth to facts is not always truth to sentiment. . . . The cruelest lies are often told in silence. A man may have sat in a room for hours and not opened his teeth and yet come out of that room a disloyal friend and a foul calumniator."

Newspapers do not deliberately sit silent and let falsehood get around through that kind of failure, but some of the results which we tolerate might as well be deliberate since they are just as damaging. When we are concerned only with seizing attention, rather than being informative, we run that risk. The old pyramid lead—the jackpot lead, or whatever you choose to call it—is only an attention seizer; that is its sole purpose. It is written with the calculated risk that the reader will not finish the story, that he will get only half the facts. We have been encouraging him to be satisfied with only half the story. We have been quite philosophical about the circumstance that Americans are a nation of headline readers. I'm afraid we made them what they are.

The newspaper clock must be changed. We haven't any more time than we ever had to put a newspaper together; in fact, we have less. Deadlines have been creeping forward. The problems of production and distribution have been given as the reasons. But lately an overshadowing reason has loomed before us, and that is television. We are told: "You must get into the home before they turn on TV."

With this I do not agree, and that is why I say we must change our clock. Disregarding the mechanics of production and distribution, we must forget that we are producing papers so that "he who runs may read." We must sit down with our reader and seriously claim his attention. We must so capture his interest and hold it that he may even forget to

press the television switch. Certainly it should not be difficult to make him selective. Are we so frustrated as to concede
that the best of the newspaper is less engrossing than the
worst of the TV screen? That is to say that the customer
tosses aside the whole newspaper to accept all of what TV
has to offer. We can at least try to make the newspaper so
interesting and important that the reader finds he has to
check the television program and say: "Only these programs
will I watch, and the rest of the time I must give to my
newspaper, if I am to be an informed and intelligent citizen."

Why should there be a limit on the time the reader spends
over the newspaper, a limit on its pulling power?

That pulling power is in our hands. You will never
increase it if you assume that the reader has so little time for
newspapers that you must pack all the information into the
first paragraph.

That's what radio and television are doing. They are the
bulletin media; they will never be anything else. But they are
beating us to the punch as bulletin media. Once upon a time,
we could win with that technique; we were Johnny-on-the-
spot, first with the news. We flung the news at the man in the
street in flashes and headlines.

You can't stop him on the street any more. He is sitting
at home in a comfortable chair and he's got all the time in the
world to read our story—provided we know how to tell it.

Our reporters have got to learn how to tell a story and
they have got to learn over again every time they sit down to
a typewriter because no two stories are alike. Each has its
own technique—a place to begin and a place to stop. There is
a certain right length to that story, and only one right
length. That length hasn't anything to do with the space left
in the page dummy you're working on.

The power of the picture has us a bit frightened. We
repeat that Chinese adage about the picture being worth a
thousand words. The image which both speaks and moves
has us paralyzed.

But the writer can lick that competition. If he knows his
business he can put wings on words that will outfly them all.
A single phrase will do it.

Pete Wellington of the *Kansas City Star* sent me a story
about a heart operation. Incidentally, the operation was
televised. The *Star's* story was clinical in its detail of surgi-
cally entering the thorax, handling the heart, placing first
one finger and then two in one of the valves, descriptions of
regurgitation of blood and of surgery inside the heart.

"I now have my finger deep in the heart; see, the heart
doesn't mind," said Dr. Bailey.

The phrase, "See, the heart doesn't mind," was so

reassuring as to make the whole story easily acceptable.

What a contrast we have here between the picture and the written word! The written word of the news artist can be not only more graphic, but infinitely more subtle. I didn't see this operation on TV and I don't know whether any of you did, but you can just imagine men in white, fearfully masked, probing in human flesh with rubber gloves and terrifying, gleaming instruments, all the more terrifying if you could only half see. That picture is unable to say: "See, the heart doesn't mind."

I have called the news writer an artist. We shouldn't scout the word artist. In its simplest terms, art is the business of selecting for effect—plus skill. You can't pick out a necktie or a piece of furniture for your home without exercising the faculty of selection—plus a degree of skill. If there is sufficient skill, you have taste.

The writer is constantly involved with the necessity of selection with skill. In [the] simplest event he is confronted with an infinite amount of detail. For tools he has only his vocabulary. He is the creative manipulator of the most plastic, the most resistant, the most mercurial and yet the stickiest substance known to man—the written word.

If you will agree that the writer is an artist, let's see where that takes us. He must immediately confront himself with certain self-imposed requirements which every artist faces, and weigh them carefully before he begins his work. The playwright has got to make up his mind whether his germ idea is a musical comedy or a social drama; the fiction writer is sunk if he tries to inflate a short story idea into a novel, and the other way around, too.

So, when your reporter sits down to his typewriter he ought to have decided upon the mood, the tone, the temper of his story; he ought to have a better idea of its length than the city editor or the copy desk; and—this is important—he ought to have just as definite ideas about the last paragraph as he had about the lead.

The lead has been a mental hazard. Its sole function really is to get the reader to the second paragraph; the only excuse for a second paragraph is to lure the reader into the third. If the writer can't get the reader to the last paragraph he is an incompetent workman and you would not, of course, call him an artist.

Recently I had a long and interesting conversation with Virgil Thompson on the principles governing critical writing. Among other things he said: "The reviewer shouldn't try to use a lot of different adjectives meaning *good*. Usually they don't mean what the writer thinks they mean. *Superb* means vainglorious; *magnificent* means extravagant or lavish; *splendid* means shiny or showy; *sumptuous* implies costliness; *sublime* means elevating or lofty. Let's put our Latin to use."

Discovering distinctions between words is one of the most stimulating experiences I know. Encourage your reporters to find them. See to it that they wear out the office dictionary. If you don't have to buy a new copy once in six months, it is being neglected. Ours is lasting much too well.

The term "good writing" does not apply only to feature writing, the extraordinary story, the big dramatic break that comes only once a year or once in a lifetime. It applies to the daily chore.

Your average reporter classifies the newspaper job in terms of black and white. Everything is either an opportunity for "swell" writing or routine. His routine is likely to be unmitigated routine—deadpan, get-it-over-with-as-quickly-as-possible routine.

It is in this area that he makes most of his mistakes. He will rewrite a clipping, errors and all, without checking. He will forget there is such a thing as the city directory. He will assume that the handout is correct and complete.

But when the old fire horse smells smoke, he is off at a gallop. He is an alert and prideful reporter. He goes dramatic—yes, sometimes even emotional. He indulges in corn because he knows that the public has a great appetite for corn.

I can support that with experience on our own newspaper. We have a requirement that a local human interest story must be provided for page one every day. We like this feature and know it has attracted wide readership. We know that some of these stories are better than others. We know that some have been gems; others, pure corn. Once in a while I run a temperature when the corn gets too bad, and [I] criticize sharply. Then the rug is pulled out from under me because the story I criticized always gets the widest public response.

I don't think that justifies indulging the very bad habit of writing down to people. These manifestations of an appetite for the phony human interest, for the verbal cliches, are the fault of the corn merchants among whom we may be counted. We may have created the taste for it. Corn begets cliches. Good writing is poisoned by cliche on the cob.

I am not satisfied with obituary reporting or, better said, with obituary writing, because when a man dies there is usually too little reporting done. We make a dive for the morgue, the clip file, the reference library, or, at most, talk with the undertaker.

The trouble with most obituaries is that they show signs

of rigor mortis before the copy comes out of the typewriter. You seldom read one that brings home the realization that the body under discussion has just stopped being a warm, breathing person.

By way of illustration: The name of Constant Lambert may not mean a great deal to us because he was, after all, a specialist, a London critic and composer. The Associated Press report of his death at the age of forty-five gave all the vital statistics and other routine data which might have fit a college professor or a railroad crossing tender. You might say that he was laid away in a ready-made suit of verbal grave clothes.

The story didn't suit me and I suggested that the obit editor refer to the *New York Times* and the *Herald Tribune*. I confess that we lifted some of the details found there. Here was one, for example: Lambert was deaf in his right ear, but was fond of saying, "I hear music easily. It is only as far as conversation is concerned that deafness affects me."

One of the news weeklies said Lambert was a "big man physically, with broad shoulders, a fleshy body and a brow-profile of Churchillian expanse."

That quotation from Lambert himself and these other little details were brush strokes toward the making of a portrait. In the obit department we need more portraits and fewer cadavers.

E. M. Forster talks of the novelist's use of what he calls round characters versus flat characters. "A round character," he says "has the incalculability of life about him. The really flat character can be expressed in a single sentence such as 'I will never desert Mr. Micawber.' There is Mrs. Micawber—she says she won't desert Mr. Micawber, she doesn't and there she is." Thus Forster.

The news writer's problem is no different, except that most of his flat characters are flat because he made them so. I can't recall ever having seen a reporter venture farther into portraiture than to name the color of a man's eyes or to refer to a woman's smile. If that's as far as he is able to go, they still are cardboard people, the dramatis personae of the newspaper puppet show.

The reporter somehow never sees a man shake the ashes off his cigar, or toy with his Phi Beta Kappa key, or even clear his throat. A hem or a haw can be a very significant punctuation mark. I have rarely seen a woman quoted verbatim and yet when a woman speaks she usually completes her sentences, rarely makes a fool of herself, and somehow manages to get her personality into the syntax. Look at Oilboat Olga.

Although most accounts referred to her quaint accent, all quoted her in conventional newspaper rhetoric. Three wire services used some variant of this deadpan identification: "A woman who said she had been nicknamed Oilboat Olga."

Newsweek quoted her: "I am having lately a nickname. I am called Oilboat Olga."

When the senators asked her if she knew with whom she was dealing in the boat business, *Newsweek* said this was her answer: "I just, after I met, or in between, or in before, whenever I met Mr. Wei, or Mr. Du, or Dr. Chen, or whatever the names of these distinguished Chinese gentlemen are, it was none of my worries to worry about them."

That sentence doesn't quite parse, but I think you'll agree that the lady got her personality into the syntax.

You can do things with an obituary, but you'd better not try to pretty up a wedding. It is God's truth that all brides are beautiful and your society editor is too smart to hit you over the head with that kind of platitude. She probably knows why women cry at weddings but she won't try to tell because it probably would be laughable in printer's ink. No, your writer can make a real person out of the funeral's guest of honor, but you've got to tell the wedding story straight. It will have to be embalmed in the language of the Juliet cap and the illusion veil, stephanotis and Lohengrin.

Is this routine? Not at all. It is formalism, but it is the formalism of the lace valentine. These things have no existance in any other form.

Alexander Woollcott was fond of quoting a reporter who said: "I counted it a high honor to belong to a profession in which the good men write every paragraph, every sentence, every line as lovingly as any Addison or Steele, and do so in the full regard that by tomorrow it will have been burned or used, if at all, to line a shelf."

There may be much less shelf lining than you think. Clippings of births, marriages, and deaths automatically go into the family Bible—or its modern equivalent. But there is a whole lot more clipping of newspaper items than that. I am astonished at the people I see at lunch or elsewhere who open a billfold and pull out clippings. They're not all comic ones about typographical errors either. They are stories that the reader liked and that he passed on with the words, "Don't forget; I want that back!"

Newspaper stories live longer than you think.

Let us try to lift the whole business out of routine. Routine doesn't exist; it is created. Routine is the rubbish and the litter of untidy, unimaginative minds. It is what you get

when a man stops thinking after he's got the lead on paper.
Thinking through—through to the end—that's the whole story.

Questions for Discussion

1. Should the newspaper do away with Five W writing altogether? Why or why not?
2. Explain what is meant by the "chronological order" approach in news writing. Why is chronological order not used all the time in newswriting?
3. Why is the surprise ending approach not used more in news or feature writing? Explain your answer.
4. What is wrong with the "inverted pyramid" form of newswriting? Do you think this is a good way to write the news?
5. Do you agree with Carl Lindstrom that the reporter should try to visualize the whole story before he begins to write? Explain your answer.

5 helping the reader understand

To write with clarity and understanding is a primary responsibility of every writer. He should use all of the devices that help the reader understand. This responsibility is especially important in newswriting because news consumers almost habitually read between the lines, misinterpret the meaning of a news story, or "half read" a story. True and precise communication between newswriter and reader is hard at best, and if the story is poorly organized, poorly written, and factually poverty-stricken, it allows, and even encourages, the reader to "half read," or read between the lines. Thus, the reader will be poorly served.

This chapter discusses a number of stylistic devices that will give the reader a clearer understanding of a story.

Signposts for the Reader

In almost every news story the characters must be *identified,* the *authority* for the news must be given, and statements often must be qualified. These are the most important signposts that guide a reader through a news or feature story.

Identification. News characters must be identified early and accurately in a news story. For example, to say "John Jones was killed in an automobile accident early today" is of little help to the reader unless John Jones is identified. There may be twenty or thirty John Joneses in the area and the reader wants to know which one was killed. How does the reporter make specific identification? He can use one or more of the following "tags":

ADDRESS — *John Jones, 2020 West Third Street.*

OCCUPATION — *John Jones, salesman for the Columbia Bakery.*

TITLE — *John Jones, Mayor of Blanktown.*

ASSOCIATION WITH A KNOWN PERSON— *John Jones, son of the mayor of Blanktown.*

RECENT APPEARANCE IN THE NEWS—*John Jones, recipient two weeks ago of the "Citizen of the Year Award" in Blanktown.*

AGE — *John Jones, 22.*

DEEDS — *John Jones, who kicked a field goal in the final seconds of the Blanktown-Oak Hill football game last Saturday, winning the game for Blanktown.*

REPUTATION — *John Jones, a front runner for the Democratic presidential nomination.*

PHYSICAL CHARACTERISTICS— *John Jones, a lean, graying lawyer from Richmond, Va.*

AREA — *John Jones, a young Blanktown man.*

There are a number of things to remember about identification.

(a) Do not run a great many identifying tags together: John Jones, 22, who lives at 2020 West Third Street, a salesman for the Columbia Bakery here and who also is the son of the mayor of Blanktown, died today in an automobile accident. Spread the identification throughout the story to give variety to paragraph beginnings.

(b) In the lead identify the news characters for the greatest number of readers. Supose a reporter in Moscow wrote:

MOSCOW—Rudolf Abel, a resident of Moscow, died of lung cancer at the age of 68, informed sources reported today.

Identifying Abel merely as a "resident of Moscow" would mean nothing to the average American reader. Most American newspapers probably would not carry the story. But suppose the reporter began his story this way:

MOSCOW—Rudolf Abel, at one time the top Soviet

spy in the United States, has died of lung cancer at the age of 68, informed sources reported today.

(c)   When identification is more important than the name of a person, use the identification first:

> A Blanktown Retail Federation spokesman recently said the Cost of Living Council has extended the deadline for businessmen to make available lists of ceiling prices for the products and services they sell.
> William A. Powers, executive vice president for the federation, said . . .

(d)   Do not identify a person by his religion, his race, or any other "tag" unless the identification is essential to the story and aids readers in identifying the news character. The following is an example of irrelevant identification:

> A Blanktown Quaker and Dogwood Junior College student convicted last month of a failure to register for the draft was given a suspended sentence with four years probation this morning here in Federal District Court.
> George Andrew Sloan, 18, was given the probation, etc.

(e)   Identification should be accurate and fair. It is bad reporting to call a man a "prominent businessman" when, in fact, he is the owner of a little-known tire shop. To call a kidnapped girl a "beautiful blonde" when, in fact, she is a rather average-looking, light-haired girl is inaccurate. To label a small-time gambler a "bolita king" may be inaccurate and unfair and it may make it more difficult for him to receive a fair trial. The point here is that a reporter should not use identifications to color a story, to make it more readable, unless the identifications are true and accurate.

Authority. Letting the reader know how authoritative the news is by telling him "who said it" or exactly where the reporter obtained his facts is important in helping the reader to understand what he reads. The source, or authority, for the news is indicated in news stories in the following manner:

> *President Blank* ordered armed government guards aboard U. S. based airlines. . . . *In a special statement,* Blank said . . .

> Israel charged for the first time Friday that

Soviet-manned SAM3 missiles had. . . . *An Israeli military spokesman* said . . .

General Motors will be struck at midnight Monday unless its $1.9-billion wage increase offer to the United Auto Workers Union (UAW) is raised, a *UAW official* said Friday.

An explosion ripped through the U. S. Destroyer "Lloyd Thomas" Friday while she was firing off the South Vietnam coast in support of Australian ground troops 45 miles southeast of Saigon, *the Navy announced* in Saigon. *A spokesman* said the explosion . . .

It is not always necessary to give the authority in the lead, or even in an early paragraph, if the source of the news is clear to the reader. Take this weather bureau story, for example:

BROWNSVILLE, Tex.—Hurricane Ella veered away from Texas Friday and pushed its 100 mile an hour winds toward the barren east shores of Mexico.

The storm shifted to a westward path in the Gulf of Mexico that would swirl its gale winds, torrential rain, and high tides ashore from 50 to 100 miles south of the Rio Grande during the night.

The reader assumes that this must be a report from the U. S. Weather Bureau. Finally, in the seventh paragraph of the story the authority for the news is given.

The center should move inland 50 to 100 miles south of Brownsville before midnight, *the U. S. Weather Bureau* said.

The reporter should follow certain rules in citing authority, in order to help the reader:

1. In any news or feature story where there is any chance at all that the reader will be uncertain about the source of the news, the source should be stated early in the story and described as specifically as possible.

Mayor Greene said today. . .
The White House is declining to answer . . .
Peter Flanigan, a Nixon assistant, said . . .
In Beirut, Lebanon, the guerrillas' Central Committee reported . . .

A Sixth Fleet spokesman declined Friday to . . .
In a broadcast heard throughout the
Mideast . . .
Chief of Police Robert A. Jones said . . .

2. Reporters should attempt to attribute news to a specific
   individual or individuals.
3. When it is impossible to name an individual as the source
   of the news, use the most specific source possible, such as:

A school board report indicated . . .
School board members said . . .
A spokesman for the Mayor said . . .
Police officials stated . . .

More and more reporters are questioning the practice of
allowing news sources to hide behind titles of this type,
however.

4. Authority for the news should be cited often enough
   within the body of the story to prevent the reader from
   becoming confused. At every point in the story where it is
   possible for the reader to doubt the source of the news,
   authority should be cited. In the following story,
   authority is given only a few times, but it is clear to the
   reader that the news comes from an official source.

WASHINGTON—Next time you get on an airplane, take a close look at the fellow next to you
reading *Playboy*. He may be one of President——'s
new force of armed guards, aimed at halting air
piracy.
The new guards will not be in uniform—and the
program is planned so passengers won't be able to
tell whether there is a guard aboard a plane where
they are riding. Many details of the program are
intentionally being kept secret in the hope that they
may make the program more effective.
The idea is that potential hijackers won't be able
to tell whether there are guards around or not.
The number of guards planned has not been
disclosed, nor has the cost of the program.
The White House is declining to answer any
questions beyond its *formal statement* that announced the plan's rough outline.
It is clear, however, that the *government* does
mean business.

Eventually as many as 4,000 guards may be used in domestic and international flights. The program is aimed at halting domestic hijackings to Cuba and international hijackings in the Middle East or anywhere else.

As a passenger, *officials say,* you don't have to worry about a jet's cabin losing its air pressure at high altitude if a shot should be fired.

Peter Flanigan, a presidential assistant, said, "A bullet can go through the skin of an airplane without a serious fall in pressure."

Qualification. Since reporters get most of their news from someone else, or from some record, without firsthand knowledge, it is necessary for them to qualify certain statements. The reporter is saying to his reader, "This is what the man said. I don't know whether it is true or not, but this is what he said." The simple use of the words *he said* is a form of qualification.

Positive identification of victims of an accident is not always possible. In many cases police refuse to give out names until the next of kin have been notified—this must be explained. If identification was made from a billfold, this should be explained. If police use the name given by a person placed under arrest and there is doubt about the name, say "the police arrested a man *who gave his* name as Joe Blow," or you could say *"the police record showed* the arrested man's name was Joe Blow."

Reporters often use *protective wording* to qualify news reports. They report that an "alleged kidnapper" made certain statements in his own defense. This is better than calling the man a kidnapper before he has been tried and convicted of the crime. Perhaps a jury will find him innocent. While protective wording does not preclude a libel suit, it does show good intent. If the newspaper is sued for libel, it would be hard for the complainant to prove malice. Other forms of protective wording include "it was reported," "the record showed," "police said," and "according to."

Another signpost that the reporter should handle with care is *time.* When identifying the time of a news event, the reporter must always consider the moment a reader will actually be holding the newspaper in his hands. If you report that an event took place "yesterday" or that it will take place "tomorrow," you may force the reader to look at the date on the newspaper in order to orient himself in time. If your story appears in a newspaper published on Tuesday, say that the event occurred Monday or that it will take place Wednesday. If the event occurred on the day of publication and you are able to get it in the newspaper that day, say the event occurred "today."

In the following leads from a newspaper published on a Tuesday, note how time is handled:

Tropical storm Laura stalled in the Caribbean Sea *today* and stood south of the Cuban coast, lashing the island with gale winds and heavy downpours. The prolonged rains brought a threat of flooding.

The body of a girl—thought to be former Oak Hill Junior College coed Sara Anne Greene—was found *Monday* afternoon near Douglasville, Ga.

Economist Herbert Greene from the University of the East will speak at Blanktown University *Thursday* night.

Bennett Newt, a Blanktown University freshman from New Jersey, was found dead in his Smithfield area dormitory, room 350, *this morning*.

Every reporter should keep in mind the "newspaper week." The newspaper week is that period in which you can identify a news occurrence by the day of the week rather than the date on the calendar. The usual rule is that if the event occurred more than a week prior to the date of the publication of the newspaper, the date should be used rather than the day of the week. If the event is going to occur a week after the date of the publication, you should use the date rather than the day of the week. The idea is to keep the identification clear and simple for the reader. For example, if you are holding in your hand a newspaper published on a Tuesday, the identifications of time should be as follows:

The accident occurred today (meaning Tuesday).

The camera club will meet Wednesday (meaning tomorrow).

The football team will return Sunday (meaning this coming Sunday).

The election will be held Monday (meaning this coming Monday).

The movie is scheduled to be shown next Tuesday (meaning a week from today).

The commission voted against the ordinance Monday night (meaning last night).

The convict was re-captured Sunday (meaning last Sunday) but he was not brought back to Blankville until today.

In every case, if you feel there may be doubt in the reader's mind about the day of the event, use the date. For example, in a story of the disappearance of a teenager, say "The girl disappeared July 15" (not "last Friday") if there is any doubt about the day of the week.

Sometimes the action is still going on when the reader holds the newspaper in his hand. In these cases the leads indicate continuation of the action, as follows:

The House is 350 to 5 for one plan of attack on cancer, the Senate is 79 to 1 for another, the President's blessing is on both, and a compromise seeker hopes to settle the dispute by Christmas.

Applications are still being accepted for a new job as executive assistant to Mayor Arthur Brown. The mayor said he hoped the position, created by the City Commission two months ago, would be filled by the first of the year.

Confidential Justice Department reports say a Hong Kong-based seamen's union is slipping Chinese Communists into the United States on espionage missions.

European and Japanese manufacturers are designing a $400 automobile that can be thrown away in a year, *Europa* magazine reported today.

How do you handle time in a story of a news event that will take place between your press time and the moment the reader will read the story? Suppose your newspaper goes to press at 2 P.M., the event is scheduled for 3 P.M., but the reader won't be reading your newspaper until 5 or 6 P.M. Most newspapers solve this problem by saying that the event "was scheduled to be held" rather than "will be held" or "was held." You can also solve this problem by "writing around" the time element, such as:

Hundreds of telegrams were pouring into Blank-town today, congratulating city officials on the opening of the new 10 million dollar jetport here.

More than 20 prominent national and state government officials, headed by Governor George A. Peters, arrived in the city last night to be on hand for the official ribbon-cutting ceremony at 3 P.M., today . . .

Making Your Newspaper Easier to Read

A few years ago, the circulation manager of the *Christian Science Monitor* put together twenty-six ways in which newspapers could be published for easier reading. His advice is still useful today. Here is the way he explained his twenty-six points:

Do you know which books have had the biggest circulation, and why? They're an amazing assortment. Yet, if you'll study them carefully you'll find they have one thing in common. They are all easy reading. Every one of them is easier to read—much easier to read—than the average daily newspaper.

Books that have had the largest circulation in the United States are the Bible, the Sears Roebuck catalog, "McGuffey's Reader," and the Boy Scout Manual.

If, overnight, newspapers became as easy to read as the Bible or Sears' catalog, you'd see tremendous changes in subscribers' reading habits.

Newspapers have an obligation to such readers. It is vital to a free press that newspapers make easy reading out of great and complex issues. It is sound public service to make news and editorials so easy to read that they compete adequately with pictures and comics for reader attention.

For easy, simple handling, I give you 26 points under subheadings:

What kinds of *words* do you use?
How forceful are your *phrases*?
How effective are your *sentences*?
Do you put power into your *paragraphs*?
Will your whole piece of copy *do its job*?

Some of the twenty-six points are simple, obvious, trite. You know them and use them. Others may tax all the skill of an Assistant Publisher in Charge of Easy Reading. Each point may expose confusion you never dreamed of.

1. *Use short simple words.* This is old stuff, you may say. But do you actually test various levels of your writing on this point? You may have a surprise in store. Take 100-word samples. Count the syllables in each hundred words. For easy reading, samples should average 135 to 145 syllables per hundred words. If samples run over 150 syllables per hundred words, look out. If they run over 165 syllables per hundred words, you are writing for college graduates. After a few "case studies" put this first point to work. Adapt it to your specific need. Put it into operation in resourceful, new ways.

2. *Use more one-syllable words.* Make them your work-horse words. Make them carry the biggest load. Use one-syllable words to cut down your over-all syllable count. Why write "agricultural-outbuilding" when you can say "barn"? Out of 267 words in Lincoln's Gettysburg address, 196 are of one syllable. More than two hundred are of Anglo-Saxon origin.

3. *Use familiar words.* Test samples of your various writers on this point. . . . As a business executive, your vocabulary is probably much larger than the average. It is probably larger than you realize. It may be upwards of fifty thousand words. But remember that your average reader's vocabulary is less than ten thousand words. The Bible uses a vocabulary of only six thousand words.

4. *Use personal words.* Use plenty of personal words. Dull, drab stories come to life when you sprinkle in a generous supply of personal words. Use in abundance such words as you, girl, mother, policeman, waitress, Joe, baby, wife, Susie.

5. *Use concrete words.* The most dignified writing needs zest, color, reader interest. Even on the financial page, in routine hearings, in annual reports to stockholders, use words that make the reader see, hear, feel, smell, or taste. Test your writers for concrete images and vivid word pictures.

6. *Make every word work.* Use fewer words. Use them with greater force. In radio or television, advertisers invest $100, $1,000 or $5,000 for each word in a commercial. They hire copy experts to choose these words. Yet undisciplined writers in other departments may write gobbledygook that costs those same companies more than their whole advertising budget. You will find a simple test convincing. Go through today's writing in your newspaper. Cross out every

Activity

unnecessary word, confusing phrase, garbled sentence, involved paragraph. On every level of your writing, the result will amaze you.

7. *Avoid technical words.* Every business has its own jargon. Different departments in the same business may have a language all their own. The technical language of the financial page. The slang of the sports page. The lingo of politics. These may be crystal clear to the user or the devotee of that page. Yet they utterly confuse the average reader. Nontechnical words are clearer. They are more familiar. They will build a broader base of readership for your financial page, your political copy, perhaps even for your sports and women's pages.

8. *Get rid of rubber stamp phrases.* Both business and newspaper writers have built up a gobbledygook of worthless cliches, worn-out phrases. Many are meaningless, dull, disgusting. Get rid of trite phrases on every level. Spot checks will show where you could stress training on this point.

9. *Put sparkle and freshness into phrases.* Give old phrases a new twist. Use concrete, specific phrases that convey word pictures. Use phrases that will help your readers see, feel, and believe.

Activity Fun

10. *Create figures of speech.* Encourage your writers to work up a storehouse of colorful new phrases. Build them into everyday writing. Feed new ones in, as old ones wear out. This is a job that requires skill. It's a job for that Assistant Publisher in Charge of Easy Reading.

11. *Use intimate phrases.* Use them in all kinds of writing. Work with those simple phrases you use at your breakfast table, with intimate friends, on the golf course. Soon you'll see how absurd it is to use dull, worn-out phrases that have lost their meaning.

12. *Use short sentences.* They are the life-blood of simple, easy-to-read writing. Try to keep average sentence length at fourteen words. Short sentences do not confuse. If a sentence runs upwards of thirty words, break it up. Make two or three sentences out of it. Variety in sentence length is good. Even an occasional sentence of thirty-five to forty words is all right. But keep the average down to fourteen if you want simple, easy reading. This takes discipline but it is worth it. Test samples of writing at every level. You'll quickly see the need for training at this point.

13. *Make frequent use of very short sentences.* Even one-word sentences are good. They're forceful. Emphatic. Arresting. In your training program, this is an easy point to put over.

14. *Use short sentences as an aid to clear thinking.* The

short, simple sentence is a working tool to help tell the difficult, complex story. In editorial writing it helps define a problem, understand it, solve it. Use short sentences to get rid of fuzzy, confused thinking.

15. *Make sentences active.* Use active verbs. Put a taboo on passives. Passives bog the reader down. They put action into reverse. I wrote this without using a single passive. With a little discipline, every writer can quit using this weak, indirect verb form. The Twenty-third Psalm and the Ninety-first Psalm are good examples of pure active verb forms.

16. *Use short simple paragraphs.* Test paragraph length just as you test sentence length. For easy newspaper reading, paragraphs should average no more than forty-two words.

17. *Use very short paragraphs for variety and emphasis.* Use long paragraphs when necessary, but use very short ones to break monotony and cut down word count.

18. *Use one-idea paragraphs.* Test sample paragraphs. Is each one built around a single idea? Can you sum up the content of each paragraph in a single phrase or sentence? Several ideas in one paragraph confuse the reader.

19. *Use one-viewpoint paragraphs.* Here, again, you can test samples. See if each paragraph sticks to one viewpoint. Note the confusion of a paragraph that opens with the "we" viewpoint, shifts to "you," then winds up with "they." Here, the editorial writer or the business correspondent is perhaps the greatest offender.

20. *Use paragraphs for action, impact, and result.* The points of greatest emphasis in a paragraph are the beginning and the end. Watch the words with which you close it. Do opening and closing words in each paragraph get over the full force of fact, emotion, or idea?

21. *Write for a specific purpose.* In simple news stories, as in features, reports and memoranda, is a writer always sure he knows just why he is writing? Whether any reader will care? Does he have a specific object in mind? A reason why? Or does he just follow a routine? Here, again, test every level of your writing. One large company used this simple test and found that more than half of all business writing was without a specific purpose. Savings on this point alone were tremendous. Are you sure that all print interests at least twenty-five percent of your readers? If not, question its value in the face of present newsprint pressures.

22. *Write to one person, one human being.* Write every story or feature as if you were talking to one man, to one

woman, to one child. Picture this one person sitting right beside you. Perhaps the reporter can learn something from the advertising copywriter in this respect. An expert copywriter talks to millions in the mass market, yet he writes to, and thinks about, one individual as if he were Uncle Elbert, or Aunt Mamie, or an old-maidish sister. Suppose you are a business or a financial writer. Talking face to face, would you say, "contingent upon the amalgamation of the subsidiary organizations. . . . "? It would be great fun to go back to a police beat and try out some of the things I have picked up through the years as a copywriter.

23.   *Talk to that person right where he is.* Talk to him at his workbench. Behind his mahogany desk. At a lunch counter. Over the washing machine. In the garden. Talk to him in his own language, in words he uses every day.

24.   *Talk to that person in his own field of knowledge.* You may know all about the subject, but does the reader? Probably not. You suppose that he knows as much about it as you do. You suppose too much. You might call this the "supposing" or "presumptive" point of weakness in writing. Do you fumble for facts because you overestimate your reader's knowledge of the subject? Take too much for granted?

25.   *Work with one basic idea.* Cover many points in a whole piece of writing but build them on the framework or skeleton of one idea. "One idea treatment" perhaps can make a complex subject easy to read about. Test whole pieces of business writing for their "one idea appeal." Can the reader grasp one single idea right at the start? Or will he flounder through a hodgepodge of several ideas, not sure which is the most vital?

26.   *Write with one viewpoint.* Shifts in viewpoint are confusing. You can do almost every kind of writing from one viewpoint or stance. With a little self-discipline, a writer can think and write almost everything from a single viewpoint. It is important, too, to keep one viewpoint in every "no" situation. The adjustment unit of a large company has proved this. In answering hundreds of complaint letters each day, its policy is "Always find the 'yes' way to say 'no'." All its letters are also from the "you" viewpoint.

Checking the Facts

Of all the lessons learned by the reporter the necessity for checking facts is first in importance. An incorrect story is of no use to a newspaper and may often get the newspaper into serious difficulty. Fact checking should become an automatic, hard-and-fast habit of every reporter. He should never rely on his memory, never take for granted the spelling of a name "because it sounded that way," never assume that spellings of names and facts are correct because they came from a public official. Look the names up in the city directory or the telephone directory. This will only take a minute, and it will help establish your newspaper as one that believes in accuracy.

Here is a short list of reference sources that may be helpful:

(a) City directory or telephone directory for checking names and addresses, business titles, and government agencies.

(b) Your own state yearbook (if your state has one) for checking names of state legislators, rosters of state departments, commissions and boards, and many other facts about your state.

(c) An up-to-date world atlas for checking names of cities, towns, rivers, mountains, and other geographical facts throughout the world.

(d) An up-to-date almanac for checking sports records, vital statistics, disasters, weather data, and thousands of other facts that have become a matter of record somewhere.

(e) *Who's Who in America* (also the regional *Who's Who* books for various professions) for checking biographical facts about important people.

(f) State and county histories for checking historical facts about your area.

(g) A good unabridged dictionary for checking word meanings and spelling.

(h) A good condensed encyclopedia for checking facts about almost anything and for providing background information.

The good reporter makes constant use of back issues of his newspaper, or morgue clippings where available. Previous stories help him fill in background information as well as check his facts.

One of the most important sources for checking facts is the public library. Unfortunately, this is a source often neglected by newspaper reporters. If they feel that they do not have time for research and checking facts, they are badly mistaken. They do not have time *not* to do it. Most public libraries, in addition to being sources of background information and facts, will provide the alert reporter with one or more news or feature stories each week. The public library, like the welfare office, serves as a kind of barometer of the social, cultural, and even economic climate of the community. Librarians in large cities report that newspaper reporters are among their best customers. Reporters in small cities and towns would do well to become better acquainted with the facilities, news and feature possibilities, and the routine of their local public library.

Errors in fact often result from one or more of the following:

(a)   The reporters' attempt to "blow up" a small story into a big one.

(b)   Failure by the reporter to interview all persons involved in an event.

(c)   A tendency by the reporter to accept dates and events from the memory of people rather than to check them in printed records.

(d)   A tendency by the reporter to use facts and quotes that develop the story he *wants* rather than the accurate one.

(e)   The reporter's own ignorance. This covers a multitude of sins. It may involve his ignorance of the community, of local government, or of some special area he is reporting.

(f)   Failure by the reporter to recognize deliberately false information from an interviewee.

(g)   A tendency on the part of everyone to jump at conclusions before all the evidence is in. A reporter should recognize this human weakness and strive to avoid it himself.

(h)   Incorrectly copying facts and figures from public records. This is an easy thing to do, and the reporter should double-check his notes against the record.

(i)   Using material "out of context," giving an incorrect impression.

Following the Style Sheet

Your newspaper's *style sheet* should be your guide for the "mechanics" of your writing. It gives your newspaper's preferences for the handling of names and addresses and use of capitalization. It also tells you which numbers should be written out and which should be in numeral form, and it explains how the newspaper wants you to handle punctuation marks. The style sheet has nothing at all to do with writing style.

If everyone learned exactly the same stylistic rules in school, it might not be necessary for a newspaper to have a style sheet. The style sheet is designed to assure consistency in the columns of the newspaper. This has two important effects. First, it makes for easier reading; second, it saves the newspaper money. If all reporters on the newspaper write an address "840 N. W. 20th St.," according to the style of the newspaper, the printers will always set it that way and thus save valuable *white space*. The readers will get in the habit of seeing the address that way and they will quickly get the meaning. If the newspaper is a jumble of miscellaneous mechanical styles, the reader's mind has to jump around, making various kinds of judgments and interpretations to clarify meaning. This is another obstacle between the reader and the meaning intended by the writer—one that stylistic consistency will help eliminate.

Not much can be said about mechanical style and the use of the style sheet. You memorize your newspaper's style and follow it. It is as simple as that. You need not argue that one style is right and another wrong. In the sentence "The speech will take place in the Alachua County Court House," some newspapers would capitalize only Alachua while others would capitalize County Court House as well. This is not a question of one style being right and the other wrong. It is simply a matter of which style a particular newspaper has decided to use.

"Newspaper English" and Style

What are the characteristics of newspaper style, the things that make newspaper writing different from magazine, radio, or television writing, from a business letter or an advertisement? Sometimes there is little difference. Present-day writers for the mass media have come up with a kind of universal style that involves language less ornate than that used during the early part of the century, language that is crisp, colorful, and concise. The major difference between much radio and television news and newspaper news today lies in the mechanics of appealing to the ear instead of the eye, or to the ear and the eye at the same time instead of to the eye only.

Someone has laughingly referred to newspaper stories as "business letters with a firecracker in every paragraph." What they mean, of course, is the tendency to use the precise language of business letters while jolting you with the human interest or the emotional impact of a situation.

Historically, there has developed a *newspaper style*. It is based on the inverted pyramid form of writing rather than the chronological form, discussed earlier. The inverted pyramid developed for two reasons. In the early days of the telegraph, if the last part of a story failed to get through the wires, not much was lost. Second, in the newspaper backshop, if the printer did not have room for the final paragraph or two of a news story, he could throw them out and the reader lost little of the story. This is still true today and it will still be true to some extent in the future when newspapers are making full use of new technological devices for producing a newspaper.

In addition to the inverted pyramid structure, other elements of newspaper style are:

(a) Use of concrete words instead of general words—for example, write, "Five thousand persons attended the rally," instead of "A large crowd attended the rally."

(b) Making one word do the work of several when it is at all possible—for example, write, "The accident occurred at University Avenue and Thirteenth Street," instead of "The accident occurred at the corner of University Avenue and Thirteenth Street."

(c)   Care not to editorialize in a news story. This means the writer never gives his own opinion of the news or of the people that make it.

(d)   Use of the impersonal point of view. The writer is an observer of life, not one of the actors. Seldom is the word "I" used. The reader is not interested in reporter Jones and his opinions, but in the story that Jones has to tell.

(e)   Use of Anglo-Saxon root words instead of Latin root words—for example, *fire* instead of *conflagration, light* instead of *illumination.*

(f)   Liberal use of attributives—words and phrases that tell who said what—for example, "The contract isn't worth the paper it's written on," the judge said.

(g)   Use of qualifying words and phrases, to report as specifically as possible—for example, write, "John Jones appeared before Judge Green on a *charge* of murder," instead of "John Jones appeared before Judge Green for murder."

When all is said and done, there are only four real requirements for a news story:

1.   It must be news.
2.   It must be accurate.
3.   It should be interesting.
4.   It should be easy to understand.

All of the elements of newspaper style are merely devices to achieve these requirements. Most are designed to help the reporter attain accuracy and clarity.

What about future newspaper style? For many years newspapers have been written and edited for people who "read as they run." Gertrude Stein is quoted as once saying that "Journalism is too immediate to be immediate." We write and print for people in a hurry.

Maybe this approach is wrong. Maybe it is time that newspaper style hit a more leisurely pace. After all, the great majority of American people read their daily newspapers at breakfast or during the evening hours, while the Sunday newspaper is read most leisurely, sometimes all day long.

There is no longer a "comic book" approach to newspaper reading by comic-book-level minds. The educational level of the nation has risen greatly during the past fifteen years. Fewer than one thousand Ph.D. degrees were granted in 1939, but more than eight thousand were awarded in 1955, and by 1970 the number had climbed to nearly thirty thousand. Many people still commute on subways and buses to their homes in the suburbs, but newsstand sales still account for only a small percentage of newspaper circulation. Home delivery is the largest and that means the newspaper today goes where people have more leisure time. The work week has become so short that the man of the house leaves home later in the day and arrives home earlier in the evening than he did thirty or forty years ago. Today, with all her labor-saving gadgets, the housewife can do in an hour or two what it took her mother from sunrise to sunset to accomplish. She can spend more time over both her morning and evening newspapers, *if they merit her interest.*

This is the challenge for the modern reporter. Whether his medium be the newspaper, radio, or television, he must not let himself get too tied up with stylistic devices or formulas. Remembering that he must be accurate, interesting, and clear, he should also strive to tell his story naturally. If that means telling it in chronological order rather than in the inverted pyramid form, by all means the chronological order should be used.

Finding the Local Angle

The reporter worth his salt is the one who can always find a local angle in every situation. These are the newsmen who make a reality out of the saying, "All news is local." All news really is local if you have the news sense to find the local angle. We might just as easily have discussed this topic under a previous heading "What is News?" for the reporter who knows what news is will easily find a local angle in most situations.

The wire service reports that come to daily newspapers, exchanges that arrive in the mail, nearby metropolitan newspapers that come to the weekly newspaper office, are all rich with ideas for developing a local angle on a state, regional, or national story. For example, a wire report reveals that the governor has just appointed a new highway commission. Listed among the half dozen names on the board is that of a local man. The alert reporter or editor will see that his paper carries a *side story* telling about the local man's qualifications for the post as well as an interview with him for his reactions to the appointment.

Sometimes the local angle is less obvious. Suppose a wire story stated simply that cement manufacturing plants in the eastern half of the United States had shut down because of a strike. The story indicated that the shutdown might last many months. The reader in your city will want to know how the strike will affect him. Will he be able to get cement to pour the new driveway he has been thinking about? Will the proposed new high school building be delayed because of the strike? Will construction of concrete highways currently underway in the area be held up? Your reader may have many questions of local meaning concerning that strike. The good reporter must anticipate those questions and answer them in a clear, accurate and interesting story.

The local angle is even less obvious in other situations. In this case the reader doesn't have any questions because he does not know the story exists. A reporter reading a magazine article about dueling in the early days of the United States got an idea for a local story. What about dueling in his own state? When was the last duel fought in his own county? These questions led to others, and eventually he developed them into a feature story for the Sunday edition.

Finding the local angle means, then, finding the point at which the story touches local readers. When an editor tells a reporter to "play up the local angle," he wants him to feature local names or places and local significance of facts. For example, an editor receives a list of five hundred students who are being graduated by the state university. Ten of the students are from the county where the paper circulates. He knows his readers will be interested in the fact that the state university will graduate five hundred students on Saturday night, but he knows they are more interested in the local youngsters who will be among the graduates. His reporter "plays the local angle" by building his story around the local graduates.

The Advance Story

People want to know details of events that are scheduled to take place. They want to know these details before the event so that they can plan their own schedules. If the event is a lecture planned in connection with a local celebration, they want to know all about it so they can decide whether to attend. They will make their judgment on the basis of the importance of the person speaking, the topic of the address, the importance of the occasion for the lecture, their interest in the organization sponsoring the program, or possibly all of these things. Thus, in his advance story of this local event the reporter needs to give details on all of these points, as well as others he thinks may interest his readers.

A high percentage of the news stories in each day's newspaper are *advance stories*. These advance stories tell the reader about future events, not in the sense of the fortune teller gazing into a crystal ball, but as a chronicler of events already planned, already scheduled, already marked on the calendar. You cannot write advance stories of a fire or of an automobile accident, but you can write advance stories on weddings, funerals, speeches, and special events.

Another more complex type of advance story is the story based upon the writer's own prognostication. This might appear to be a "crystal ball" story, but it differs from clairvoyance in that the writer's story comes from background knowledge, keen observation, and discussion with many persons. A writer predicting the outcome of a football game or an election should reach his conclusions in a logical manner so that the reader can follow the writer's reasoning and either agree or disagree with him. This type of advance story should result from exhaustive research, tireless interviewing, and thorough fact-gathering, but never from guesswork.

Follow-up Stories

Follow-up stories for a new edition of your newspaper, or for the next day's edition, must include two important elements: new developments and enough of the original story so that those who read the first story will readily identify the news characters and the events. For example, if the original story was about two children lost in the mountains, the follow-up might read:

> GATLINBURG, Tenn.—Two young children who wandered from their family campsite in the Great Smoky Mountain National Park shortly after noon yesterday have been found, exhausted but unharmed.
> Park rangers found the youngsters, Rodney Tims, 8, and Paul, 10, huddled under a rock ledge about two miles from their parents' camp. . . .

The story would continue with details of the search, statements by parents and the youngsters, as well as statements by the park rangers. The lead could be handled in many ways to be more dramatic—such as a description of the youngsters huddled under the rock ledge and their statements on being found—but in any case the story should immediately tie in with the previous story's details.

Another kind of follow-up story is one that appears months, or even years, after the original story. Such a story might be the anniversary of a major disaster, retelling the story for those who are unfamiliar with it or who have forgotten the details. New elements in such a story might be facts about rebuilding in the disaster area, changes in the lives of persons affected by the disaster, or statements by persons involved. A common story of this type is about missing persons who disappeared under mysterious circumstances. Follow-up stories usually tell what police officials have been doing about the case, actions of relatives and friends, and full details from the original story.

Questions for Discussion

1. What are the reasons for and against racial identification in every news story?

2. How is fairness applied to identification in a news or feature story? If the reader is more interested in a news character if you call her a "dangerous blonde" or a "gun moll" why not stretch the truth a little and call her that?
3. What are the arguments for and against using such "authority" words as "a person close to the governor," "a Navy spokesman," "the mayor's office reported," or "a source in the governor's office"?
4. What does "protective wording" protect?
5. What are your pet peeves about news reporting? Where do you think reporters fail to carry out their responsibility to be accurate?

6 the art of interviewing

The interview is the basis of most reporting. This chapter will help the reporter who must rush away to an interview at a moment's notice, as well as the reporter who must arrange a number of interviews over weeks, or even months, for an investigative story.

Interviewing is an art, a profession, an opportunity, a challenge, sometimes a frustration, but more often an inspiration, and a reward to the writer.

On his first interview the beginning newsman finds that he has many questions—and few answers. Where should he begin? How does he arrange the interview? What should he ask? How will he be able to get the interviewee to talk? Should he take notes? Should he use a tape recorder? How long should the interview last? How should he handle a belligerent interviewee? How should he conclude the interview?

Preparing for the Interview

The reporter who gets an assignment at 2 P.M. to interview a political figure at the airport at 2:30 P.M. may have little or no time to prepare for the interview. Unless the reporter knows the interviewee's background, the results are usually sad: a story full of small talk, neither entertaining nor informative.

Recently, a newspaper sent one of its beginning reporters to interview a university president on the occasion of his tenth anniversary as the head of a large state university. He began the interview by asking, "Mr. Jones, how long have you been president of this university?"

The president was kindly but firm. "Young man," he said, "obviously you have not done your homework." He got up from his chair, concluding the interview. "When you have some intelligent questions, call my secretary and we'll arrange another time."

The reason for the interview may well have some bearing on the kind of preparations necessary. If the reporter is seeking a personality interview, he will need to find out all that he can about the person himself. He should consult his own newspaper files and *Who's Who* books. There may be magazine articles written by or about the subject. If the subject is a politician the reporter will need to know his political leanings, his voting record, his performance in office, his hobbies, and his position on various matters.

If the interview is with a businessman, and the reporter is seeking a story on his business success, he will want to know all about the background of the business, the company's policies, its successes and its failures. If the purpose of the interview is to obtain the interviewee's opinions on various matters, the reporter still needs to know about the subjects of the interview as well as a biography of the person to be interviewed.

Some Do's and Don'ts in setting up an interview:

(a) If possible, call the interviewee beforehand and arrange a time for the interview to suit his convenience. Let him set the time and place, but indicate times that would be convenient to you.

(b) Never ask the interviewee to come to you.

(c) Tell the interviewee about your newspaper and, if possible, about the nature of the interview you are seeking. You might send him a note before the interview, stating some of the questions you plan to ask, particularly if he needs to do some research of his own in preparation for the interview. (Some reporters disagree on this point, saying the interviewee should not be tipped off ahead of time concerning the nature of the interview. Others insist that a better interview will result.)

(d) Tell him something about yourself, especially if you have a reporting speciality that ties in with the subject of the interview or the profession of the interviewee.

(e) Appear on time and end the interview at the designated time, unless the interviewee obviously wants to prolong the conversation.

Ground rules should be arranged, if you know the interviewee well enough to suspect that trouble may arise, or if the subject matter for the interview is touchy. Here is an example of what can happen without ground rules:

During the course of an interview an interviewee repeatedly went "off" the record and "on" again. At the end of the interview it was difficult to determine what had been said that the reporter could use. When the story appeared in the newspaper, the interviewee complained that he had been misquoted and threatened to bring suit.

Before leaving an interview, the reporter should pin down what has been said on record. Better still, he should insist at the outset of the interview that everything said be on record and that if the interviewee does not want something in print he should not say it. An occasional "off the record" in an interview is fine for background purposes, but it should not be overdone. Both the interviewer and the interviewee should have a clear understanding of what is to be reported.

There is nothing wrong with making arrangements for the interview through a third party. Sometimes the interviewee is too busy to be contacted in person. You may arrange the interview through his secretary, his wife, or a public relations aide. There are certain advantages in contacting a public relations officer: he may be able to provide you with much material about the interviewee and his office or company ahead of the interview. Availability of this material, however, should never stop a reporter from researching the subject himself. He should never allow prepared material provided in this manner to color his interview or dictate its direction.

Be Ready with Questions

The reporter who must prepare for an interview at a moment's notice should at least assemble a few questions in his head on the way to the interview. If more time is available, a list of specific questions should be prepared. Some reporters jot these down on a note pad, others prepare them in typewritten form in the order in which they will be used. Still others type their questions on a 3 x 5 card, or cards.

How many questions should you ask? That depends upon the nature and importance of the interview. Some reporters use only a few questions to get the subject talking, others prepare a list of a dozen or more questions, and still others who are preparing long features may come up with a hundred or more questions, many of which will not be used. Here are a few Do's and Don'ts:

(a) Don't allow your list of questions to turn the interview into a formal question and answer session that has no warmth or personality.

(b) Don't be afraid to ask controversial or delicate questions.

(c) Don't ask questions that are already answered in printed material available to you ahead of the interview. You might want to elaborate on answers already made public but don't repeat the same questions.

(d) Do prepare intelligent, well thought-out questions for which there are no obvious answers.

(e) If you work better this way, prepare a few key questions and let the direction of the interview dictate other questions.

Point (c) requires special emphasis. Too many questions, asked one after another, can spoil the result. A good interview should have warmth and flow smoothly and naturally. If your list of prepared questions makes for stiffness, don't use every question on the list. The reporter must be flexible during an interview so that he can take advantage of his interviewee's mood. The list of questions should remind you of important questions but should not dictate the entire interview.

Mechanics of the Interview

Should you take notes, use a tape recorder, or neither of these? Many successful interviewers go to an interview with a list of memorized questions and no visible writing materials. Such reporters conduct their interviews without writing a word and then go to some quiet corner immediately after the interview and put on paper everything that was said, before they forget the subject matter.

Some interviewees are suspicious of reporters who use this method, and may refuse to talk because they fear the reporter will not remember what they said and misquote them. Others will talk more freely under such circumstances. Some interviewees react favorably to a taped interview and others do not. There is no pat answer to this question. You must play it by ear. Sometimes the answer lies in the research done about the individual. The more you know about him, the better you can decide on the mechanics of the interview.

If you have time, and the interviewee is amenable, a tape-recorded interview will produce the best results. The attitude of the interviewer has a lot to do with the reaction of the interviewee to the use of a tape recorder. If the interviewer gives the impression that he wants to tape the interview so that the interviewee cannot back down or challenge the story at a later date, the interviewee may not be responsive. If the recorder is used unobtrusively, with tact—the unit placed casually upon the table and then ignored—the interviewee is likely to react favorably. Don't make a big deal of the machine. You might explain that you are using the recorder to protect him, to prevent being misquoted. If the recorder proves to be an obstacle, and you are doing the interview against a deadline, turn off the machine and proceed without it.

Tone of the Interview

What is the best approach for the interviewer to use in an interview? Should he come on strong, with probing and searching questions and an air of belligerency? Should he keep the subject on the defensive throughout the interview? Should he keep asking embarrassing and impertinent questions so that the subject is off balance most of the time, answering angrily, but with good copy?

That is one way to do it, and some reporters use this method, particularly with extroverts who don't mind saying what they think.

Most interviews are more successful, however, in a relaxed atmosphere, with the reporter using a "soft sell."

The hard sell should be used only by the truly professional interviewer who knows his subject well and knows how far to go. Certainly, the beginner had better adopt a friendly attitude. Honey still catches more flies than vinegar.

Breaking the Ice

In many interviews you won't have time to break the ice. The hour or hour and a half set aside for the interview (it could be only fifteen or twenty minutes) is not long enough to waste time on small talk. But some of this is necessary. The interviewee should be reminded of the purpose of the interview. If he is the only person you plan to interview for your story, tell him so. If others are to be interviewed, tell him that too, and explain why.

A friendly, interested manner is best. Most persons are flattered because you, or your newspaper, feel that they have something to say. They will react favorably toward a reporter who appears to be genuinely interested in them and their work.

Many interviewers make a special effort to find out about the special interests or hobbies of the persons they are assigned to interview. Questions concerning these make good icebreakers. The purpose of such questions is to get the interviewee in a talkative mood, to establish a relaxed, informal climate between the reporter and the interviewee. If the interview takes place over a period of several days,

during which the reporter spends all of his time with the
subject, observing his various moods and lifestyle, the
icebreaking period will take longer. There the reporter needs
to establish a friendship that allows for mutual respect and
confidence. Such lengthy interviews are not uncommon,
even in the newspaper business, when reporters are
preparing in-depth pieces or Sunday magazine features.
Long interviews are quite common in the magazine business,
especially when the writer is doing a profile on a famous
person.

In most newspaper interviews the icebreaking period
may consist simply of the reporter giving his name and the
reason for the interview—then he launches into his questions. In such cases it is all the more important that he research the inverviewee and the subject beforehand, and have
a clear idea of exactly what he is after and what, exactly, the
interviewee is expected to provide.

Handling the Interview

Managing the interview sometimes can be difficult. The
subject may spend precious time on topics that add nothing
to the interview. However, these topics are sometimes more
productive than those pre-established by the reporter. In
such cases pursue these new avenues. If the interviewee
rambles on about definitely unproductive topics, the reporter
should bring him back to the main subject of the interview by
saying simply, "Mr. Jones, we didn't finish our discussion of
the new committee on environmental problems that you are
setting up. Just how do you propose to go about this?"

Attitude of the Interviewer. The reporter should be
confident and look the interviewee in the eye. A shifty-eyed
reporter, who slouches in his chair and gives the impression
of not knowing what he is doing, will quickly destroy any
confidence that he might have developed at the beginning of
the interview. Informality is fine, but it can be carried to
extremes. The reporter who instantly calls the interviewee by
his first name when they have just met may kill the interview
at the outset.

Good interviewing is, in a way, good salesmanship. The

reporter "sells" himself and his newspaper by correctly pronouncing the name of the interviewee and conducting himself in an alert, professional manner.

This is not to say that many good interviews have not been obtained by amateurs. High school and college students often obtain interviews that professionals could not obtain because the students approached the interviewee in a frank and honest manner, admitting they were terrified but capitalizing on their youth and enthusiasm. Even for the professional, honesty and frankness are good assets.

Refusal to Answer. What do you do when the interviewee refuses to answer a question important to the success of your interview? Be persistent. Keep coming back to the question. Explain why the answer is important to you and the readers of your newspaper. You can point out that failure to answer a certain question will be apparent to readers and that the interviewee could be more damaged by such an omission in the story than by his answer. If all else fails, you can try to get the answer from another source.

Handling Your Questions. Questions should be specific and clear. Use easy questions first to relax the interviewee. After the proper mood of informality and relaxation has been established, use the more difficult questions. Don't try to trick the interviewee into answering a touchy question. Subterfuge may produce an answer, but you may be in trouble when the interview appears in print. Frankness and honesty are still the best approaches to sensitive matters.

You will quickly discover that it is impossible to ask your questions in a particular order. The interviewee may anticipate a question that you have reserved for a later moment. In answering one question he may answer several on your list. The reporter must be alert and not ask questions where answers have already been provided.

Don't Let the Interviewee Confuse You. If an interviewee's answers are not clear, don't accept the answers until you understand clearly what he has said. Some interviewees will be intentionally vague. Pin them down until you have a clear, understandable answer. If you fail to grasp a point, your readers will also be confused. Most interviewees do not mind additional questions to clarify what they have said.

Ask Why. Today's readers want to know the "why" of almost everything. Don't forget this important question during the interview. The "why" is particularly important for in-depth pieces that go behind the news.

Miscellaneous Tips. Should you indicate to the interviewee what you don't know and expect him to fill in the answers? The answer is both yes and no—it depends upon the circumstances. If you are dealing with sensitive subject matter, a little knowledge on your part may bring out all the details you don't know. If you tell the interviewee beforehand what you know, he might not fill in what you don't know. Time and again reporters have gone to interviews with a little knowledge, their questions having convinced the interviewee that they knew the entire story. In such cases they did not hesitate to discuss the entire matter.

On sensitive matters, where do you begin? Go to the top. Seek out the head of the organization. Lesser officials will most often refuse to talk.

When do you talk to more than one person? If you are doing a profile, you may want to talk to secretaries, relatives, friends, and even opponents, as well as the subject of the story. If you are seeking opinions about a particular subject, talk to as many individuals as possible in order to get a well-balanced story.

What about the person who is willing to talk but does not want to be quoted? This happens all the time. If you can handle the material so that it is meaningful and clear without directly quoting the person, do so. Otherwise, seek the information from another person who will allow you to quote him.

The interviewer should not monopolize the conversation. His main job is to get information, not show off his own knowledge. On the other hand, good interviews develop well when the interview becomes a kind of dialog between two parties.

Closing the Interview

As mentioned previously, end the interview on time. Do not overstay your welcome unless the interviewee seems eager to continue talking and you feel further conversation will be profitable to you. If your time is limited, and you must end the interview, do so graciously. Occasionally, the interviewee has nothing else to do and he is so wound up in his subject that he will ramble on forever. How do you get out of this kind of situation without hurting his feelings? Different reporters have different methods. Probably the simplest is to rise, look at your watch, and say that you have another story to cover or a deadline to meet.

Postinterview Contacts

Should you offer to let the interviewee see the story before it is published? Should you contact him by telephone during the writing process to check on the accuracy of some details? Should you promise to get him a copy of the newspaper containing the story when it is published?

Generally speaking, the answer should be no to all of these questions.

Dates, names, and statistics should be checked with the interviewee before you leave his office. But if something does come up when you are writing the story, by all means check with him to get the correct information. If you should ever agree to let an interviewee see your story before it goes to press, have a clear understanding that he will check it for facts only. The style of writing is your own. If an interviewee insists on seeing your story before he will grant an interview, you must decide whether the interview is worth this extra effort, and whether you want to risk compromising your own integrity as a writer and reporter just to get the interview. Most of the time you will decline the interview.

Summary

The following interview techniques developed for student reporters by the School of Journalism, University of Oregon, summarize many of the points made in this chapter.

Preparation for the Interview. Find out all you can about your interviewee, before you speak to him. Ask somebody. Look him up in *Who's Who* or wherever else he may be written up. Get into your mind his exact offices or distinguishing features of his career. Pronounce his name over to yourself several times until it comes to your lips easily and naturally.

Find out all you can about the subject on which you are to interview him. It is better to ask somebody who knows than to depend upon scrapbooks or reference books, but where it is practicable, do both. Read a magazine article on the subject where one is obtainable.

Where the interview is of a general nature (not about a definite theme determined beforehand), make a general outline of questions of the different fields in which you think the interview might be productive. Memorize this outline, and do not end the interview until you have tried out questions in all fields.

First Part of the Interview. Start by explaining whom you represent and what you want. Address your interviewee by name in practically every sentence. Look him in the eye, and if you take notes do not constantly look at your notebook. *Look interested,* and *be interested* in everything he says. Do not do much talking yourself in the first part of the interview; your main purpose is to encourage your subject to talk freely and interestedly while you are sizing up him and the subject. Little expressions of interest, approval, or curiosity are all that is necessary in this part of the interview. Yours is a thinking role, not a talking role, in the first part of the interview. This part ends when you have made up your mind what kind of story you want and can get from your interviewee. The second part consists of getting it.

Second Part of the Interview. You have your hint of a possible story from the first part of the interview. But it is only a hint. Your newspaper training will tell you what details you will have to add before it becomes a readable and complete story. Ask questions calculated to make the story complete in all its details. Make sure that you have the WHO (both names and identifications), WHAT, WHERE, and

WHEN exactly. But bring out the most interesting sides of the story. This part of the interview ends when you feel that you have the complete story with all the details and dramatic incidents necessary to you as a writer.

Third Part of the Interview. The last part of the interview is a process of verification and of going over ground to make sure that nothing has been overlooked. This part is somewhat tedious to your subject, but you will usually be able to hold him to it by the argument: "So long as it's going to be printed you surely want to see that I don't get anything wrong." In this part of the interview use your notes openly, repeating your understanding of the story to your subject, asking, "Is that correct?" and entering corrections and additions to your notes. Go over with special care every date, number, and the spelling of all proper names. Run over in your mind all possibilities of further information from your subject in other fields besides the one which has just been productive. The last question of all should be verification of the interviewee's name and its spelling.

General Warning. It is usually ruinous to take up these different phases of the interview in any order other than that above. To begin with the tedious and vexatious manner of the third part would put your interviewee out of humor and likely spoil your story. If you put off activities listed under "preparation" until after the interview, you will miss the opportunity to ask about interesting things you may have learned from the interviewee. To begin with part two before you have given the interviewee the free range advised in part one will often give you the story you started out to get instead of the important different story the interviewee may have when he is talking freely. The first part of the interview is generally awkward and difficult if you have not preceded it with the work labeled "preparation."

Remember—there are three different attitudes corresponding to the three different parts of the interview. You have three different purposes in mind, three different phases of action.

Remember, remember, remember—look your interviewee in the eye at all times, appear interested, *be* interested, and address him frequently by his name.

Even if you master all of these techniques and advice, do not make the mistake of thinking that you will be an accomplished interviewer. Interviewing is a skill you learn from experience—sometimes hard, bitter experience. These tips from the experience of many professionals will certainly help, but the accomplished interviewer has developed a personality that causes people to like and trust him. To begin with, he must sincerely like to talk with people. He becomes like a practical psychologist who can play upon the moods and sensitivities of people in the same way a skilled musician plays his instrument. He learns to push ahead in one direction and to slow down when an interviewee begins to bristle.

Questions for Discussion

1. Why wouldn't the best kind of interview technique be one in which the reporter used a tape recorder and then simply typed up the interview the way it came off the tape?
2. If the person to be interviewed is the U. S. Secretary of Labor, where would you go to obtain information about him prior to the interview? What kind of information would you seek?
3. If the person to be interviewed is the mayor of your city, where would you go to find information about him?
4. Is there anything wrong with allowing a public relations man to set up an interview for you with his boss?
5. Discuss the practicality or impracticality of allowing an interviewee to see a copy of your interview before it goes to your editor.

7 common news story faults

The writing errors that creep unnoticed into news stories can be categorized under a few general headings. Those listed here do not include all errors that reporters make, but they are the more obvious faults that disturb newspaper readers. The good reporter should compile his own list and hope that as he learns to avoid them, he will no longer need the list.

Unanswered Questions

Never leave the reader with a lot of unanswered questions. For example:

PINE KEY, Sept. 10—Bait house operator Sam Sloan outguessed the Gulf of Mexico Monday to rescue a 27-year-old River Town bank teller who was swept out to sea by a strong current and stranded, for 20 hours.

Sloan said he joined the search party looking for Sara Anne Smith shortly after she was reported missing by her husband George Sunday evening.

Small boat owners, fishermen, the Coast Guard, and the Florida Marine Patrol searched most of the night without success until Sloan figured out Monday morning where the currents might have swept Mrs. Smith.

"He was familiar with the currents and winds in

the area," said Tom Andrews, a driver for the Roberts ambulance service in River Town. "After he got his bearings straight, he practically went right to her."

Sloan, however, said there really wasn't very much to it. "Let's say, with the grace of God and a little mathematics we went right to her," he said.

Mrs. Smith dove off her husband's boat a few miles off Silver River Sunday afternoon when she got hot while sunbathing, Andrews said.

He said the current swept her out to sea and when she called for help from her husband, he could not reach her.

"He was an excellent swimmer," Andrews said. "He was a swimmer in high school, and it took him six hours to fight his way back to the boat."

It was nearly dark when Smith reached the boat and called for help on a citizen's band radio, Andrews said.

Mrs. Smith was taken to a River Town hospital after her recovery and was reported in good condition there.

Sloan said that the real credit for her rescue should go to all the searchers whose activity and flares in the night gave Mrs. Smith hope enough to stay afloat in the 20-foot depths about 20 miles from shore.

"The girl told me after I picked her up if it hadn't been for the activity and light of those boats she would have given up," he said.

The reporter has left his reader with the following unanswered questions. Where was Mr. Smith when his wife was swept out to sea? Was he also swimming in the water with her, and if so, why was he not swept out to sea with her? If he was on the boat when his wife called for help, how did he get into the water? Why didn't he crank up his boat and go to her assistance? Was the boat disabled? The writer of a news story must anticipate all the questions his reader will ask and have the answers in the story.

Unknown Characters

Readers dislike having even one "unknown" character wander into a news story. For example:

WASHINGTON, April 9—The House Wednesday approved a $230 million-a-year pay raise for 850,000 "blue-collar" government workers despite a warning that it would cost 40,000 of them their jobs.

"This Congress has voted sizable pay increases for its classified workers and sizable increases for its military personnel," said Rep. David N. Henderson (D-N.C.), whose House Manpower and Civil Service Committee drafted the bill. "It's only fair that we do the same for our wage board workers."

Wage board workers, mainly involved in maintenance work, receive salaries based on the prevailing pay for workers in private industry doing comparable work. The Henderson bill would raise the maximum amount their pay could be above that of local workers in comparable jobs from four to twelve percent.

In one nonrecord vote, the House rejected 61-40 a Derwinski effort to repeal a provision that now allows labor markets outside the local area to determine a prevailing wage.

That law, enacted in 1968 but only implemented last month, has resulted in nearly $103 million in retroactive pay for blue-collar workers, according to Derwinski.

In this story, when the reader reaches the name Derwinski he will stop and reread the entire story to find out who he is. He may even read it a third time before giving up in disgust. The unwritten rule is that the writer must identify completely every single character he introduces into his news story—at the time the character is introduced.

Lead Disagrees with Body of Story

Beware of writing a lead that promises something the body of the story does not produce. The most common fault of this kind is the lead that says, for example, seven citizens have been given distinguished service awards, with the body of the story listing only six persons. In any story that lists persons or events, check the body of the story against the number in the lead.

Carelessness in Reporting Names

One of the unpardonable sins of reporting is the failure of a reporter to use the name of an organization exactly as it should be used: the way the organization is officially known or the way it is legally recorded. All too many reporters assume that if the name is approximately correct, that is sufficient, but a good reporter is not satisfied with a near miss. For example, how many times has a department, school, or college been incorrectly identified in a newspaper? The "School of Journalism and Communications" may be referred to on campus as the "School of Journalism," but that is no reason for a newspaper to refer to it in such a way. The correct title should be used.

If the correct name for a newspaper is *The Blanktown News,* it should be referred to in print that way and not merely *Blanktown News.* The same should be true for use by the newspaper of company designations in your city.

Readers are inclined to feel that if the newspaper and the reporter are not accurate in minor details, they will not be accurate in matters of more importance.

The reporter must be aware, of course, that if the style of his newspaper calls for a different handling of the name of a newspaper, for example, he will need to follow his own newspaper's style. In this book, you may note, names of newspapers are used in accordance with the style recommended by the University of Chicago *Manual of Style.*

Failure to Apply Common Sense to Facts

Not long ago a reporter in a medium-sized town was covering a joint city-county meeting where the main business of the evening was consolidation of the city and county jail systems. A statement by one official that the consolidation would cost a "mere fifty million dollars" was noted by the reporter and used in a news story the next day. Actually, the official had meant to say "fifty thousand dollars," and the members of the two commissions understood that he *meant* fifty thousand dollars, so no one corrected him. If the reporter had thought twice, he would have realized that the combined total budget for both the city and county did not even come to fifty million dollars and that this was therefore an outrageous figure.

One safeguard a reporter can take at the end of a meeting is to check and double-check facts and figures with news sources before the story is written.

A reporter was assigned to write a story on a class reunion at the local high school, based on a publicity handout. According to the handout, fifteen thousand persons were expected to attend the reunion. The reporter rewrote the handout into a half-column story, using background information obtained from the oldest living member of the class. It was a good story, with local color and history, but the writer marred the story by including the fifteen thousand attendance figure from the handout. Fortunately, the newspaper's copy editor caught the error, pointing out to the reporter that the high school had graduated five hundred persons that particular year, and that even if all returned for the reunion—with their wives, husbands, and children—the attendance could not possibly reach fifteen thousand.

Failure to Question Statements by News Sources

The newspaper business is no place for the gullible or naive reporter who accepts facts, figures, and opinions from speakers, interviewees, and government and business officials without question. All too frequently, reporters are either too lazy or too apathetic to ask questions challenging the material they get. The easy way is to write the story the way it is told to you and not question the facts. Here is the way one reporter began a story:

GAINESVILLE, Jan. 5—Jerome C. Curtis, gubernatorial candidate, today called upon all the citizens of Florida to back his program to bring clean water to the state.

"Let's act together now before it it too late," he told a state convention of high school teachers. "We've got enough good highways for the present. What we need now is to clean up our rivers and streams. If we dropped just one road project, like the expansion of State Road 25, we could have the money to stop all pollution in the St. Johns River," the candidate said.

A second reporter, skeptical of the candidate's remarks, cornered him after the speech. The conversation went something like this:

REPORTER: Mr. Curtis, you said enough money could be

saved from the State Road 25 project alone to clean up the St. Johns River. In round figures, just how much money would be saved if that project, the State Road 25 project, were dropped?

CURTIS: I understand the State Department of Transportation has twenty-five million dollars budgeted for that project.

REPORTER: Actually, Mr. Curtis, the Department's budget for that project is only fifteen million.

CURTIS (sputtering): Well, young man, I am sure you are wrong. I read the figure in a magazine just the other day.

REPORTER: Do you have the exact figures on just what it would cost to free the St. Johns River entirely of pollution?

CURTIS: Why, yes, certainly. Just what I said: twenty-five million.

REPORTER (pulling some notes from his coat pocket): These federal figures released this week indicate that it will take ninety-three million dollars to do the job. Where did you get your figures?

CURTIS (red-faced and confused): Well, now, maybe those figures I used are a bit off. I'll have to recheck that. Just leave that statement out of the story, will you, please?

This reporter quoted the candidate's exact words to the convention of teachers and then, in a background paragraph, reported the figures used by the Department of Transportation and the federal government.

One of the greatest needs in reporting today is for reporters to look behind statements made in handouts, to probe deeply into facts and figures and reasoning used by public figures and candidates for public office, and to cross-question news sources in a lawyerlike but courteous manner.

Distortion of the News

Distortion in a news story can be intentional or accidental. Either way, both the newspaper and the reader suffer: the reader because he has failed to get the truth and the newspaper because it has opened a credibility gap between itself and its readers. The irony of intentional distortion is that while its purpose is to build circulation or to gain some kind of favorable position for the reporter or the publication, it destroys, at the same time, the confidence of readers in the reliability and integrity of the press. Distortion takes many forms:

Poor Choice of Words. The following lead gives a distorted picture of the news because of a single word:

> *Even* little children are protesting the war in Vietnam these days.
>
> Children, marching alongside their mothers and carrying tiny American flags. . . .

The word "even" gives the impression that everyone is protesting this war. The story is further distorted by the fact that the children referred to in the second paragraph actually included only two children of one family, a five-year-old boy and a four-year-old girl, alongside their mother.

Consciously or unconsciously, a reporter frequently reveals that he has "taken sides." For example, he has in his own mind convicted a defendant by reporting that the defendant "stood there, *brazenly* telling the jury that he did not commit the crime."

A reporter can favorably slant a news story by calling one candidate for public office a "leader" and another a "party boss." Public officials can be described as "under fire," or said to be "passing the buck," but such terminology is unfair unless the writer can document such ascriptions by explaining, on the one hand, how a person "under fire" is being criticized, or, on the other, what actual behavior leads to the conclusion that a person has evaded responsibility.

Take this example from a feature story:

> My wife fell in love with the old ceramics shop. She spent most of the weekend there, painting some beautiful clay urns and wall plaques she had bought at a most reasonable price. The atmosphere was friendly, and the worktables were available as though they were in your own art studio.

The writer is "plugging" the ceramics shop when he says the urns and wall plaques can be bought at a "most reasonable price." The statement would have been more objective if the writer had written, "bought at what *she thought* was a most reasonable price."

There are other ways to handle such a statement. The writer could have eliminated altogether the phrase "at a most reasonable price," and ended the sentence with "bought." Or, he could have given the price paid for the objects, allowing the reader to decide whether or not the price was reasonable.

A man's character could well be ruined, intentionally or unintentionally, by an untruthful description of the way he left a legislative committee meeting. He could be described as "slinking" from the room, "walking like a man in a dream," "tottering as though he had taken a beating," or "with a dazed expression on his face."

Distortion by Tone. News stories can be distorted in varying degrees by the tone of the writing. A serious action by public officials can be made to appear ridiculous if the story is written with a tongue-in-cheek approach. Humor, in its place, is permissible in a news story. If a humorous tone contributes to character assassination or erosion of confidence in government, just for the sake of humor, then it is out of place.

A state university attempted to stop the drinking of alcoholic beverages in its football stadium by not allowing fans to take containers of any kind through the turnstiles. One newspaper reporter laughed off the whole matter when he concluded a paragraph of his story with these words: "and the outlawing of outside liquids ranges from 100-proof booze to coffee containers and any kid's lemonade jug."

The reporter is saying to his readers, "Look, how ridiculous can they get? They won't even allow a little kid to take lemonade into the stadium!"

Another reporter told how the campus police had little to do in the old days, "when things were normal," except to get people in their right seats and prevent overanxious fans from blocking the aisles. Now, he writes, the police must "watch from binoculars for people drinking or sipping from sunglasses." He points out that the administration of the university no longer will allow fans to carry any kind of container into the stadium. "It does not matter if it contains water, Gatorade, or goldfish. Containers are not allowed in the place."

Of course, all of this is written in the name of innocent fun, to gain rapport with fans who read the newspaper. But the serious intent of the regulation—to prevent drunken brawls and drunken fans from disrupting the enjoyment of the game for others—gets lost in the "fun."

Distortion by Half-Truths. Check your news or feature story to see if it distorts the truth by not telling all of the facts or failing to analyze facts properly for the reader. For example, one reporter, without any explanation whatsoever, threw the following sentence into a feature story: "Migrant workers and their families often go hungry while the federal government subsidizes rich farmers for growing nothing."

This is a clear example of an oversimplification of a most complex problem. The government pays subsidies to poor farmers as well as rich farmers. And there are many reasons given by agricultural economists for maintaining the farm subsidy program.

Another writer, attempting to describe what he thought was a national bellicose attitude, wrote, "Military men are given awards for their ability to kill. Obviously, 'Thou shalt not kill' means little to us."

These statements, when considered as bare bones, are misleading. From one point of view, military medals are given for valor, often to men who *save* lives on the battlefield. If the writer had desired, he could have found countless instances in everyday life where men have fought and died to protect and preserve the commandment, "Thou shalt not kill."

Men can be slandered and ideas discredited by bringing together two unrelated events. For example, a state legislator was attacked because of a report that he failed to vote for "an adequate corporate tax" but did vote for a tax on "cane fishing poles used by the poor." It might follow that the legislator was a protector of the rich corporations and a foe of the poor man, but this could not be deduced solely from his vote on these two bills.

Quoting Weak Authority. Attributing news facts to such will-o'-the-wisp authorities as "persons in a position to know," "a well-informed official," and "one close to the inside story," and writing that such and such a situation is the "general belief" in the community could lead to distortion of the news. These attributions may result from lazy reporting, or they may be the only kinds of attribution that a reporter is able to get in an important news situation.

The point here is that such weak attributions should not be used if it is possible to get more specific ones, and in no case should they be used to distort the news and thus mislead the reader.

Suppose a Washington correspondent writes that "farm interests *reportedly* want to chop down their property taxes, etc." or that such and such a story has reached the "strong rumor stage" in the halls of Congress. Unfortunately, this kind of wording could be used to "color" a news story. "Farm interests" may not be trying to get their taxes cut at all, but one person's opinion, attributed in a news story to such an abstract source as "interests," could give readers the impression that an attitude or opinion expressed by one is common. In this same way, an opinion expressed by one person could be inflated in importance by saying that it is in the "strong rumor stage."

It should be noted, however, that it is more desirable to write that something is a rumor than to lead the reader to believe that it is an official statement or a known fact. If a statement is pure gossip or rumor, you can lessen its impact by branding it as such.

Opinion in the News. Editorial opinions in a by-lined news story are tolerable because the reader knows who is doing the talking. Editorial opinion quoted from news sources is fine because the reader again knows who is doing the talking. But editorializing in a news story without a by-line tends to color the story and may either confuse the reader or cause him to disbelieve everything the newspaper reports. Here are some examples:

> George Rogers, the University of Blanktown professor who was one of, if not the most, qualified of ten persons seeking board seats, was trounced by Paul Ellis.

> Smith and Green were the bottom-most candidates and many voters must not have bothered to

look down for their names. Something should be done so this is not repeated.

Such uncalled-for tactics in arresting and bringing innocent persons into court are the marks of a police state.

How can a reporter detect opinion injected by him into his own news stories? He should ask himself these questions:

Has he written what he *knows* or what he *thinks?*

Can he detect, or will his readers be able to determine, which side he has taken or which one he favors?

Can he underline words that slant the story in one direction or another?

What is the *real* purpose of the story—to inform readers or to present a point of view?

Distortion by Identification. One of the most irritating newspaper practices, in the eyes of readers, is that of assigning a general identification to a major news character when he should be more specifically identified. For example:

The trial of a Blanktown University professor, accused of hitting a River Town police officer in the face and touching off a disturbance during an antiwar demonstration two years ago, will continue this morning following an all-day session yesterday.

The case against Milton A. Sweeney is expected to go to the jury before noon, following final arguments and summations scheduled to begin this morning at 9 o'clock.

However, Sweeney was not a professor. He was actually a graduate teaching assistant working on a Ph.D. in philosophy and teaching in an English course. So, you say, what is all the fuss about? Doesn't the general public refer to *all* persons who teach anything at a college or university as "professor"? What harm is done?

In this particular case, newspapers throughout the state kept referring to Sweeney as a "Blanktown University professor," despite the fact that a wire service story had correctly stated that Sweeney was only a teaching assistant and did not have faculty status at the university. People around the state were inclined to say, "Did you read about

that fool professor at Blanktown University? No telling
what these professors will do." The university was harmed,
and all professors were harmed.

People who knew the truth had more proof for the old
saying, "You can't believe anything you see in the
newspapers."

This kind of shoddy reporting distorts the news.

No one is seeking to protect professors—or admirals, or
anyone else with a title—and no one is asking newspapers to
protect them. No one is asking that the university not be
named. All that the public wants is the truth. No good
reporter should lower his standards to the informal level of
the general public in the handling of facts or the identification of news characters.

Stories with Inaccurate Details

A news story should not contain details that are
inaccurate or obscure because they are poorly presented,
only partly presented, or cloaked in ambiguity, thus causing
the reader to jump to one or more wrong conclusions. For
example:

> The 30-year-old man found hanging in the Blank
> County jail died in the presence of three other men in
> a six-by-eight foot cell.
>
> Ralph Albert Wiggins, an inmate being held on a
> charge of possession of marijuana, was found dead
> early Monday morning, hanging from the bars of his
> cell door. A torn sheet was used as the instrument of
> hanging, according to a sheriff's office spokesman.
>
> Dr. Wilbur A. Smithers, Blank County medical
> examiner, was unable to release information on the
> deceased without permission from the state at-
> torney's office.
>
> Clouding that explanation is the fact that
> Wiggins was not alone in his cell. At the time of his
> death, three other prisoners were also inside the cell.
> They said they were asleep and saw nothing.

This story creates a number of doubts from the
beginning. Were the three in the same cell as the man who
hanged himself? The lead of the story simply says that they

were *in* a six-by-eight-foot cell. It is not clear that all four men were in the same cell. This point is cleared up in the final paragraph. But the reader might not reach the final paragraph or the final paragraph could be dropped in the makeup process. There is another problem. The story says the man died in the "presence of three other men." Later the story says the men said they were asleep and saw nothing. Was the hanging "in the presence of" the men if they were asleep? The reader wonders if the man was murdered by the three men, if he was allowed to hang himself without anyone attempting to stop him, or if he did actually commit suicide.

If the reporter is going to "tell it as it is," all he can say at this time is that the man died in a cell containing three other prisoners, all of whom said they were asleep and saw nothing. This should be told in the lead and not put in a later paragraph.

Inaccuracy of detail often stems from the fact that a reporter will sometimes get the right information but interpret it in terms of his own prejudices. For example, five different correspondents for metropolitan newspapers in a university town picked up a story concerning a youngster who was thrown out of high school because he refused to cut his long hair. The boy's father was a retired Army master sergeant. At the time of the incident, the father was completing a master's degree in education at the university and planned to enter a theological seminary later that year. As a graduate student in the university's college of education, he taught several sections of a beginning course, but was not a bona fide member of the teaching staff.

One correspondent identified the father as "former army officer." This information shades the truth since a master sergeant is not strictly an officer, but a noncommissioned officer.

Another correspondent identified the father as a "professor of education." This was completely untrue since the man was not even an instructor. He could have been identified as a graduate teaching assistant in education.

A third reporter identified the father as a "staff member

at Blanktown University," and in a later story referred to him as a "Blanktown University professor." None of these identifications was true.

The fourth reporter said the father was "a local minister, working on an education degree at the University." The "local minister" tag apparently stemmed from the fact that the man had done some lay preaching in a local church; however, he was not an ordained minister.

A fifth correspondent identified the father as a "faculty member of the Blanktown University College of Education."

Minor inaccuracies of this type are causing readers, public officials, and others to charge that the "liberal" press is out to destroy everybody and everything.

One-sided Stories

The one-sided news story, whether in a television or newspaper report, is unfair, unprofessional, and even dishonest. If a television cameraman photographs only that part of a mob scene showing the mob being attacked by policemen and not that part showing police officers being attacked, he has produced a one-sided view of events. When a newspaper reporter describes a mob scene he should tell the whole story and not focus on a single aspect.

The confidence of readers in the integrity of newspapers and the accuracy of news accounts has been more often shaken by reporters who tell only one side of a story than by any other journalistic sin. The so-called credibility gap between newspapers and their readers can only be widened by the reporter who devotes an entire news story to a single news character who makes serious charges that go unanswered because the reporter does not allow any refutation by responsible individuals.

Let no one misunderstand: the guidelines of fairness stated here are on the one hand not easy to follow. On the other hand, if a reporter does not consistently try to be fair, his stories are likely to be misleading. Possibly you can think of a hundred actual news situations in which it would appear to be impossible to relate both sides. What about the news report of a speech in which the speaker advocates one side of a controversial issue? You must report what he said, the way he said it, but you can also, if necessary, use a side-bar to give the other side in a subsequent issue.

There is another way to be unfair which infuriates many readers. Sometimes a reporter will devote nine-tenths of a news story to one side of a controversy and end his story with a sentence or paragraph on the other side. This is called a "fair and objective" article. The one sentence or paragraph may be adequate, if that is all it takes to report the opposition, but the chances are it is not adequate.

Exaggerated Stories

High standards of newsgathering and newswriting prohibit the practice of pumping up a few rumors into a full-fledged news story that is all out of proportion to the importance of the event. There was a day in American journalism when premium salaries were paid to reporters who could "expand" a handful of facts into a column of type. This is not to say that newspapers today do not value the reporter who can take a breaking story and, by adding background and informed interpretation, come up with a whiz of a story that clarifies and enhances the reader's understanding of the event. But "inflating" and "rounding out" are two different things. In the former the reporter is guilty of reporting a mountain for a molehill, doing violence to the entire concept of fairness and objectivity in the news.

A reporter's efforts to build a "bigger and better" story than is warranted can be dangerous. Here is an example:

A reporter's wife noticed a few bubbles in a glass of water taken from her kitchen faucet. She told her husband, who called the municipal water plant to find out about the phenomenon. A voice at the other end of the line dismissed the whole matter with the comment, "Maybe some detergent has gotten into the water supply."

Without checking further, the reporter wrote a half-column story beginning:

What is causing bubbles in the Blanktown water supply these days?
A check with officials at the Municipal Water

Plant brought forth only a "guess" that the bubbles are caused by some kind of detergent.

The reporter went on from that point to speculate on how the detergent might have penetrated the water supply, and raised a number of questions concerning what else "might have seeped into the city's main well."

The story created a small panic in the city. The public utility phones were jammed with calls from frantic and irate citizens who wanted to know what the hell was going on and why the city was not doing something about the "poisonous" water supply.

When the facts were known, it was revealed that a small break in a pipeline had allowed air to get into the system. For a short time some customers did have bubbles in their water. No detergents or any other harmful substances were found.

Failure to Qualify Statements

Sometimes a news story is inaccurate and harmful because a reporter uses an interview statement out of context, to the extent that the statement misleads the reader. If the statement was qualified by its original context, it may have an entirely different meaning. Sometimes a reporter deliberately pulls statements out of context. More often he does it through ignorance of the subject or sheer laziness in putting together a good report. A statement of correction and apology by the newspaper may be the consequence.

Suppose the public utilities man in the above story had said, "Maybe there's some kind of detergent in the water supply, but, on the other hand, we've been having some air leaks in some of our pipes and that could account for the bubbles." The reporter might have deliberately ignored the second part of the statement and reported only the speculation about the detergent, because it was more dramatic and he knew the story would get better readership. Bad journalism? Certainly.

Here is another example of "news" resulting from some statement out of context:

Re-election of Governor Brown was predicted today by Dr. Fred A. Powers, Blanktown College

political science professor and president of Political
Poll, Inc.

Professor Powers, for more than twenty years
one of the leading political analysts in the state, said
in an interview his predictions were based on a
month-long study by his opinion polling organization of voting habits in every precinct in the state.

The remainder of the story included facts and figures
from the professor's study, but it never mentioned that the
professor had also said he was predicting re-election of the
governor *only if* he achieved a majority of the votes in the
first primary. The professor did not flatly say that the
governor would be reelected. Later the newspaper published
a correction and an apology.

Stories That Lack Clarity

Actually, all of the faults already listed contribute to lack
of clarity in news stories, but some special sins of
commission and omission affecting clarity need to be mentioned at this point.

Strange Terminology. Reporters often use language in
their stories that is familiar to the news source but not
commonly known to readers. For example:

Nearly 25 percent of all oceanfront property in
Blanktown Beach is composed of streetends. There
are 46 of them shown on a city map, but one, at 15th
Avenue North, has been abandoned since the map
was last revised.

Sea Gull Beach has 19 streetends 75 feet wide,
but of varying lengths because the strand, which
parallels the bulkhead line, does not run the entire
length of the city.

Turtle Beach also shares one streetend and a
ramp with Blanktown Beach at Moonrise Avenue,
and another with Surfside Beach at the east end of
Surfside Boulevard.

Surfside Beach has another 14 streets deadend-
ing at the bulkhead line, including ramps at 7th and
15th streets, which are impassable for cars because
of storm damage.

The streets are 60 feet wide, and measure about
300 feet from Seagrape Avenue to the sea wall.

North of Surfside Beach, the City of Greenville

has five public accesses to Neptune Beach, with parking areas each.

One—access No. 4—has a ramp to permit driving on the strand itself.

In the first place, try to get the beachend streets to add up to forty-six. The figures just don't add up. Possibly the reporter assumes that persons living along the ocean understand what this story is all about. But maybe they don't know at all what he is talking about. What does the reporter mean by one street was abandoned? What precisely is the strand—is this a street running along the ocean, or is it the beach itself? What is the "bulkhead line," and what is the difference between it and the sea wall? All of these terms need to be explained for the story to be perfectly clear.

Lack of Adequate Background. A continuing story that lacks background each day makes no sense to a reader unless he has been following the series from the beginning. Even then he may not remember important details. Each day the reporter must bring the story up to date for the reader who is seeing the story for the first time, and then add the new facts. These stories, for example, are not clear because they lack backgrounding:

BLANKTOWN, April 10—Whether 16-year old Anthony A. Kino will be allowed to return to his high school classroom will be decided today by the Blank County School Board.

Young Kino, son of City Commissioner John P. Kino, was expelled from Blanktown High School last week after Principal Roy A. Smith had failed over a period of weeks to get the youth to cut his shoulder-length hair and conform to the school dress code.

BLANKTOWN, April 11—Expulsion of Anthony A. Kino from Blanktown High School by Principal Roy A. Smith was upheld by a 3-2 vote of the Blank County School Board yesterday.

At the close of yesterday morning's session of the board, City Commissioner John P. Kino, the boy's father, told members of the board that the case was not closed. "I intend to take this matter all the way to the Supreme Court, if necessary," he said.

BLANKTOWN, June 3—Declaring that Anthony A. Kino had not exhausted all administrative
appeals, a circuit court judge today refused to hear a
case brought by the youth's father to get the 16-year-
old Blanktown High School student reinstated in
school.

The case was brought by a Blanktown City
Commissioner on behalf of his son, who has been out
of school since April 5.

Assuming that each story is complete and that no
further details were provided, each story leaves a number of
unanswered questions. But the second and third stories are
completely inadequate because each fails to explain why the
case went to the school board and then to the circuit court.

Poor Story Organization. Stories often are unclear
because story organization is so jumbled that the reader is
unable to find any logical pattern. A rambling, confusing
story can result from lack of paragraph unity and/or from
paragraphs arranged in an illogical manner. For example:

The deceased was active in civic affairs, having
served as president of the Blanktown Kiwanis Club,
of which he was a charter member. During his high
school days he was an All-American quarterback. In
1960 he ran for mayor of Blanktown but was defeated
by a small number of votes. He is survived by his
widow, Mrs. Mary Ann Coles.

Mr. Coles served on the Blanktown Boy Scout
District Council for more than 20 years, and was
United Fund Drive Chairman for the county for two
years. As an All-American high school football
player he helped Blanktown High School win the
only state championship in its history. He served one
term in the state legislature five years ago. Also
surviving him are two sons, Harry F. and Glenn J., as
well as five grandsons.

The story would be clearer if all of Mr. Coles' civic
achievements were discussed in one paragraph, his football
triumphs in a second paragraph, and his list of survivors in a
third paragraph.

"Loose" Writing. The need for "tight" writing is more
critical today than at any other period in history. The

amount of news available for the average newspaper has multiplied a hundredfold in the years following the first American newspaper which advertised that it contained a "glut of occurrences." As frequently as possible use words that are so loaded with meaning they can replace entire phrases. For example:

Don't write:	*Write it:*
Blanktown's Conservation Club will hold a meeting tonight for the purpose of electing a new president.	Blanktown's Conservation Club will meet tonight to elect a new president.
The main speaker at the Conservation Club meeting will be Cary O. Thomas, who has chosen as the subject for his talk, "Winning Against the Wilderness."	Cary O. Thomas will speak to members of the Conservation Club on "Winning Against the Wilderness."
They were united in the bonds of holy matrimony just minutes before their automobile was involved in an accident at the corner of Bluff and Pine Streets.	They were married just minutes before their automobile was involved in an accident at Bluff and Pine Streets.
The judge made a statement that the bail was being set in the amount of $500.00	The judge said bail would be $500.00.

Today there is competition between every written word and something else. People don't have to read what you write. They can watch television, go to a movie, take a walk, ride in the family car, or do any of a hundred different things. The man who receives your newspaper doesn't *have* to read *your* news story. To capture and hold attention today you must be brief. People today often "read on the run." How do you learn to write with brevity?

Watch Your Articles. The articles involved here are *a, an,* and *the.* Sometimes these articles clutter up writing and make it hard to understand. In the statement, "I saw *the* book on *the* table," *the* is important because it tells us that a particular book in question is on a particular table. In the sentence, "I saw *a* book on the table," *a* tells us that some book was seen, not a pencil or an ashtray, or that one unparticular book was seen.

In the examples above, articles have some particular meaning in each sentence. Now look at the following sentences:

It is a part of the clock.
It is part of the clock.

Leaving out the *a* in the second sentence creates punch and brevity.

Wordiness. The best way to learn "tight" writing is to go over your finished writing with a heavy pencil, underlining combinations of words which can be replaced by a single word. Write the one word above the phrase it will replace. Here are a few examples:

The committee arrived at a conclusion.	Poor
The committee concluded.	Better
When he got through with his work, he went home."	Poor
When he finished his work, he went home.	Better
The boy fell off of the cliff.	Poor
The boy fell off the cliff.	Better
There are no jobs at the present time.	Poor
There are no jobs at present.	Better
The color of the house was green.	Poor
The house was green.	Better
The reason he was unhappy was because he had no money.	Poor
He was unhappy because he had no money.	Better

Sometimes writers say that an event will take place at "10 A.M. this morning." "Morning" is unnecessary because A.M. means morning. Verbosity often occurs because writers fail to think about the meaning of words. This last sentence could have been written, "Much wordy writing occurs because writers fail to think about the meaning of what they write," but it would have taken three more words.

Short Sentences. Short sentences do not necessarily result in brevity. Let's take an example from a "reader" for children:

I saw the cat.
The cat was black.
The cat was sitting on the fence.
The cat was watching me.

Those four sentences total twenty words. The writing is monotonous and boring. Rewrite the sentences: "I saw the black cat sitting on the fence watching me." Now there are only eleven words and the sentence says the same thing. "Shortness" is the result of editing out unnecessary words. It does not result from breaking up one sentence into several and repeating key words.

Redundancy. Writers sometimes use redundant expressions in both speaking and writing. Here are some examples:

As a *usual* rule.
Round *in shape.*
Small *in size.*
Consensus *of opinion.*
Cooperate *together.*
Form a *joint* partnership.

Look at your own writing. You may find many expressions cluttered with unnecessary words because you failed to think.

Thatitis. One way to achieve brevity in writing is to eliminate unnecessary use of the word "that." Overuse of the word has been called *that*itis by some writers. Here's an example:

Dear Mr. Jones:

In answer to your letter of this date, it is our pleasure to inform you *that* the accommodations *that* you requested for the Easter weekend have been set aside for your use and *that* it will be our pleasure to serve you in connection with the convention *that* will be held at our hotel at *that* time.

If you need to make changes in this reservation for any reason prior to the meeting, please send details and at *that* time we will do our best to provide you with the accommodations *that* will suit your new needs.

You may rest assured *that* our staff personnel are geared to the efficient handling of any convention needs *that* might arise and *that* we are all most eager to serve your association.

The above letter from a hotel manager contains the word "that" ten times in a 135-word letter. The letter is wordy; the language is stilted and a little pompous. The ten instances of "that" are not in themselves faulty, but the wordy phrases they create make the letter too long. Here is the letter, rewritten:

Dear Mr. Jones:

The room which you requested for the Easter weekend has been reserved for you. Should you wish to make any changes in your reservation prior to your convention at our hotel, please let me know. Our hotel staff people are geared to the handling of conventions of all sizes and we shall do our best to make your convention a success.

Write in a Straight Line. Brevity results from clear, uncluttered thinking which allows you to write "in a straight line." If you want to say, "The cat crossed the street," you say just that. You don't say, "The cat, it crossed the street," or "The cat it the street crossed."

Yet some people are inclined to write that way. They write all around an idea instead of straight to it. Watch for awkward expressions in your writing:

Tommy, he went to the store.	Poor
Tommy went to the store.	Better
The car it got stuck in the mud.	Poor
The car got stuck in the mud.	Better

In the following example, the cat never made it across the street:

Another story which shows news value, but also

human interest which the *Kansas City Star* wrote a long feature on is one on wartime marriages.

What the writer really wanted to say was:

A long feature in the *Kansas City Star* on wartime marriages is a good example of a story with both news value and human interest.

Stay on the Track. Sometimes it is hard for a writer to stick with a central subject—he forgets the intent of his story and allows himself to stray far afield. Writers need to ask themselves, Is this material germane to the subject? Am I sticking to my subject? What has this got to do with my topic?

Keep It Simple. Here is the foreword to a new magazine recently on the newsstands:

The world of today is a world abounding in contradictions, a world beset with commotions of the gravest kind. Ominous winds and clouds sweeping across the international arena portend invariably unfathomable changes or vicissitudes; international problems ever give rise to unnumerable diverse schools of thought. Confronted with such a situation, it is therefore incumbent on us that we must, in regard to the different or sometimes even completely contradictory views, form our own opinion, our real understanding of the arguments, before we can avoid falling into the pitfalls of credulity and blind conformity.

This writer is trying to say that we live in a complex world but that we must nevertheless form opinions and have a real understanding of issues.

Failure to Be Concrete. Have you ever considered how much misunderstanding is caused by writing and speaking in general rather than specific language? Concrete language is as important as brevity in news and feature writing. If you were to write in a feature story, "A glass of water is one sign of an advanced civilization," your readers would naturally assume that you were talking about a glass of *drinking* water. Even so, the statement is too general because you force your reader to make an assumption. "A glass of drinking water," would have been more concrete.

If you were to write simply that a scientist went to his laboratory for a glass of water, you could throw a number of obstacles in the way of communication. Did he go for distilled water, tap water, hot water, cold water, salt water, or heavy water? The reader cannot see the glass of water, or taste it, nor can he ask the scientist what kind of water.

Concrete Words. Challenge every *key* word you use to see if it is the most concrete word you can find for the job. *Gun* is a general word; *shotgun* is more concrete. *Weapon* is general; *broadsword, dagger,* or *rapier* are more concrete. *House* is general, but words like *cottage* and *cabin* are more concrete.

Don't use abstract words without explanation. If you write, for example, "He was fond of his liberty," you are not being concrete. What kind of liberty do you mean? Do you mean constitutional liberty, such as freedom of the press, freedom of speech, or freedom of religion; or do you mean that he likes to steal away from home nights? To say that a person is "dishonest" is to be general. What is the nature of his dishonesty? Does he cheat, lie, or steal?

Concrete Ideas. The writer should try to *think* concretely. Instead of saying, "He was in trouble with the law," the writer needs to report the exact nature of the trouble. Advertising copy often tells you nothing:

We offer you full and complete protection for your home at the lowest cost in history. Our company is backed by some of the largest insurers in the world, so we feel you are safe when you do business with us. Also, we guarantee our contract with you.

This sounds great, but it actually offers only generalities. You don't know the nature of the "protection." You don't know the name of a single large insurer backing the company. You don't know the nature of the contract, and you don't know the nature of the guarantee.

Here is another example of writing that cheats the reader:

I believe in integrity in government. I believe in good schools. I believe in the preservation of our natural resources. I believe in helping the farmer and the small businessman. When I am elected your representative, you have my word that I will do all these things. On this promise I stand or fall.

What is "integrity" in government? What makes for good schools? What needs to be done to preserve natural resources, and how can the farmer and the small businessman be helped? This candidate has avoided specific issues and hopes to ride to victory on generalities.

Questions for Discussion

1. Edit a piece of newspaper copy to find examples of wordiness or lack of clarity.
2. Edit a paragraph in a textbook for clarity of thought. See if you can rewrite the paragraph to improve a reader's understanding of it.
3. Is most newspaper copy brief and to the point? Is it too brief?
4. Can brevity destroy reader interest? Why, or why not?
5. Do you believe newspapers deliberately "color" news stories?

8 how to achieve reader interest

Dullness is a cardinal sin in writing. Creating and maintaining interest is the main ingredient in the success of underground newspapers and the so-called new journalism. In responsible journalism, however, making interesting copy should not overtake the necessity to be accurate. Interest is often just a matter of the writer's attitude. The reporter must say to himself, This is a difficult subject. How can I make it interesting as well as informative and accurate?

All too frequently, reporters pound out a story without ever thinking about how they can make the story more readable, more human, more in tune with the interests of their readers.

In the following pages I will discuss a number of techniques to achieve reader interest. Not all will work for every story, but the reporter should get into the habit of trying various devices so that every story is not written in the same straightforward, dull, factual style.

The Matter of Attitude

How you approach the assignment is important. Two reporters, from different newspapers, were assigned to cover a rummage sale by a local parent-teacher group. Each repor-

ter went about his task in a different way. The resulting
stories clearly reveal how each reporter's attitude governed
his reporting.

The first reporter used the telephone to contact the
chairman of the rummage sale committee. The story read:

Members of the Parent-Teacher Association of
the Southside Elementary School earned $133 Satur-
day at a rummage sale held to raise money for school
needs.

Mrs. Thomas J. Mooney, chairman of the rummage sale committee, said the money "will probably
be used to buy drapes for the student lounge."

This is the third rummage sale held by the school
this school year. Members of Mrs. Mooney's committee are: Mrs. Albert A. Jones, Mrs. Roger C. Clarke,
Mrs. Sven Y. Edwards, and Mrs. Carl B. Yeager, all
mothers of Southside students.

The second reporter went to the rummage sale. He poked
around among the articles being offered for sale, interviewed
each of the mothers on duty, observed customers making
purchases, and turned in the following story. It appeared
with a by-line in the Sunday edition.

Santa Claus shows up in the strangest places.

No one saw the bearded old gentleman at the
Southside Elementary School rummage sale on West
Union St. yesterday, but he was there. A barefoot
boy, his legs slightly blue from the wet December
wind, knows he was there.

Amid the hustle and confusion of the sale, one of
the mothers saw the boy rooting through a box of
shoes, marked to go at ten cents a pair.

"Find a pair you like?" she asked kindly.

"Yes, ma'am," the boy replied, "but I don't have
any money."

The mother thought quickly. "Why, you came
just at the right time," she said. "It just happens that
we need someone to clean this place up a bit. If you'll
just pick up the scraps of paper around here, you may
have the shoes."

The chores were quickly done and the shoes
changed hands. A pair of socks was added for good
measure.

Rummage sales—there is one nearly every
Saturday on the Johnson Company parking lot

behind the store—are good barometers of the financial climate of Blanktown and Blank County, according to the PTA mothers. They reveal what the cost of living has done to pocketbooks of many local residents.

Local church women and PTA members who conduct many of these sales say they frequently turn their heads to allow thinly clad men and women an opportunity to walk out with a needed dress or coat they have stuffed under a tattered jacket.

Parents with large families are the best customers. At yesterday's sale total receipts were $133, made from sale of men's suits at $2, women's dresses from 25 to 50 cents, shoes at 10 cents a pair, and children's clothes from 5 to 50 cents. A good, warm overcoat without holes went for less than $2.

Many families were "winterized" for less than $5. When the money was not available to buy everything a family needed, extras were thrown in at no cost.

These local rummage sales produce all kinds of benefits to the community, say the people who conduct them. By offering needy persons warm clothes at a low price, the sellers help keep up public morale. The buyers do not feel that they are receiving charity. They pay for the clothes with hard-earned money. The schools, in turn, use the money for worthy causes.

Mrs. Thomas J. Mooney, chairman of yesterday's sale, said the money earned by her committee "probably will be used to buy drapes for the student lounge."

Regardless of whether you consider the above story good or bad, at least the writer tried to bring people into his article. The first writer used names in his story, but the second reporter turned those names into warm, thoughtful human beings, engaged in a public service project.

The Human Touch

The interesting writer often tells his story in terms of people. Most news is about people, but frequently the reporter is faced with a story about a new tax law, full of facts and figures and legal terminology, a story about a new school, or a new bridge. Even if the reporter writes such a story in terms

of the facts alone, he can follow-up with a story telling
readers how the new law, school, or bridge will affect them.
He does this by interviewing readers affected by the new
development and getting their viewpoints. In the case of the
new tax law, he can use a statistically typical family to show
how the tax will affect most readers.

The reader can be further brought into the story by using
a personal address style. One writer wrote a story on the use
of chrysanthemums for decorating the home in this fashion:

> If you're thinking about using mums for holiday
> arrangements, it's possible to place potted mums in a
> copper or brass kettle and use them as your center-
> piece. . . . Don't feel like a failure if the chrysanthe-
> mum you bring home from the grocery store or florist
> isn't everlasting.

Marjoe Creamer, of the *St. Petersburg* (Fla.) *Times,* set
out to do a story about the appearance of a lawyer's office for
the home section of her newspaper. She could have dryly
described the office; instead she spiced up the description
with comments by the attorney:

> Attorney Anthony Battaglia feels that a profes-
> sional office should emanate warmth.
>
> "You've got to make a client feel comfortable,"
> he said.
>
> In redecorating the office of Parker, Battaglia
> and Ross, Battaglia "took basic red and went on from
> there."
>
> He used the color in the carpets to warm the
> reception room.
>
> The same red carpet follows into Battaglia's
> rather unusual office that features a wall of Zyrian
> stone, which Battaglia said frankly "was a lot more
> trouble and cost a lot more than we planned."
>
> As with most of the walls in the office complex,
> the three remaining walls in the attorney's room
> have dark paneling. Against them, and displayed in
> frames matted in red, are keys from all over the
> world, either collected by Battaglia or sent to him by
> clients.
>
> "I started the key collection as a hobby. I would
> bring a key back from places where I had business.
>
> "I started a key book as a reference to where I'd
> been. It would also remind me of the name of the
> hotel. Then my clients started mailing me keys.

"Now I have keys from all parts of the earth."

Those from Amsterdam and Tokyo are special prizes. And one large key from Fallsburg, N.Y., is purportedly to a room that George Washington slept in.

Battaglia's office doors slide in response to controls electrically operated behind his desk or from outside.

"If there's a power failure while the door is closed, I just sit here," he commented. There are no windows in the room. "If there's a fire, I have an ax to help me get out."

There is more to the story, but this gives some idea of how the writer put it together.

Another St. Petersburg reporter was sent to cover the opening of a new cafeteria. She told the entire story through quotes of conversations among people around her—without identifying anyone—but allowing people to reveal their personalities through what they said. Facts about the opening were sprinkled in brief paragraphs throughout the piece.

Letting People Talk

The use of conversation is a good way of getting people into the news. The use of direct quotes in a story is important. Not only do they prevent a story from looking dull, they help give the reader a better idea of what a news character is like. They make the story more believable, and they can add sprightliness and interest. There are some pitfalls to avoid:

1. Don't make a person appear foolish or stupid unless there is a reason for it and your newspaper is prepared to defend a possible libel suit.
2. Don't include quotes just to have quotes in the story. The conversation or statements must be natural and add something to the story.
3. Don't quote people out of context to the extent that the story is inaccurate.

A paragraph-by-paragraph comparison of the two stories that follow illustrates the importance of conversation in making a story sparkle:

SARASOTA—Karl Wallenda, who set a world's record in 1970 by walking a 1,000-foot-high wire across Tallulah Falls, Ga., expects to break his own record in England next year.

The Great Wallenda, as he is booked in show circles, revealed that the British Broadcasting Company has invited him to walk across an even longer gorge in the English Midlands.

At his winter home in Sarasota, Wallenda said he understands that the English gorge is not as deep as the 750-foot Tallulah Falls gorge but that it is longer and deep enough.

He will make the walk without nets or other mechanical devices.

The location of the gorge has not been revealed. Wallenda turned down a previous selection because the gorge was not long enough and because people could not get to it. Wallenda explained that he cannot perform without an audience.

At 66, Wallenda appears to be in wonderful health. He has the energy of a youth, which comes through in his effervescent personality and his almost childlike restlessness. Unable to sit in one place very long, he was up and down during a recent interview. He seems to need several chairs in a room so he can move from one to another to satisfy his restlessness.

Wallenda admitted that he had some misgivings about that dangerous Tallulah Falls walk. The day before the walk he received a letter from a woman who urged him against trying the dangerous feat. Wallenda said the woman wrote him that she had talked with God and had been told that he was going to fall. The tight-wire artist explained that he believes such things and that such statements disturb him.

During the 17 and one quarter minute walk, Wallenda stood twice on his head at the spot where he was directly over the deepest part in the gorge. He explained that people who walk on a tight-wire don't like to look down but when he stood on his head he had to look down. He said when he looked at the tight-wire—really a cable one and eleven-sixteenths inches in diameter—his eyes wanted to focus on distance below. He said he looked down the 750 feet and wondered how crazy it was for him to be up there.

Wallenda returned to his feet and walked the rest of the way, tense and not without fear, but he never doubted that he would make it. At the end of the cable he was given a martini to settle his nerves. He explained, however, that the martini was only water. This disappointed him.

Notice in the second version of this same story how the writer used conversation in just the right places to add to the portrait of Wallenda:

Sarasota—Karl Wallenda, who set a world's record in 1970 by walking a 1,000-foot-high wire across Tallulah Falls, Ga., expects to break his own record in England next year.

The Great Wallenda, as he is booked in show circles, revealed that the British Broadcasting Company has invited him to walk across an even longer gorge in the English Midlands.

"I understand the English gorge isn't quite as deep as the 750-foot-deep Tallulah Falls gorge," said Wallenda at his winter home in Sarasota, "but I have been assured it is longer and that the gorge is deep enough."

He will make the walk without nets or other mechanical safety devices.

The location of the gorge has not been revealed. Wallenda turned down a previous location because the gorge "wasn't long enough" and because "people couldn't get to it."

"I cannot perform without an audience," he said.

At 66, Wallenda appears to be in wonderful health. He has the energy of a youth, which comes through in his effervescent personality and his almost childlike restlessness.

Unable to sit in one place very long, he was up and down during a recent interview.

He seems to need several chairs in a room so he can move from one to another to satisfy his restlessness.

Wallenda admitted that he had some misgivings about that dangerous Tallulah Falls walk. The day before the walk he received a letter from a woman who urged him against trying the dangerous feat.

"She wrote me she had talked with God and that I was going to fall," Wallenda said.

"I'm a believer. Such things shake me up."

During the 17 and one quarter minute walk, Wallenda stood twice on his head at the spot where he was directly over the deepest part of the gorge.

"People who walk the high-wire don't like to look down—but when I stood on my head I had to look down," he said.

"I was looking at the wire—well, it was a cable, one and eleven-sixteenths inches in diameter—and my eyes wanted to focus on the distance below. Suddenly, I'm looking down 750 feet and I said to myself:

"'Karl, you're crazy; what are you doing up here?'"

Wallenda returned to his feet and walked the rest of the way tense and not without fear, but he never doubted that he would make it.

At the end of the cable he was given the "world's largest martini" to settle his nerves.

"But it was only water—it was in a dry county," he said disappointedly.

Handling Description

The trouble with most descriptions of people in newspapers is that they consist almost entirely of enumerations of physical traits. For example, here is a paragraph from a Sunday feature:

At 72, he is short with brown eyes that look through black frame glasses, dark hair that has receded and left a shiny bald spot on top, and a slender figure that's beginning to bulge slightly in the middle. Martha is a chunky lady of 64, with buoyant good humor.

In the preceding paragraph two persons are described, a man and a woman, but in the case of each, the picture is rather flat. The pictures are flat because there is no motion. Think hard about a very close friend. Can you imagine that friend as completely immobile? Aren't you more likely to think of the way he walks, the way he talks, how he carries himself, his mannerisms? When you first see a person, you are likely to be struck by something unusual about him, or an outstanding feature. It may be his hair, his deepset eyes that give his face a tragic look, a hump on his back, the ramrod straightness of his frame, and so forth. Starting with this one characteristic, you fit other characteristics into a general picture of the person.

You might do it another way. You might get a general picture of the person, such as shabbiness. Then you look for details to verify your impression that he looks shabby. His shoes are scuffed and unshined. His trousers are baggy at the knees, and two of the belt loops are missing. Even though he wears a necktie it is soiled. His blue shirt is wrinkled and looks "slept-in."

Good description of people should have the following characteristics:

1. It should have some kind of order or pattern to it. You should not describe the person haphazardly. You begin by telling the reader how the person looks generally or by describing an outstanding feature. Then you add the details that complete the picture.
2. Good description requires a keen eye that never misses a single detail in a person's face, his clothes, or his surroundings. As Mr. Lindstrom said earlier in this book, most reporters never see the ashes fall from a man's cigar, or a man twirling his Phi Beta Kappa key.
3. Good description has such sharpness of detail, such movement, such personification, that every reader gets a clear mental picture. Your goal should be to make the reader see what you see, smell what you smell, hear what you hear.
4. Good description should have motion to it. Describe people doing characteristic things, unusual things, interesting things, things that will bring them alive for your readers.

How do you describe places and things? The need for a pattern in this kind of description is just as necessary. You don't, for example, list everything in a room or tell your readers exactly where every article of furniture is placed. You begin by giving the readers your dominant impression of the room, adding the details later. If you are describing an outdoor scene you can begin by describing the foreground, then the center, and finally the background. Or you can describe the most impressive feature of the scene, adding details that help accentuate that part of the scene you found to be the center of interest.

Try using verbs and adverbs instead of adjectives when describing people, places, or things. You can write, "These were sad men," or you can picture the sadness like this: "The men we met walked slowly by, unsmiling, with downcast eyes."

You must be aware of your *observation point* when describing something. The reader cannot see you and will not know whether you are at the bottom or top when you begin describing a hill. You should write, "As I approached the bottom of the hill, I saw. . . ," and "From the bottom of the hill you could see. . . ."

Figures of Speech

Few reporters seem to remember their English composition classes and their emphasis on figures of speech. Descriptive writing can be made to glow with proper figures of speech, but it can also fall flat on its face with improper ones. The most common figures of speech are *similes* and *metaphors*. Similes are comparisons—usually introduced by the words "like" or "as"—of places, objects, or persons that are unlike, but which have some similar characteristics. For example, "The lilies along the walk looked like slender candles." Metaphors also compare, but the comparison is implied. In the above description of the lilies, if the statement had read, "The lilies along the walk were slender candles," this would have been a metaphor. In a newspaper feature about the Castro family, of Castro Convertibles sofa fame, Molly Sinclair of the *St. Petersburg Times* used the following figures of speech:

They've got convertibles that *jump up, down and sideways* at their Ocala ranch. . .

When a fly *slipped* into the house, Bernard took after it with a swatter.

Life for the Castros hasn't been *lined with mink,* however.

People *flocked* into the store and stood in line to buy.

But, for all their wheeling here and dealing there, the Castros keep a *tight rein* on their furniture business.

The writer who attributes human qualities to an inanimate object or to an idea is using *personification,* another figure of speech. These can be either similes or metaphors. For example:

Simile: The fog sneaked into town like a thief in the night.

Metaphor: When I opened my shutters, the fog stood outside, a silent stranger. The wind, a madman, tore at my throat.

The trouble with similes, metaphors, personifications, and all other figures of speech is that writers and speakers use the same ones over and over until they become trite and lifeless. We speak all too often of the "lap of luxury" and the maid who is "pretty as a picture." We often spoil figures of speech by mixing them up in such a way that they are unbelievable or ridiculous. For example:

The cold wind was a madman who burned my face like a torch.

Point of View

The writer's point of view is important to readers. As mentioned earlier, the reader needs to know the physical location of the writer. If the writer is in a train moving at sixty miles an hour, the reader should know so that he can evaluate what the writer says. If the writer is describing a subway crowd during a rush hour, the reader wants to know if the writer is observing the scene from a station platform, the middle of a crowded car, or from the ticket seller's booth.

Sometimes a writer will write from a vantage point which is actually impossible for him. For example, the reporter who wrote the news story about Charles A. Lindbergh's departure for Paris in a single engine airplane in 1927 described the takeoff in great detail, including how the pilot looked and felt as he sat in the plane's cockpit, struggling to get the heavily loaded "Spirit of St. Louis" off the ground. The writer *imagined* how Lindbergh felt.

Every newspaper writer should be thoroughly aware of the problems created by prejudice as a *point of view*. A reporter who dislikes dogs will have a tough time being objective in a news story about a dog attacking a child. He may describe the animal as a wild, vicious, man-hating beast, whereas the dog may have attacked because it was startled and feared for its own safety.

An outdoor reporter sent to cover the opening of a new highway through a national forest might picture the highway as an intrusion on the forest animals and therefore ecologically unwise. Another reporter, with a different point of view, might write about the benefits to city dwellers, now able to spend their weekends in the coolness and serenity of the deep woods. Which reporter is right? Probably both. How can a writer write interesting descriptive copy and yet remain objective? You cannot, of course, be completely objective, but you can be honest and responsible as a writer—be aware of your own biases.

Once you move from straightforward description to evaluative description your point of view has emerged. For example, you may describe a girl as having blue eyes; another writer might say that she has blue-green eyes, and both will be objective. If, however, you describe her eyes as "blue pools of laughter," you have made a subjective evaluation. Another writer, less favorably inclined to the young lady, might describe the same eyes as "blue pools of blankness."

Narrative Techniques

The difference between the news reporter and the writer of fiction is that the one deals exclusively with fact, the other with imagination. But that is no reason for the newswriter to write in a dull and colorless manner. He has as much opportunity as the storyteller to use certain narrative devices to enhance the interest of his story. The principal devices are:

The Narrative Beginning. The narrative beginning can be either an action beginning, one that puts the reader in the middle of the main event of the story, or one that sets the scene for the story. It might also describe a main character.

Here is an example of an action beginning, written by Sheila Moran for the Associated Press:

NEW YORK—"I'm looking for coke. I'm looking for coke," said the slim, long-haired young man in silver-studded bluejeans, to anyone in the crowded discotheque who could hear him above the blaring music.

A mod, hippie type sidled up to him at the bar. "Hey, man, I've got some smokin' coke," he said.

The character-development opening is used frequently for stories that are wholly or partly biographical. The following example was written by Michael Widmer for United Press International:

BROCKTON, Mass.—His neighbors knew Heinrich von George as a pleasant man who kept to himself, but others saw the unemployed father of seven as a talker who bluffed his way through life.

Behind these contrasting guises lay the rumblings of internal conflict of a proud man unable to live up to his dreams of success.

Chronological Order. Chronological order—relating events in the order in which they occurred—is a natural storytelling device. The use of chronological order carries with it a sense of orderliness that appeals to many readers. But this is not a device to use in every story; in fact, the success of a writer depends largely on his ability to determine when chronological order should or should not be used.

Singleness of Effect. One criterion of success for a fiction writer is his ability to produce a single, sustained, and predetermined effect. The fact that an effect is predetermined does not necessarily mean that the article will be exclusively subjective. Objectivity is largely a result of the writer's integrity. You may, for example, set out to write "A Day at Grand Canyon." Suppose you are most strongly impressed by the sheer size of this natural wonder, and want to leave this impression with your readers. You have predetermined the tone of the article, and you will use words throughout the story that emphasize again and again, the vastness of the canyon. Singleness of effect is, then, the tone, or mood, that pervades the article. Here is an example from Charles Dickens:

These were all foreshadowings of London, Tom thought, as he sat upon the box, and looked about him. Such a coachman, and such a guard, never could have existed between Salisbury and any other place.

The coach was none of your steady-going, yokel coaches, but a swaggering, rakish, dissipated London coach; up all night and lying by all day, and leading a devil of a life. It cared no more for Salisbury than if it had been a hamlet. It rattled noisily through the best streets, defied the Cathedral, took the worst corners sharpest, went cutting in everywhere, making everything get out of its way; and spun along the open country-road, blowing a lively defiance out of its key-bugle, as its last glad parting legacy.

A tone of light-hearted gaiety is produced by the imagery in the writing. The coach is likened to a person, carefree, light-hearted, swaggering, and rakish. Such words as "swaggering," "rakish," "dissipated," "noisily," and "defiance," all give the desired tone.

Theme. The theme, or central idea, of a novel might be to show what happens to a family consumed by greed. In nonfiction articles, for example, an in-depth report for the Sunday newspaper or a magazine piece, the theme is often explicitly indicated in the title or headline. "The Imperiled Everglades," written by Fred Ward for *National Geographic,* is based on the idea that the Florida Everglades are indeed in peril.

The theme may be a point of view that the writer has adopted after intensive research in a subject. Objectivity in this case depends upon the honesty and conviction with which the writer adopts his point of view or "theme." If he adopts a theme only to be controversial and therefore arouse interest, without any concern for the rightness of his position or the direction of the facts, then he is not being true to his profession and does not deserve to have reader support.

Point of View. In description the "point of view" is the implied or stated physical location of the writer. In narrative writing "point of view" is synonymous with person, or the grammatical mode of relating the story. The reporter can tell his story in the first person mode to emphasize that he has personally experienced the events being described. The chief disadvantage of this technique is that the reader might look upon the writer as being boastful. An advantage is that the reader may feel he is getting a "truer" account because it is from one who has participated in the event or was an eyewitness.

News writers often adopt the device of the story-within-a-story, where, for example, the mode is shifted from third to first person. Chaucer's *Canterbury Tales,* a story of travelers who pass the time during a trip by telling tales, is an example from literature. The reporter might include in the middle of a factual article about the poaching of alligator hides an anecdote, or "little story," to illustrate a point. Such an anecdote would give dramatic impact to the article if, for example, it were a real-life situation, full of action and danger, written in the first person.

The writer can also assume an omniscient point of view. Here is an example beginning a story about strange crosses that appeared in the windows of a church:

> The black minister stands beneath the cross in the the window of the church, wondering aloud why it exists and pondering the possibility of a miracle—the Cross in the Glass.

Apparently the writer knows what is in the mind of the minister. In fact, the reporter had talked with the man and was told that he had thought about the possibility of a miracle as he looked at the mysterious cross in the glass. In the description, quoted earlier, of Lindbergh's takeoff for Paris, it might seem as if the writer were omniscient since he described the cockpit and the attitude of Lindbergh while the plane was in the air—when it was otherwise impossible for the writer to see into the cockpit or study the pilot. In fact, the writer had examined the cockpit prior to takeoff and had interviewed the pilot just minutes before his journey.

Finding an Angle

Finding an angle for a feature story or an in-depth news article means that you must point the article in a specific direction and keep it pointed. You attract and keep readers by limiting your subject. Every editor is familiar with the writer who says, "I'd like to do a story about the poor people of our city. What about it, boss?"

The editor is likely to reply, "Everybody wants to write about poor people—and everybody does. What do you have to say about them that is different from what was said last week? Are there more poor people or fewer? Are the people poor because they want to be poor or don't they have a choice? What's your angle?"

What is your angle? That is the question every editor asks. He wants to know what is new, different, or unusual about the subject you have chosen. You don't write about the Florida Everglades—you write about "The Imperiled Everglades." A reporter can write a piece on "Juvenile Delinquency" and he will probably wander all over the subject because it is too general. He can limit the subject somewhat by writing about "Juvenile Delinquency in Blanktown."

Color Words

Some writers have said that an interesting writing style must have vitality, force, and variety. Each of these characteristics is achieved in part through the writer's choice of words. When we say that a person writes "colorfully," we often mean that he writes with imagination, with variety, with emphasis, and with emotion; that is, it has a certain amount of action in it. Much of this is achieved with "color" words, or "charged" words. These are words that carry an extra load of meaning.

In the next few paragraphs I am going to discuss color words as words useful in colorful writing, in writing that holds the reader's attention. Sometimes the term "charged words" is used to mean words that are deliberately put into sentences to distort their meaning or to develop negative emotional reactions. Consider the sentence, "These three men were the fat cats of the church and always traveled together as though for mutual protection." The two words *fat cats* are "charged" words in the sense that they arouse negative feelings about the men. They are also "color" words in that they make the writing colorful and interesting. All I am talking about in this section is the need for the writer to make a conscious effort to select words that will make his writing colorful and interesting.

Colorful writing is best described by example. The examples below describe the setting up of a circus.

BRADENTON—The Clyde Beatty-Cole Bros. Circus came to town this week.

About midnight Wednesday, it all began with trucks, cars and trailers pulling onto Bradenton's filled area by the river, just northwest of U.S. 301 and Manatee Avenue, a vacant acreage with nothing but a few sprigs of grass sticking above the ground.

The tents started going up at daylight. Lions roared, dogs barked, horses neighed, elephants trumpeted, and the sounds of people at work could be heard.

Men pulled on ropes to haul the big pieces of canvas into place and soon the Big Top was up. One by one other tents were put up, each to house its part of the show. Soon the world of the circus had been created.

This world affects all the senses. There was the music of the calliope, the smell of cotton candy, and all the odors from the various food stands.

This first example is a matter-of-fact account that fails to stir the reader very much. Compare it with this story written by Electa Wells for the *Tampa* (Fla.) *Tribune:*

BRADENTON—So, you think you've never seen a miracle. Well, one happened right here this week— the Clyde Beatty-Cole Bros. Circus came to town. That's a special kind of miracle with magic and excitement all mixed in together.

About midnight Wednesday, it all began with trucks, cars and trailers pulling onto Bradenton's "million dollar sand pile," the filled area by the river, just northwest of U.S. 301 and Manatee Avenue, a vacant uninteresting acreage with nothing but a few wiry sprigs of grass and sand spurs poking through the white sand and shell.

With the light of dawn, the sound of stakes being driven into the ground could be heard. There were other sounds too, lions roaring, dogs barking, horses neighing, elephants trumpeting and the sounds of people at work.

Huge pieces of canvas were hoisted into place by strong men pulling thick ropes. There it was—the Big Top with its banners flying in the breeze. Other smaller tents popped up, one by one, each to house its own segment of the great show.

Within six hours, scores of workmen had created a complete little world—unlike any other. An absolute nothing was transformed into a bustling, exciting place for all to come and enjoy.

A circus tickles all the senses. The music of the calliope stirs the imagination of the young and warms the memory of the young-at-heart. The sweet smell of cotton candy and the pungent aroma of onions mingle with the smells of hot dogs and hamburgers, popcorn, and peanuts.

One of the major differences between the two stories is choice of words—and the way in which they are used. In the second story the writer uses such color words as "miracle," "magic," and "excitement." Instead of a "few sprigs of grass sticking above the ground," the picture is sharpened by a "few wiry sprigs of grass and sand spurs poking through the white sand and shell." The sprigs of grass become "wiry" and they "poke" rather than "stick" upward. The ground in which they are found is no longer merely ground, but white sand and shell. The pieces of canvas become "huge" and the ropes "thick." The Big Top is further described with banners flying in the breeze. The other tents are not merely "put up," they "pop up, one by one."

The second story also has action, vitality, and enthusiasm. It stirs the reader so that he appreciates the circus by means of all his senses. He sees, smells, hears—and almost tastes and touches—the Big Top and its activities.

Visualization

Fortunate is the writer who has trained himself to visualize his entire story before he begins to write. This kind of writer sees the whole story in his mind's eye. His powers of visualization allow him to see his beginning, the theme of his article, the various parts as they will look when they are linked together, and the ending that will tie up the article like a string around a package.

Another way to define visualization is to say that it is the way a writer perceives his story. In the circus story in the preceding section dealing with color words, one writer apparently saw his story as "just another assignment," one that had been written over and over. The writer visualized the story as just a dull recital of a few facts. In the second version of the same story the writer was excited by the circus, capturing some of its magic, as though the circus were being seen for the first time.

If a writer visualizes his story with fresh eyes, with enthusiasm, with interest, and with honesty, he will be able to make the story "come alive" for his readers. If he perceives the story in an uninteresting and dull fashion, it will turn out that way for his readers and the newspaper will be unable to make it appear interesting through the magic of typographical treatment.

Putting It All Together

Now let us see how the advice in this chapter works in a single story. The example, "My Story, from the Heart," is by Jack McGuire, from the magazine section of the Jacksonville (Fla.) *Times-Union.*

In a few moments they will put me to death. That's what it amounts to really, and it will be accomplished by means of an electric shock administered by the surgeon. Later, with another jolt of stronger voltage, he plans to shock me back to life.

Now, my wheeled stretcher-cart rolls the last few feet along a hushed corridor and trips the mechanism which activates automatic sliding doors ahead. We enter the bright, aseptic world of the operating room. I am partly anesthetized already from a needle slipped into my arm before I began the journey on the cart, and apprehension and fear have given way to euphoria. Now, other things are done to me, and the room with its bright lights grows vague, and I'm falling slowly into a warm, misty eternity. . . .

It began on an ordinary Thursday a year ago, after a quick lunch and a rush back to the office for an important meeting. A slight case of indigestion, it seemed, nothing more. But annoying enough so that I asked to be excused from the meeting. My colleagues were conventionally sympathetic, and a 7-Up and a Rolaid provided by my secretary made me feel better. I dismissed the incident from my mind.

Two days later my wife, Betsy, and I climbed the stairs to see a basketball game. I was suddenly aware of pain that grew in intensity with each step. Rising from the base of the breastbone, it fanned across my chest to reach a crescendo as it raced down both arms. With it came cold fear.

Heart!

Doesn't every man in his midforties feel, with any sharp chest pain, the same flash of panic?

Heart!

But I had been given a clean bill of health only two months before after an expensive medical going-over.

Somehow I made it to the arena's top deck. But the attack took my breath away and slammed me into my seat, dizzy with fear. I sat with head bowed as Betsy went to telephone for help.

By the time she returned, the pain had dissipated, and I found that if I sat motionless, it could be contained. That, coupled with the news that the doctor Betsy had called was on vacation, brought me some sort of perverse cheer and made it easier for her to exact a promise: Should the pain return, we would go immediately to the nearest hospital! Reassured, she held tightly to my arm as we left the game early and headed for home.

Next morning, I slept late, had a light breakfast, read the Sunday papers. I felt fine. Fine, except for a nagging fear that kept picking its way up to the conscious level.

Suppose it's my heart giving me a message? But that physical . . . from head to toe? Besides, there's no way I can afford a heart problem. A wife and two small sons to support, a home, two cars, a color TV set. I'm in a tough, demanding business, running my own public relations agency. It needs me. Take away me and there won't be a business.

"Why don't you take a walk?" Betsy asked. "It's a lovely day."

"I don't feel like a walk. I never walk."

"But it's such a nice day. Maybe that's what's wrong with you. Maybe you don't get enough exercise."

"There's nothing wrong with me. Besides, I'd feel stupid taking a walk."

"Lots of people take walks. People take walks every day."

I slammed the paper down. "All right. I'll take a walk. I'll take a goddamn walk."

I carefully showered and shaved, dressed slowly, and with misgivings, left the house. But it *was* a nice day, a very sunny and bright, very beautiful, not-cold-at-all-for-January day. A good idea, taking a walk. Best of all, there was no pain.

After I had gone about half a block, I increased the pace, walking briskly. Brave. Bold. Testing. What a beautiful day.

"Oh my God!" came out as much a prayer as an exclamation as the first pain hit with an impact that froze my feet to the winter ground. "It's here again. Only this time, dear God, how it burns. My chest, my arms . . . my God."

Dr. William Kerr was waiting for us at the emergency room. He was short and slight of build. His graying hair made him look older than his 37 years. He walked with a limp, a constantly painful reminder of a crippling attack of polio in his senior year at high school. Now, with a crisp efficiency, he took charge.

In a moment I was in a hospital robe, stretched on a bed. Somebody stuck a needle in my arm. I was bone-tired and aware that a numbness was beginning to spread. I could hear a voice coming across an expanse of corridor. It came closer, emanating from a white blur moving alongside. White clothes, white face, coming still closer, whispering in my ear.

"You're lucky," said the voice. "You've either had a heart attack, or you're about to have one. You're lucky. You're in the right place either way." And everything melted away.

I awoke in the coronary care unit, a symphony of meticulous precision. Wires linked me to electric heart-monitoring equipment and the slightest signs of distress would bring the comforting presence of cardiovascular specialists. There was time now to assess the damage and more important, its consequences. In spite of what my surroundings implied, I felt strangely at peace. For the moment, at least, it was somebody else's problem. Not really mine.

On Friday, February 6, after two weeks of bedrest, X-rays, and endless testing, I got the good news from Dr. Kerr that I would be celebrating my 46th birthday, the next day, at home. I had waited anxiously for this meeting—loaded with questions.

"Unequivocally . . . ," he began and held for a dramatic pause, ". . . you can never smoke again."

There was no discussion on that point. By coincidence he had adequately covered the first item on my list.

"Let's get to diet," he continued, his manner slightly pedantic. "Eighteen hundred calories on a low-cholesterol, low-fat diet." He paused to study notes on a pink sheet of paper.

I interrupted with a question, "When can I go back to work?"

"I'm letting you go home tomorrow because it's your birthday. You take it easy this weekend. Stay home all next week, up and around if you feel like it, but stay in if it's cold outside. Then, by the following week, you can start working half days."

"When can I go back full-time?"

He sat staring at me without an answer. I was uncomfortable under his scrutiny.

"How about sex?" I asked.

"One or two times a week," he said with stoic professionalism. Pausing again to look at his notes, he added, "And without vigor."

I laughed, tears suddenly streaming down my cheeks.

"What's so funny?" he asked. "I was just thinking," I said, "my wife will be thrilled with the increase."

He laughed, too, and I wondered if it gave him the same relief it gave me.

A moment later he was serious again.

"Now, the important part," he said. "So far you've been lucky. You're going to be asked to do certain things, and I hope you have the guts to do them. I'm going to tell you about some other people who came to me with the same condition as yours, who could adjust to their new condition—and some who couldn't."

"About my condition," I asked, "just what is wrong with me? Did I have a heart attack?"

"No, there's been no heart damage we can find. The pain you described when you were first admitted suggests angina pectoris."

Angina for "pain" and pectoris for "chest muscles." That much I knew. But these were just the symptoms, and I wanted to know the condition. Dr. Kerr explained that he was proceeding on the strong presumption there was some deterioration of the arteries that fed blood to my heart. Deterioration in the form of "blockage" possibly caused by a build-up of cholesterol, a fatty deposit clogging the artery and reducing the blood supply to the heart.

He continued about the necessity of changing my life-style. No more work at the office on weekends, no night work unless absolutely necessary. Regular vacations. Time off for sports and a hobby. A program of mild but daily exercise. Good, clean living. A time to become the All-American boy—at age 46.

"Well," he said, "do you think you can do it?" He didn't wait for my answer. "Most people say they can, but they don't make it. Oh, they have good intentions when they leave here, with memory of the pain so recent. But once back in the world. . . ." His voice had a shrug in it. "If you do come back," he concluded, "there won't be much doubt on the prognosis."

In the months that followed, I reported at the hospital regularly as an outpatient. Vague chest pains still occurred if I walked at all fast, but nitroglycerin pills quickly brought relief. I had dropped 10 pounds and now weighed in at 145. My cholesterol count was within acceptable limits, blood pressure normal. By June 24 I was off all medications but the nitroglycerin, had been working full time for a long stretch, and was in good spirits. That morning I arrived at the hospital for something called an exercise tolerance test.

The pretty, blonde technician dabbed the cold, pasty stuff on my chest and attached the rubber suction cups of the EKG machine. I climbed onto the electric treadmill, she started it, and I began to walk, slowly.

Gradually the machine's speed increased, and, as I walked faster to keep up, this time without any nitro pills, pain fanned out over my chest and ran in steady waves down each arm.

"Stop," Dr. Kerr ordered. "Get off."

"I'm okay, Doc. It's not that bad."

"Get off," he snapped.

I got off and stretched out on a cold, hard cot, breathing heavily.

"Where are your pills?" asked Dr. Kerr.

"In my suit coat there, but I don't think I need one."

He had difficulty opening the fancy gold box shaped like an old fashioned watch. I took it from him, pushed the spring lock, put a pill under my tongue. In a moment, the tiny pellet had dissolved, entered the bloodstream and was dilating the blood vessels and bringing relief.

Later, in Kerr's office, he explained what had happened. "Your electrocardiogram was positive," he said. "It indicated a coronary artery disease. But we've gone as far as we can go with this kind of testing. I want you to call Dr. Thomas Murphy. He can tell you about a test you can take there that can help in further diagnosis."

So I was right back where I'd started in January. Facing the unknown again, this time at St. Francis, the third hospital in less than a year. Me, who had never set foot inside a hospital as a patient since World War II in France in 1944. My depression couldn't have been deeper, I thought. But it could.

"You're the surgery patient, aren't you?" It was an orderly with long sideburns and steel-rim glasses doing the asking. "I'll probably be the one to prep you."

"What the hell you talking about?" I demanded. "I'm no surgery patient. I'm here for a test."

"You're in for an angiogram, aren't you?"

"I guess that's what they called it, but no one said anything about surgery."

"That's what it is, man. Surgery."

I waited anxiously for the cardiologist. In our first brief meeting, he had told me little about the impending test. This time, though, I had questions.

St. Francis' Dr. A. Gerald Rothenberg (his friends call him Jerry) has a quick smile and a friendly manner. Like most members of the hospital's "heart squad," he is young, approaching his midthirties. He has black hair, dark eyes, heavy eyebrows.

"What's this about surgery?" I asked him.

"It's not really a surgical procedure," he said, "although the hospital may refer to it as that, perhaps as minor surgery. Let me explain what's involved."

A long, thin tube, a "catheter," was to be inserted into an artery in my groin and shoved upward through it into the aorta, the large blood vessel above the heart. Dye would be injected into the tube and, by following the dye's flow with X-ray equipment, doctors could see if there was blockage of the coronary arteries, as suspected. The test would be carried out under local anesthesia, so I would be conscious all the while. In fact, if I wanted to, I could watch on a television monitor because a videotape would be made of the test for further study if needed.

Quite a show. Me, live on TV, and with instant replay.

Was there danger?

"There's always some risk in any medical procedure," Dr. Rothenberg said. Then he gave me a form to sign.

"What's this about heart attack?" I asked.

"This thing is written for all types of cases, many in a lot worse shape than you, so there is that element of risk," he replied. "But in any emergency you'll have the most experienced and specialized help at hand."

Rothenberg and his partner, Dr. Edward Pinsel, presided during the cine coronary arteriography. At the start, I felt a slight tingling sensation in the groin, caused, I suppose, by the introduction of the catheter. What seemed like a few moments later, Dr. Rothenberg said, "We're about one-third done."

Impossible, I thought, we'd barely started.

"Now," he said, "I'm going to inject the dye. You'll feel a hot flash all over your body, but don't be alarmed. It will last only for a moment. Ready? Here goes."

There was an explosion of amazingly intense heat that seemed to start in my chest and then rush to every body opening in a stampede to escape. "Record," he said, and I could hear a loud whirring noise like a motor starting. On the TV screen I could see moving lines, like squirming black snakes, but they meant nothing to me.

At one point I began to laugh.

"What's the matter?" Rothenberg asked.

"It tickles, whatever it is."

"Okay," he said. "Laugh."

The same procedure was repeated. He injected the dye, said "cough" to me and "record" to someone else. There was no sensation of heat this time.

Finally he said, "Okay, it's over. You did a good job. You were a real help."

Dr. Thomas E. Murphy, 37, chief of heart surgery, settled his 6-foot-1-inch, 180-pound frame on a gray steel desk. He was smiling. But he had asked that Betsy be present for what he was going to say.

Now he said it in three words.

"You need surgery."

Quietly, he explained why. There were definite indications of a blockage of the left anterior descending artery. That meant, he said, fatty deposits had accumulated inside the affected coronary artery and were impeding the flow of blood to the heart. Exertion or stress resulted in chest pain. So surgery was unavoidable. Major surgery. Open-heart surgery.

"Open-heart surgery," I repeated, stunned. "When? When will it be?"

"That's up to you," he said. "I'd suggest as soon as possible."

The possible consequences of delay?

"It's like this," he said. "A giant thumb is resting on your windpipe, one that could choke off your life without warning. You know guys your age, friends of yours, who have a check-up one day and go out the next for a round of golf, and zap, they drop dead. The mortality rate with a first heart attack is 33 percent. The second, 50. Not many have a third. Unless you want other opinions, and there are fine coronary centers—St. Luke's in Milwaukee, Cleveland, Houston—my suggestion is, we don't delay. As soon as we can fit you into the schedule, we operate."

"Okay, as soon as possible," I said numbly.

There it was. Resolved. I'd taken longer, lots of times, to decide on the color of a new tie. Yet here I was, agreeing almost instantly to place my life, literally, in the hands of this young man.

Most of the adult life of Tom Murphy had been prologue to the medical drama in which he was about to perform. As director and costar, he came well-prepared for his role.

It was only after 12 years of medical training that he and his wife Jane, the nurse he had met and

married while an intern, could celebrate the hanging
of his own shingle. The happy event, in the summer
of 1970, had been preceded by hard schooling at
Notre Dame and Northwestern, internship and
residency, and further residency at Memorial
Hospital in New York and New York Hospital. Then
Vietnam, where he was chief of surgery at the 91st
Evacuation Hospital.

A heavy influence on the young doctor's success
was his association in New York with Dr. C. Walton
Lillehei, celebrated savant of heart surgery whose
improvement in the heart-lung machine alone should
be enough to earn him a niche in medicine's Hall of
Fame.

As chief resident in cardiac surgery at St. Luke's
in Milwaukee, Dr. Murphy studied under Dr. W.
Dudley Johnson, a pioneer in open-heart techniques
and in the intricate and life-saving bypass operation.

The coronary artery bypass graft, a procedure
first pioneered about four and a half years ago, and
an operation Tom Murphy has performed some 100
or so times since, has saved thousands. Yet, less than
a century ago, medical science had resigned itself to
the fact that the chest, like the abdomen and brain,
was a "sacred temple" that could never be violated by
a surgeon's knife. Operating on the heart was too
ridiculous even to contemplate. But now I was sub-
mitting myself to a team of bold, young infidels—and
I prayed to God they would successfully violate my
temple.

A week later I was back in the hospital. It had
been a hard week for all of us—for Betsy and me, a
week of fear of what was ahead. For our boys, Mike,
11, and Matt, 9, seven days of strain.

Dr. Murphy came that afternoon to explain—
this time in careful detail—what was going to
happen.

A six-inch section of the saphenous vein would
be removed from my thigh. I could get on quite well
without it, he assured me, since it moves only about
10 percent of the blood in the leg back to the heart.
"As a matter of fact," he explained, "it's the vein
often removed in surgical treatment of varicose
veins."

Then the real operation would begin. My chest
would be opened, and I would be connected to the

heart-lung machine since a "motionless dry field" was required. This meant that my heart had to be not only stopped but bloodless—"dry." The machine would do the living for me, in effect, pumping the blood through my body while my heart, in effect, was dead.

Two electrodes, touched to the heart, would reduce its action to a quiver. Later it would be completely stopped when blood to the coronary arteries was cut off by a clamp on the aorta. Two ends of the saphenous vein (about the diameter of a soda straw) would be sewn into the incisions in the aorta and in the coronary artery below the blockage.

My heart would be restarted with the second electric shock, and they would disconnect the heart-lung machine. Then, if all was well, blood would course through the bypass, bringing new nourishment to my heart.

With a pencil, Dr. Murphy traced the course of the anticipated plumbing job on a life-size model of the heart.

"I never realized it was so large," I said.

"It's not," he said, touching my chest with an index finger, "when you've got to work in there."

The weekend was one of preparation. Nurses came at all hours to give injections or draw blood. Each vital function was checked—breathing, kidney function, liver—to assess the risk.

A young man with red hair and a handlebar mustache introduced himself as an inhalation therapist. He brought with him a machine he said was designed to aid in breathing following surgery. He demonstrated it and cautioned me that failing to follow instructions would mean risking pneumonia, which might well prove fatal. Folding a pillow in half and holding it tightly against his chest, he showed me how to cough. "It's extremely important that you bring up the mucus which will form, or you could be in serious trouble," he said. "It's going to hurt to cough, you'll feel like your sutures are bursting, but it's got to be done."

Another man, this one in pajamas and a robe, came to call. He was my age, with graying hair and a slight Spanish accent. He was extremely cheerful as he described what I was about to face. He was there because he had undergone the surgery himself.

According to my visitor, Dr. Murphy would cut

through my sternum, or breastbone, with an electric saw. A mechanical retractor would hold the rib cage open to display the membranous sac enclosing the heart, the pericardium. Once Murphy had cut through this final barrier, the naked heart would be exposed to view.

"You won't feel a thing," my visitor insisted. He opened his pajama top to reveal a just-healing incision that started at the top of the breastbone and traveled down the middle of his chest to the upper abdomen. At inch-long intervals were stitches of heavy black thread. The whole thing looked like a giant zipper.

He had hoped to cheer me, obviously. He had failed.

Alone, I lay back and closed my eyes. Suddenly, I became aware of someone new in the room. It was a priest, white hair and a pale face in sharp relief against the jet black of his cassock.

We talked quietly about my immortal soul. Was I prepared for death? No, I said, and no words of his could prepare me. There would be no confession. No purging at the end.

He was a kind and gentle man. Understanding.

But if there was to be a final consolation, it would have to come from somewhere else, not from his ministration. I had turned away from formal religion years before. The philosophy that had carried me through the past several years, one day at a time, would have to serve me now.

When the priest was gone, I walked to the end of the corridor to the chapel. There in the quiet shadows I lit a candle and knelt to pray. It was a short prayer, learned in a time of adversity years before, and one that seemed appropriate now:

"God grant me the serenity to accept the things I cannot change; the courage to change things I can, and the wisdom to know the difference."

Time moved swiftly. It was the last day before surgery. The final lung-breathing tests had been completed at the heart center. An orderly had left a replacement container of pHisoHex so that I could continue the required series of "preop" showers, its cleansing powers supposedly washing away all traces of bacteria. He would be back to administer an enema and to shave me from the ankles to neck.

Lots of things began to go through my mind. *If*

*only there would be a delay. No. No delay. But why,
dear God, did it have to be me?*

I closed my eyes, determined to hold back the
tears as I went over it in my mind: The pain as the
scalpel slit my skin. The sting of new pain as it cut
deeper into my chest—to open my heart—to bare my
soul. Oh, no, no, please God, oh, sweet Jesus! *Mary,
Mother of God, intervene for me. Let all of this be a
dream.*

"Mr. McGuire?" The hand on my shoulder shook
me gently. "I'm Miss Kruppa. I operate the heart-
lung machine, and I've come to tell you about it."

Staff nurse Arlene Kruppa, tall and blonde, wore
a white lab robe over a surgical gown. She had been
in surgery most of that day, but if she was tired, she
didn't show it. She explained how the machine, "a
type of bubble-oxygenator," would take over the work
of the heart and lungs, bypassing them to allow an
almost dry and inactive heart.

Morbidly curious, I asked what were the tolerable limits of her infernal machine. How long could it
keep me going?

About four hours was the answer, and even
within that time there was the possibility of deterioration of the red blood cells, with resultant anemia.
Almost certainly I would be given extra blood.

I pressed on. How long could the brain survive
without its precious supply of blood, before there
would be permanent damage?

Four minutes. An absolute maximum of four
minutes. I was sorry I'd asked.

There were no reassurances at parting, no "don't
worry, everything will be all right," not even a "good
luck." Just "I'll see you in the morning," and she was
gone.

Surgery itself, and the period immediately after,
are blocked from the patient's memory by blessed
oblivion. My first recollection is of a nurse's voice
shouting my name, "Jack, Jack, Jack," over and
over. It seemed important I answer, and suddenly I
was fully conscious of my surroundings. It was over.
Over at last. I had made it. I thanked God. I had
made it.

What had taken place? The same climactic scene
that has illuminated millions of screens in countless
TV dramas, when the patient hovers perilously like a

drunken tightrope walker on the thin line between
life and death? Where a wobbly line on a monitor
precipitates a flurry of feverish activity and a close-
up of the surgeon's widening eyes and sweaty brow?

No, nothing so prosaically dramatic. What had
happened was the coming together of ten skilled and
dedicated people who for five hours in a small room
performed their well-rehearsed roles in a delicate
operation. To the patient, a miracle. To them, routine
cardiovascular surgery.

Betsy was shocked at the sight of me on her first
visit to Intensive Care. In such a surgical experience
a patient collects some uncomfortable but essential
accoutrements. Before she arrived, they had removed
the urine catheter. But a tube up one nostril and
another taped into my mouth remained, along with
two chest drains. Adding to my "man from Mars"
look was another length of hose, an intravenous tube
or IV, that would drip nourishment into an arm vein
and in an emergency could be used for high-speed
delivery of medication into my system.

You get used to things, though, even a tangle of
tubes sticking out of your body, and my early come-
back was rapid. Within two days the intubation tube
had been removed from my mouth, resulting in a
feeling of great relief and a sore throat. The IV tube in
my arm and the chest drains were gone. I was transferred to a regular room, and except for heavy ban-
daging of my chest and thigh, there were few
outward reminders of what had taken place in surgery. There were others, though.

Every four hours the inhalation therapist would
arrive, and I would be subjected to the painful process
of breathing deeply of a bitterly pungent mist hissing
from a plastic tube—inhaling and exhaling for ten-
minute periods, to break up mucus and open lung
passages. The acrid result was that all food tasted as
though my taste buds had been sandpapered into
uselessness. And after each session, I had to force
myself to cough. Painful as the coughing was, there
was something worse, a moment when Dr. Murphy,
detecting an excessive amount of trapped mucus,
without warning put one arm behind my shoulder to
brace me and with his free hand plunged a hypoder-
mic needle directly into the trachea below my Adam's
apple. Hard coughing and expulsion of the viscous

fluid was the immediate and dramatic result. I learned he'd devised the diabolical procedure in Vietnam to relieve choking Vietnamese soldiers who didn't understand his shouted command to cough. All over Vietnam there must now be men who can't speak English who know painfully and precisely what "cough" means.

Complete recuperation was slow and hurtful in its own special ways. I, who had often wondered how a narcotic addict ever let himself get hooked in the first place, found myself waiting anxiously for my allotted dosage of pain-killing morphine. Sleep was measured in two or three hour periods broken by racking chest pain brought on by any attempt to get into a comfortable position. Reading was difficult since my vision blurred periodically (something to do with the after-effects of the heart-lung machine), and the TV set had to be shared with a roommate whose interest seemed to be confined to the Cubs and the news.

Visits by friends were physically and emotionally tiring, and while the nurses offered a momentary distraction, most of the time they were poking needles or pushing pills into me. Then, there were those cups of orange-colored liquid—a deceptively appetizing looking substance with the vilest taste imaginable. Mostly I managed to get it down, but once I failed. Spectacularly.

"I can't," I told this nurse. "I just can't drink any more of that stuff."

"But, you must," she insisted. "This is important medicine. Come on now, be a good boy." With that, she cupped one hand around the back of my neck and lifted the cup to my lips.

"Please, please," I protested. "I can't."

I was right. She tipped the cup into my mouth. I swallowed desperately, and the fluid went down, only to rebound in a magnificent orange cascade over her crisp white uniform.

How fast memories began to fade in the days that followed. One vivid reminder of how fortune had smiled upon me came in the middle of a long and lonely night. I was awakened by a changing commotion in the hall and looked out the open door to catch a glimpse of men and women running at breakneck speed, pulling and pushing a cart loaded with medi-

cal equipment. My roommate, who got up to investigate, came back with the news.

"A nine-nine," he said dramatically. "Emergency in Cardiac Care."

The next morning a nurse told me that a man
recovering from the same type of surgery I'd been
through had died in the night.

Eleven days after the operation I was discharged. What signaled my final freedom—
literally—was a tug at my heart. The doctor simply
grabbed a wire that protruded from one of the two
wounds in my belly and pulled it out. He explained
that during surgery the wire had been plunged
directly into my heart so that it could be attached to
an external pacemaker in an emergency.

My breastbone, laced like a holiday turkey with a
stainless steel wire, had begun to knit. Each day for a
week, I had walked slowly back and forth from my
bed to the chapel in anticipation of the three-mile
daily hike that would be required when I got home.

Miraculously, or so it seemed to me, the operation
had been accomplished with only my own blood. Dr.
Murphy considered the risk of hepatitis from an
outside source far more dangerous than the anemia
caused by the loss of my red blood cells.

At home I began my daily walks.

The O anemia had drained my energy, and each
movement was painful, but I took them cheerfully.

The walks, the quiet days of recuperation, gave
me a chance to reflect on where I had been and
consider where I must go. Dr. Kerr had been right. I'd
been lucky. I still am.

I feel physically fine. I walk five miles without
tiring. I've completed a set of tennis lessons and can
hardly wait for spring.

Just as important, mentally, I'm learning to
apply the lessons adversity and desperation have
taught. I've turned over more of my business load,
many of the things I used to think no one could
handle but myself, to my associates. My family,
which needs and wants me, gets more of me.

These long months since those sliding doors
opened for me have been a time of reevaluation, for
new emphasis—a time for life.

The author of this Sunday feature article has used

narrative techniques throughout. For a beginning he uses a bit of action from one of the most dramatic moments in the story, then flashes back to the chronological beginning to tell the story to the end. This is a device used frequently in fiction writing.

The story is told in the first person by the main character. It was noted earlier that one disadvantage of writing in the first person is the danger of alienating readers who may feel that the writer is too boastful. Such is not the case in this story. The subject matter is so dramatic that readers are not aware of the first-person device. They do not feel that the writer is too boastful. Instead, the first person enhances the believability of the experience.

The article moves at a rapid pace to a climax, the moment when the operation begins. In fiction, this movement to the climax is called "the rising action." After the climax, the difficulties of the characters begin to disappear, and the story reaches a point where all problems are solved. This movement is the *dénouement*. It occurs in this story in the final few paragraphs.

Is there colorful writing here? Right from the beginning! The opening sentence will undoubtedly urge the reader on: "In a few moments they will put me to death." There are such phrases as "hushed corridor," "aseptic world," "warm, misty eternity," The first heart problem "grew in intensity," "fanned across my chest," and produced "cold fear."

Time after time in this article conversation is used to advance the action toward the climax:

> Gradually the machine's speed increased, and, as I walked faster to keep up, this time without any nitro pill, pain fanned out over my chest and ran in steady waves down each arm.
> "Stop," Dr. Kerr ordered. "Get off."
> "I'm okay, Doc. It's not that bad."
> "Get off," he snapped.
> I got off and stretched out on a cold, hard cot, breathing heavily.
> "Where are your pills?" asked Dr. Kerr.
> "In my suit coat there, but I don't think I need one."

The meeting between doctor and patient after the first hospital stay is much more dramatic when it is reported in the actual words of the two characters. If this portion of the story had been told otherwise, even in the first person, it would have failed as high drama.

Questions for Discussion
1. Analyze Jack McGuire's article to discover other narrative devices used by the writer and not discussed above. Prepare to defend your points.
2. Is the McGuire article written objectively or subjectively? Discuss your answer.
3. Point out the *reporting* contained in the McGuire story. Explain how you think the facts were obtained.
4. What is the theme of the McGuire article? Explain your answer.
5. Could a reporter not actually receiving a heart operation get this same kind of story? How would he go about it? Do you think Jack McGuire actually experienced the events in his story?

9 depth reporting

Newspaper editors in the 1970s are asking for more "reporting in depth." Let television and radio have the news scoop. Let them skim the cream off the news. Let them have the headlines. Let's encourage the newspaper reporter to probe beneath the surface of news events, to leave no stone unturned as he grubs for facts.

One editor says depth reporting simply makes readers aware of all aspects of a given subject by giving them all possible information, including background and atmosphere. "We also try to make them aware of the impact and importance of the matter at hand," he adds.

Another editor says depth reporting treats a story with a kind of thoroughness, detail, and background which neither the five-minute radio nor the half-hour television newscast can provide. "Depth reporting," he says, "tells the reader not only what happened, but why it happened."

A third editor says, "Depth reporting to us means reporting that gives the newspaper reader the entire story. It is exhaustive, it is well organized, and it is backgrounded. It is designed to answer all the questions the intelligent, interested reader would ask, but it would not burden him with extraneous matter or superfluous detail."

A fourth editor says he believes the term "depth

reporting" is an overworked term for complete reporting. By "complete reporting" he means simplified reporting of complicated subjects, but he also means digging to get facts obscured by two different factions.

Still another editor says, "To me, depth reporting has never meant anything but good reporting. On the fast-breaking news story, it is complete accuracy plus the interesting angles, the sidebars, the quotes that give your paper some color, and facts the opposition doesn't have. It comes from training reporters and editors to go after the 'extra' fact, to ask the additional questions that bring out the complete story. Otherwise, a reporter is always writing right up to the edge of his knowledge—and sometimes beyond. And it shows."

Another type of depth reporting, this same editor says, is the explanatory story that accompanies or follows a breaking news story.

A sixth editor explains depth reporting in these words: "Depth reporting, in my dictionary, means going into a news development and explaining its significance now, why it happened, and what may be expected to result—written interestingly, possibly accompanied by photos that help tell the story."

This editor goes on to explain that the story can be presented in one shot or in a series over consecutive days, or it may be told primarily with photos accompanied by a short story and cutlines. "In other words," he says, "I believe depth reporting does not involve methods of presentation so much as it does purpose."

Another editor points out that reporting "at length" should not be confused with "reporting in depth." He explains, "Usually there are two ingredients which make depth reporting possible: sound planning in anticipation of the news and vigorous execution while the news is fresh."

This editor points to the need for "team effort" in handling a depth story. He says, "The planning can be confined to the brain cells of one person but in most of today's newspaper offices it calls for a team effort. Planning calls for imagination and anticipation, not only of what the story may contain but also what the reader may want to know about it. The execution calls for complete understanding of the tools of the modern newspaper and a willingness to use these tools to their maximum. It also calls for flexibility."

An eighth editor feels that "depth reporting," "analytic reporting," "interpretative reporting" are all the same, because in each the writer attempts to get and present all the facts of a situation or personality. The editor explains further:

"The essence of the so-called depth story is that it deals in explanatory facts and not in explanatory opinion. Too many papers and reporters fail to make the distinction, with the result that extended editorials are presented as interpretative stories."

Another editor says he dislikes the term "depth reporting," and would prefer to call all such reporting just "good reporting." He says a depth story is one written in such a way that, after reading it, there are no questions left in the reader's mind about exactly what happened, what brought it about, what would be the proposed remedy or action, and what, based on common sense or the opinion of qualified observers, will be the probable result.

Still another editor says that a depth story is reporting which goes beyond mere parroting of what the principals in the story may have said, a mere chronicling of surface events, a mere presentation of facts as they appear at first glance, but delves instead into enough of the origins, the logic, the pressures, and the interests involved, that the reader understands not merely who and what, but how and, more importantly, why.

An eleventh editor says the phrase "depth reporting" means thorough backgrounding of an event or personality without sacrifice of objectivity. It cannot be mere expression of opinion and remain reporting, he says. "To me there is nothing new about the concept except the name applied to it. And the name, I fear, has been appropriated as an excuse for bad habits which have nothing to do with either reporting or depth."

A twelfth editor says he believes one of the greatest problems in today's society is the reader's unanswered questions. For years, he says, it has been the rare newspaper story which does not raise as many questions as it answers. Concerning a definition of depth reporting, he writes: "Frankly, I have no precise definition or descriptions. I do know that there are a great many stories which do not lend themselves to direct matter-of-fact reporting. There is often more under the surface than is showing. In depth reporting it is our job to mine that subsurface material and relate it to the overall picture."

Another editor says, "The average news story generally stops short of a penetrating exploration of all the facets of a news event. But reporting in depth requires the ability to see a connection between, for instance, the *where* and the *why*. To understand *why* an event occurred, the *where* may be vitally important—for instance, in a story about crime in a big city slum area, political immaturity in the topsy-turvy Congo, or aggressive foreign policy in the Soviet Union. The subjects of crime, political immaturity, and foreign policy take on new meanings in these special environments."

A fourteenth editor says, "There's no magic or mystery to depth reporting. It's basically a matter of digging beneath the surface and coming up with the facts that aren't immediately visible, but which nevertheless contribute to an understanding of the story.

"It's obvious, for example, that there's an increase in the number of young people who get married while still in high school, and to print a story to that effect is straight, unadorned reporting. But when you begin to explore the underlying causes, the social or economic pressures behind the trend, the problems created by such youthful partnerships, then you've stepped over into the realm of depth reporting.

"Even in the sports pages there is depth reporting, in the signed column that singles out the key play and analyzes the reasons behind a favored team's unexpected defeat, in the dressing room sidebars that convey the attitudes and reactions of the players."

A few years ago, Lloyd Wendt, at that time Sunday editor of the *Chicago Tribune,* explained his views on depth reporting in this way.

Reporting in depth means answering questions that may not have occurred to the reader. It means anticipating him. And it means satisfying yourself, whether you are reporter or editor, that you have made your report as complete, as accurate, and as lucid as you can. It doesn't necessarily mean—as many writers think—that the story must be unusually long.

Depth reporting means expanding the "what" of the story—supplying background details that make the event fall into place as a meaningful part of history. It means careful attention to the "why"—explaining important motivations of the people involved. These things, plus clarity in the writing, make the story more interesting and understandable. They are the elements that make depth reporting more and more essential to today's newspaper.

Another definition of "reporting in depth" comes from Gerard Harrington, former managing editor of the *New Haven* (Conn.) *Journal-Courier:*

As I understand "reporting in depth" it is reporting based on extensive research. The story contains detail (perhaps social, economic, or political) uncovered by investigating conditions preceding and contributing to a single news happening—which in itself could be reported in ten inches of type.

As a practical matter, this kind of job requires a series of three or more articles. I cite a classic example:

Let us call the behavior of the New York City youth gangs a single news happening. (It's the same violent story each time it's printed, always in the same pattern.) the *New York Times*—and other papers—report these in their surface aspects every time the police get into the situation.

Then, at one stage, Harrison Salisbury of the *Times* did a masterly research job, dredging up tons of material on family incomes, foreign backgrounds of parents, status ambition affecting underprivileged boys, aggressive abuses against property in new housing developments by boys and girls living in them, and many other details related to the superficial, obvious fact that these kids are roaming with lethal homemade weapons and are dangerous.

The Salisbury series included interviews with officials and with unofficial persons constructively concerned with this problem, and I believe Salisbury himself drew some conclusions on causes (as he is entitled to do under a *New York Times* by-line).

A few months ago in New Haven, a man was taken from

the county jail to a hospital, with certain injuries which might have indicated violent treatment. He died.

The autopsy showed that the cause of death was acute alcoholism. The man had been locked up alone in a cell, the sheriff having decided that his behavior was much too irrational to let him mix with, and annoy, other prisoners and so cause disturbances.

Impartial investigation showed that the man had injured himself a number of times by hurling himself at walls and on a cement floor.

As a single-shot news story, that was all there was to it. Nobody hit the unfortunate man. He killed himself with more liquor than his system could handle.

However, this newspaper put a mature, capable reporter to work on a so-called "depth" project and later printed a series of stories on conditions which will probably produce similar misfortunes unless corrected.

We found, of course, that there is no real provision for housing and treating alcoholics. The jail is antiquated and overcrowded (nobody denies it). Chronic alcoholism is extremely expensive to taxpayers and to the economy as a whole. Normal people are almost completely unconcerned with the personal tragedy of the alcoholic—who is dismissed as a useless bum.

All this background material was printed as a series. There was some private and public acclaim. The mayor appointed a committee to look into it. Whether or not anything else happens, it was, for our purposes, "reporting in depth."

Large papers with serious financial sections do a good deal of depth reporting in analyzing the condition of industrial corporations. They dig into production and market situations and other factors which ultimately affect earnings, and produce stories which are intrinsically interesting in addition to being valuable for investors.

Nowadays, the meetings of editors' and managing editors' associations hear at least one clarion call for more interpretative writing (which both wire services fondly call "interpretives"). The demand is for more background in writings on foreign affairs, national politics, and other large events.

There has been an improvement in this field, although sometimes it seems that stories run too long to be manageable when a real whiz is filing the stuff. There is also a lot of counterfeit "interpreting" which is produced by writers doing their own speculating as to causes. From Moscow such a flight of fancy might be made to appear objective and legitimate by the prefix "Western diplomats believe. . . ." London is also another dateline where the opinions of "diplomatic resources" seems to have a remarkably austere authority.

I think depth reporting requires a little scope. Mr. Luce can't do it in *Time* but does it admirably in *Fortune,* and now and then in *Life.*

The New Yorker has a record of great distinction in this field, dating back to its founding in 1925. A formidable accomplishment was Edmund Wilson's fascinating story of the discovery of the Dead Sea Scrolls, which appeared complete in one (very thick) issue of *The New Yorker.*

Other remarkable jobs have been A. J. Liebling's discussion of the Hearst newspaper empire shortly after W. R. Hearst, Sr., died. The same Mr. Liebling did a notable discussion of eating in France since 1924 in another series.

The New Yorker could well be recommended to anyone wishing to study the depth treatment of current stories.

Depth Reporting Assignment

Not long ago the managing editor of a metropolitan newspaper in the South assigned a reporter to do a story in depth on all aspects of food additives and environmental health. The managing editor's memorandum to the reporter was simple:

Explore every possible facet of the subject. There are not many experts on separate phases of the subject. You must get to know their specialty as well as they do. Then, when we combine the result of our research we will have to be able to put for the first time into one package information that will be of real public service.

After he had been on the reporting job for some six months, the reporter turned in the following memorandum to his managing editor, accounting for his time:

Time totaling about seven weeks has been spent intermittently during the last six months, and several more weeks will probably be spent by a reporter assigned to a project on the whole field of environmental health.

Chemicals in foods and cosmetics, air pollution, water pollution, and radiation aspects will be covered in what will likely be three or four series of articles.

The project has involved combing a range of literature,

including scientific articles, records of congressional hearings, some federal and state laws, magazine and newspaper
stories. It has included visits to most of the following agencies and will include the rest before it is completed:

The U.S. Department of Agriculture in Washington and
Beltsville, Maryland; Food and Drug Administration; U.S.
Public Health Service; VPI, the state land-grant College;
state health departments; state agriculture department;
state board of pharmacy; state water control board; state
commission of game and inland fisheries; state fisheries lab,
and city agencies.

It has included interviews with scientists, veterinarians,
feed men and farmers and will include physicians and a few
legislators and farm commodity group representatives.

There has also been some correspondence with regional
offices of some of the federal agencies.

The project has taken the reporter into most parts of the
state as time and scheduling available from spot news work
permitted, as well as to Washington and Beltsville.

In order to explore every facet of the subject, this reporter
had traveled to the nation's capital and into almost every
sector of his own state. He had reviewed state and federal
laws covering his subject and had explored all of the printed
material he could find on additives and environmental
health. He had visited more than a dozen state, federal, and
city agencies connected in some way with his subject, and
had interviewed everyone he thought could offer expert
testimony on the topics being researched.

At the end of ten weeks of work the reporter had become a
"temporary expert" in the field of food additives and
environmental health. He had determined to leave no stone
unturned in his research on the subject and had become so
"filled" with the subject that the writing job was easy.

A depth reporting assignment may appear mysterious
and difficult to the beginning reporter; the following questions and answers should help clarify how such an assignment can be handled:

Q. How do you know where to start? On this food additive
story, for example, where would you begin?

A. You begin by reading everything you can find on the

subject. You "background" yourself in this way so that you know which questions to ask when you begin talking to the experts.

Q. Do you get into public documents, and if so, how do you know what to look for?

A. Many depth stories, and investigative stories discussed in the next chapter, lead reporters into public records. Many times records at first sight seem barren of information for the story. But don't stop digging prematurely. A reporter examining all of the records having to do with the building of a large bridge sifted through thousands of invoices and expense vouchers before uncovering illegal expenditures. Methodical examination of invoices and vouchers, day after day, paid off in a front-page story. Sometimes you don't know what to look for, but you must look at every document you think might have some bearing on the subject.

Q. How do you get access to public documents? Don't some public officials try to stop you when they think you are looking for something to pin on them?

A. First, you should know all there is to know about your own state public record laws telling you which documents are public records and which are not. Then, if a public official tries to keep you from seeing a document, you can quote him the law. If that doesn't work, and the story is important, your newspaper can take legal steps to force the official to turn over the records.

Q. After you have read enough background material and looked at all of the pertinent documents, how do you approach the experts? Do you tell people what you are after and identify yourself, or do you try to fool them into giving you information?

A. The direct approach is best. Identify yourself and most people will tell you what you want to know. They will even go out of their way to be helpful. (See the next chapter, on Investigative Reporting, for further advice.)

Q. This kind of story seems too intangible. Take the food additives story, for example. The reporter had nothing to begin with and he had to create something right out of the air, so to speak. Nothing had happened. No one had made any statements on the subject. No one had been poisoned by food additives. So how does the reporter get a lead on this story in the first place?

A.   In this case the assignment came from the managing editor, who may have come up with the story idea from any one of a number of places. The idea might have come from an overheard conversation. It might have come from a paragraph in a news story, a column, or an editorial. It might have come from a magazine, or it might have come from a comment by his wife at breakfast. You said the reporter had to "create" the story "right out of the air." A depth story is a *news* story and you don't fabricate any part of it. The depth story is built upon fact. While this story that you are creating "out of the air" is something that did not "happen" like an event, it must nevertheless be truthful and believable.

Q.   How do you get people who are suspicious of you or who just don't want to be interviewed to talk?

A.   Sometimes every method fails, but read the chapter in this book on "Interviewing."

Q.   What are the most important things to remember about depth reporting?

A.   Patience and digging will pay off. You may plug away at a story over a period of months—going back to it between regular assignments—but eventually persistence and research will pay off.

Analysis of a Depth Story

Quoted below is a background article on a hospital in Minneapolis, Minnesota. The article was written by Victor Cohn, *Minneapolis Tribune* staff writer, as the introduction to a six-part series on a hospital and its problems.

It is an ugly place. It is a pile of old bricks and ancient mortar. It is patched and primped just a little.

It is an ugly place in the heart of Minneapolis, and it dispenses some of the finest medicine and surgery in the United States.

It is Hennepin County General Hospital. And the assessment of its care is not local pride speaking, but the opinion of some of the country's toughest medical inspectors, who must visit it.

General Hospital is in crisis. It could die.

Within five years, unless some steps are taken that some Hennepin County politicians call "impossible," its doors could begin closing. That this could happen sorely puzzles the national medical leaders who know it, and it puzzles local medical leaders who, almost to a man, consider that we cannot do without it.

They give one main reason. It provides a large share of our very best doctors.

Statistics show that 45 percent of all specialists in Hennepin County had all or part of their advanced training at General. Twenty percent of all general practitioners in the county and 10 percent of all doctors in the state interned at General.

General Hospital is many things. It is an emergency - burn - poison - suicide - mental health - acute disease - kidney disease - contagion - disaster - poverty care center for this area.

It can be all of these things because it has, night and day, 48 of the nation's brightest interns and 66 residents (M.D.s past their internship, studying specialties), working under 49 staff specialists, and 334 Minneapolis and suburban doctors who donate their time.

General's interns, rotating among various services, are one-third of all the interns and 47 percent of all rotating interns in Minnesota. It is rotating interns who tend to go into general, family, or private practice, versus teaching or research, the goal of many young M.D.s at a training center like the University of Minnesota Hospitals, across the river.

Doctors tend to settle, many studies prove, not mainly where they go to medical school but where they complete their last training, whether internship or residency.

This was strongly recognized by a 1965-66 Health Manpower Advisory Commission, financed by the Hill Family Foundation. It was created in response to demand for a second medical school in Minnesota, a school that could cost from $30 to $50 million.

Two legislative committees are now considering this demand, or what other steps to take to improve our doctor supply. Support for a new General

Hospital, which might cost $10 to $20 million, has not been considered.

But Dr. Ivan Fahs, the Hill study's staff sociologist, recalls, "We weren't concerned about expanding medical schools alone, but with expanding internships and residencies. A doctor finishes his training. He's in debt. He takes a look at the nearest opportunities! If we want doctors, we must expand, not shrink, our good training programs."

Doctors already are becoming scarce, as anyone learns who asks for an appointment. U.S. demand for medical care is expected to increase 26 percent by 1975, while the doctor supply (even with thirteen new medical schools) increases 16 percent.

"If General Hospital closes," warns Thomas P. Cook, executive secretary of the Hennepin County Medical Society, "patients here will feel the impact very quickly, when they try to find a doctor. Isn't this a fine time, then, to talk about closing one of the nation's finest facilities for training doctors?

Why then is General Hospital in imminent danger?

It cannot operate indefinitely in its aged plant, and the money either to rehabilitate it (if really possible) or replace it is not in sight.

Moneyless Minneapolis, which until 1964 operated the hospital as Minneapolis General, long ignored the situation. Then Hennepin County took it over, but only under a legislative deal providing that: (1) suburbanites can only be taxed for the hospital to the extent that they use it (training their doctors is not considered "use"); (2) there must be a countywide referendum before any new hospital is built.

Non-Minneapolitans actually make up 26 percent of all bed-patients, 23 percent of emergencies, 16 percent of out-patients. All these figures have been increasing.

Minneapolitans, however, still must pay more than four times as much as suburbanites toward the $12.8 million 1968 budget. Forty-eight percent of this will come from Medicare and other government payments. City residents' property will still be taxed 14.02 mills; suburbanites 3.2.

The budget (up 22 percent over 1967 largely for salaries) will still allow only some $300,000 for maintenance and equipment, and $350,000 for urgent remodeling.

A 1965 study, one of many, found this outdated plant "totally inadequate." But Medicare and other government programs have raised a new point; is a new public hospital needed in a day when most of us can get government or insurance-paid care in private hospitals?

The Planning Agency for Hospitals of Metropolitan Minneapolis (PAHMM)—with the blessing of Hennepin County's Commissioners—therefore has ordered a new study by Booz, Allen and Hamilton of Chicago to tell us: (1) is the hospital still needed? (2) if so, what kind of building plan would be prudent?

The study cannot be ready before fall. But the county commissioners, by 3-2, voted a building referendum for November. This is far too early, believe most observers, for any real consideration of the study's findings.

If a referendum fails, there may not be another chance.

"Those interns and residents come from the top of their classes at the best medical schools," explain General's supporters. "General is one of only three large hospitals in the whole U.S. that have never failed to fill their intern quotas."

"This is solely because of its reputation. Medical students now can be independent. Let the word get around that this hospital is on the way out, and the intern supply could dry up."

Hospital supporters hope the referendum will at least be postponed until there is time to examine and debate the new study's findings.

They ask also, "Need there be a referendum at all? There are none for other county or state hospitals. Private hospitals just build and add the cost onto their patients' bills."

Changing the referendum requirement would require legislative agreement.

Many medical observers also ask: "Shouldn't a new General get some state building support, for training state doctors?"

But the questions raised by some who doubt the need for a new building are: "Why not phase out General completely in a day of growing and improving private hospitals? Couldn't they do all it does?"

To try to answer this, we need to take a close look at all that General does.

Does the above story meet the criteria set down for depth reporting by editors quoted in this chapter? Let's examine the evidence.

1.   Does the story attempt to make the reader aware of the importance and impact of the hospital situation?

The fact that the newspaper devoted seven articles to the subject and gave the stories prominent display helps impress the readers with the importance of this subject. On the other hand, the entire tone of the article quoted here is designed to have an impact upon readers. From the words, "General Hospital is in crisis. It could die," the story proceeds to relate in depth why the hospital is in crisis and why it could die.

2.   In a depth story you should tell not only *what* is happening but why it is happening. Does this story qualify in these respects?

About half the story tells in depth what is happening at General Hospital and the remaining half explains why these things are happening. The writer asks his readers the question, "Why then is General Hospital in imminent danger?" The answer is given in five points, covering nine paragraphs of the story.

3.   A depth story should give the reader the entire story. "It is exhaustive, it is well organized and it is backgrounded." Does this story qualify?

The story used for this example is merely a background story that sets the stage for six more parts. Even so, this story is complete in itself. It is an exhaustive report on the problems at General Hospital. The facts are documented and backgrounded.

The remaining stories in the series confine themselves to telling readers how important the hospital is to them.

Story One carries the headline "General Hospital Serves the Sickest and Poorest." Story Two concerns itself with "Young M.D.s: Priceless Asset at General Hospital." The third story headline says "Heart Surgery—Real Drama in High Pressure Chamber." The headline for the fourth article reads "Emergency Room—Where Staff at General

Excels." Story Five has this headline: "Troubled Minds Can Unwind Despite Unlovely Atmosphere." The headline for the sixth story says "General Replaces Family Doctor for County's Poor."

4. The essence of the story is that it offers explanatory facts, not explanatory opinion. Does this story qualify?

It is true that the reporter begins with a viewpoint that the hospital is in crisis and could die. One could argue that this is only his view. The difference is that the reporter amasses facts to support his viewpoint. He uses statements by doctors and quotes from various reports to support his statement that the hospital is in a critical situation. The story is certainly one of explanatory facts and not explanatory opinion.

5. Does the story raise more questions than it answers?
6. Does this story dig beneath the surface and reveal facts that are not visible to the average citizen?
7. Does the story answer questions that might not have occurred to the reader?
8. Has the writer of this story unearthed some interesting facts?

These are just some of the tests you might apply to any depth story you write for your newspaper.

Depth Stories Can Be Short

Some reporters, and some newspapers, seem to believe that length defines the depth story. Length, however, has nothing to do with depth. Nor does the fact that a news story is labeled, "A Report in Depth," or some such wording, make it a depth story. Many rambling, boring, "thin" articles have been pawned off as depth articles by having the label "in depth." But the old public relations adage applies here: You cannot whitewash a black crow. Art work, fancy headlines, and typography can make a poor story *appear* to be important, but discriminating readers will find it out every time. The depth story whether long, short, or otherwise, must meet all criteria quoted in the first part of this chapter.

Depth Through Teamwork

Some of the finest depth stories in American newspapers are being written by teams of reporters, each member writing a portion of the story. A good example is a twenty-page section of the *Kansas City Star* entitled, "The Negro's Role in American History." This section was written by nine staff members of the *Star,* each contributing an article in depth that tied in with the general theme of the section. The result was enough copy to make a small book.

At the *Minneapolis Star* two reporters and an artist teamed up to produce a series of depth stories that revealed the true state of "Poverty in Minneapolis." The stories resulting from this teamwork appeared as a series in the newspaper and later were reprinted in a separate twenty-page tabloid section.

Teamwork by the *Kansas City Star's* science-medical editor, Phillip S. Brimble, and two other writers, Rosaline K. Ellingsworth and Michael J. Satchell, resulted in an eight-page section entitled, "Medicine: Breakthroughs and Barriers." The series required weeks of research, travel, and interviewing by the three writers.

A report totaling more than thirty thousand words was produced by the *Akron* (Ohio) *Beacon Journal.* "Kent State: The Search for Understanding" appeared as a special report in an eight-page section of the newspaper. Concerning the report, the editor of the section said, "It is as accurate as hard work and an honest regard for the facts can make it, yet it cannot be called complete: the dimensions of the incident at Kent State University are too enormous, the humanity too complex, ever to be fully reduced to writing." Members of the Knight Newspapers team who prepared the report were Gene Miller of the *Miami Herald;* Julie Morris, John Oppedahl, William Serrin, William Schmidt, and Lee Winfrey of the *Detroit Free Press;* Helen Carringer, Pat Englehart, James Herzog, and Jeff Sallot of the *Beacon Journal.*

Surveys Provide In-Depth Stories

The *Miami Herald's* news department conducted a survey to discover what members of Dade County's black community thought and felt. *Miami Herald* officials believe it is the most comprehensive survey of its type ever undertaken by a daily newspaper. The project was conceived and planned by Philip Meyer of the *Herald*'s Washington Bureau. He was assisted in drafting the questionnaire and writing the resulting in-depth series of articles by Juanita Greene and George Kennedy, *Herald* staff writers.

Landon Haynes of the *Herald*'s Market Research Division designed the sample so that every black fifteen years old or older and living at a fixed address in the survey area had an equal chance of being interviewed. According to officials, this probability sampling allowed the results to be projected onto the entire community, within a small margin of error. The 530 interviews were obtained from an original sample of 635 persons for a response rate of 83.5 percent.

Mapping and survey facilities of the Dade County Planning Department, aerial photos of the County's Housing and Urban Development Department, and information gathered by the interviewing staff were used to establish perimeters of selected black communities. Every block containing 50 percent or more black families was included in the sample area. The interviewers were selected from applicants supplied by various civic and local agencies. Field work was periodically checked by follow-up interviewers.

The data were analyzed at the Harvard Computing Center, using punched cards prepared from the question-naires by the *Herald*'s Data Processing Department.

Academic consultant on the project was Peter Natchez of the Department of Political Science, Yale University. Also giving advice and suggestions were Dr. Thomas Tomlinson, research psychologist, U.S. Office of Economic Opportunity; Dr. Thomas Pettigrew, professor of social psychology, Harvard University; Dr. David Coslin, sociologist, Russell Sage Foundation; Dr. Albert Gollin, research associate, Bureau of Social Science Research; and Irwin Bupp, Department of Government, Harvard.

Out of all this work came eleven stories profiling Miami's blacks. The stories later appeared in a fifty-six-page book called "Miami Negroes: A Study in Depth."

Today, newspaper reporters have new tools which can provide fascinating data for depth stories. They can obtain professional help in designing questionnaires and survey techniques, and computer services for analyzing data from almost any nearby University. The newspaper's own computers will probably be used more and more to help the newsroom.

The kinds of depth reporting being done by the *Miami Herald,* the *Kansas City Star,* the *Minneapolis Star* and the *Akron Beacon Journal* are examples of what is being done by newspapers all over the nation. Research is finding a new role in the newsroom. In the future, the reporter who wants to advance in the journalism profession must learn new ways to use the new techniques and tools now at hand and yet to come.

Questions for Discussion
1. Explain your own definition of "depth reporting."
2. Assume that you are news editor for your local newspaper. Discuss one idea for a depth story for that newspaper.
3. Do you have any public record laws in your state? If so, explain what they are and how they work.
4. How can an assignment editor keep coming up with good ideas for depth stories? How does he stimulate his own thinking along these lines?
5. Give an example of teamwork in the development of a good in-depth story.

10 investigative reporting

What is investigative reporting? Neale Copple, in his book *Depth Reporting,* says it is a valuable tool of depth writers. "There is no opinion in truly investigative reporting," he says. "It resembles a scientific approach. Fact is laid upon fact. No conclusions are drawn until the facts themselves form a conclusion."

Charles and Bonnie Remsberg, in an article for *Writer's Digest,* describe investigative reporting as master detective work. "No writing specialty has the potential to produce a more spectacular impact—or requires more patience and imagination—than investigative reporting. Often, in its purest form, this art requires not only that the writer be a clear communicator but that he be a master detective as well. He starts with only the hint of a story and, in the face of intense opposition, carefully pieces together elusive facts through numerous interviews and a dogged search of obscure records. In investigative reporting more than in any other form of writing, is the obligation to seek out 'the truth.'"

K. Scott Christiansen, investigative reporter for the *Albany* (N.Y.) *Knickerbocker News-Union Star,* describes investigative reporting in an article in *The Quill* in this way:

"As I see it, investigative reporting involves the gathering of important secret information which somebody is determined to keep secret. That somebody can be the President of the United States, the university administration, the coach of the New York Mets, the local dog catcher, or just about anyone or any group.

"Investigative reporting requires the individual reporter, or team, to dig up this secret information in complete detail, overcoming whatever barriers may be placed in the way. He must then arrange it into something meaningful and digestible and convey it through fine writing. These are formidable tasks. As a result, it is often the most expensive and time-consuming kind of reporting, and very often, the most crucial and controversial."

The editor of *The Christian Science Monitor,* Erwin D. Canham, also writing for *The Quill,* says, "News in the past has been more event-oriented. It is getting to be more and more situation-oriented. We have been the slave of the event, the servant of time alone, and we have wasted a lot of time just waiting around for things to happen. Investigative reporting about situations is much more rewarding, gets much deeper into significance and validity than merely covering an event. Nothing can more effectively restore the credibility of a newspaper in a community than the uncovering of some situation which badly needs exposure."

To summarize what these experts are saying:
1. Investigative reporting is a *way* of reporting, a way of reporting that makes it a tool for the depth writer.
2. Investigative reporting is master detective work.
3. Investigative reporting is the art of digging out information that someone wants to keep secret.
4. Investigative reporting is situation reporting rather than event reporting, although events may be involved.

Neither investigative reporting nor its technique is new. Both date at least to James Franklin, editor-publisher of the *New England Courant,* and his smallpox inoculation crusade in 1721. Only the term is relatively new, and sometimes it is not even applied to stories of an investigative nature. Some newsmen today talk about "muckraking," meaning journalism that pries and probes until the truth comes to light. Morton Mintz, reporter for the *Washington Post,* told the newsmen attending the 1972 A. J. Liebling Counter-Convention in New York City that "muckraking should not be any more than reporting."

Is investigative reporting crusading journalism? Not necessarily. In fact, Gaylord Shaw, member of an eleven-man team of reporters in the Washington Bureau of the Associated Press, reported in *The Quill:*

"We on the team are not crusaders. Our business is information and not reformation. Sometimes team stories lead to steps to correct an injustice or clean up a messy situation. When this happens, we view it as a result of a clean-cut documented story—not a constant, one-sided carping in the news columns.

"We believe this cool, dispassionate approach is essential for two reasons: First, we write for newspapers and broadcast stations of all political persuasions. We should not survive if AP members thought we were slanting our copy. Second, we think the American public prefers a straightforward presentation of documented facts, rather than a mixture of facts and opinions. And it is, after all, the public we serve."

Then how do you distinguish between investigative reporting and depth reporting? You don't. Remember, investigative reporting is a tool of the depth writers. Thus, when we talk about investigative reporting we are talking about reporting *techniques,* which will be discussed next.

Investigative Reporting Techniques

Investigative reporting techniques probably vary as much as the personalities of reporters engaged in this kind of effort. Some are brash and cold as a fish eye, while others use the soft-sell approach. All are endowed with infinite patience and determination. Ray Brennen, whose exposés and investigative stories have brightened newspapers and magazines since the days of Al Capone, says investigative reporting techniques are probably not a great deal different from any other type of reporting. (He probably meant that they weren't much different from any kind of reporting that *he* did because his reporting always seemed to smack of detective work.)

The investigative reporter works much like a police detective or research analyst. He spends hours, days, and weeks reading government records of all kinds, hoping to find another link in the chain of evidence he is forging for a story. Much of this kind of investigation is routine, dull, and uninteresting, but often the reporter finds a jewel of information hidden in the most inconspicuous of dusty records, one that caps off his story or sends him off in a new direction.

What sets the reporter on his way? Often it is bits of information missed by other reporters. Often it is a nose sensitive to news, that tells him all is not right in an official report or document.

Any investigative reporter can tell you how *he* went about covering a particular story but few will attempt to tell you exactly what you must do on *every* story. Situations differ, and each story calls for particular, appropriate techniques. However, the experts all agree that certain techniques are common to most investigative reporting.

Begin with the known. Find out all that is known about the person or situation you are investigating. Information that your turnpike authority is not regularly audited may send you off to find out all there is to know about the turnpike management. Then go to the "unknown," such as the piles of yellowed expense vouchers.

Verify on your own. Do not accept without question information given to you—verify it yourself. Remember the 1971 Attica, N.Y., State Prison riot, and all the reporters who accepted false information without question.

Documentation and record keeping. Make copies of every document or record from which you take information. These are necessary for your own protection and may eventually have to be produced in court. You should be able to back up every word in a story with evidence. Interviews, telephone calls, and documents should all be recorded in duplicate or triplicate and stored in safe places. Get affidavits. Take witnesses along on some interviews. Use tape recorders for interviews and telephone conversations.

Cultivate contacts. A considerable part of the time an investigative reporter spends on a story may be spent finding people who can help him. These contacts may include private investigators or police detectives who can instruct him in a particular investigation.

Avoid cold trails. Give the principals in your story a chance to give their side of the story—but talk to them last, after you have all the evidence. If you see them too soon, tracks can be covered.

Make a legal check. Many newspapers insist that investigative stories be checked by their legal staff. Sometimes lawyers can make suggestions that will strengthen your story.

Keep yourself above reproach. Once a reporter becomes involved in an investigation of wrongdoing he is likely to be investigated himself. He may also be the target for pressures of various kinds. Even members of his family may find themselves threatened in one way or another. A Florida reporter who won a Pulitzer Prize for public service for his newspaper recalls that during his investigations frequent telephone calls were made to his home in the middle of the night. When his wife picked up the receiver all she heard was the clicking of a revolver chamber. There are two schools of thought on how far in the background an investigative reporter should keep himself. Some newspapers believe that their investigative reporters should remain completely behind the scene. Others want them plainly visible. (This is somewhat like identifying a battlefield medic with a red cross.)

Keep quiet. An investigative reporter on a story should not talk a great deal about what he is doing. He should be tightlipped, like any other kind of investigator handling a delicate matter. In the first place, his investigation may turn out to be fruitless. Secondly, loose talk about his progress on a case may be used against him.

Investigative Reporting Raises Problems

Investigative reporters all agree that their activities give rise to a number of important questions for which there are no easy answers. Some of these questions are:

Should the investigative reporter work with the authorities or on his own? If he works on his own, without the investigative power of the police, for example, he may end up in trouble, perhaps arrested for an illegal maneuver. If he works with the police his case may move slowly, maybe not at all, depending on the interest of the police and the manpower they are able to afford. In many cases, investigative reporters can proceed only so far without calling in the police or other authorities. When that point is reached, they do call for help. Reporters are often prevented from seeing certain records and must turn to authorities for legal help in prying the records loose.

What about undercover techniques to get a story? In other words, can you use disguises, false credentials, assume a false identity? Investigative reporters disagree on the answer to this question. Some feel the direct approach is best, that you should not attempt to deceive anyone or adopt any kind of subterfuge in order to get the facts for your story. Others feel that the end justifies the means. Which way to go? This is a moral judgment you and your newspaper must make.

Do I pay for information? Most investigative reporters do not, saying they do not trust the person who talks for money.

What do I do with a negative report? Suppose that you are investigating a rumor that a public official is stealing public funds but you find no evidence. If you had found evidence, the story would have been printed. Do you write a story saying the official is not a crook? The answer to this question depends upon the circumstances. If the investigation was a quiet one, there would be no reason to clear the official's name because it had not been stained. On the other hand, if the investigation were widely known, the newspaper would have a professional obligation to clear the official's name.

At what point in the investigation do I identify myself as a reporter? Some investigative reporters say they do so from the beginning, it being a policy of their newspapers. Others say they wait until they have enough information to use as a pry to get more information. Still others say they delay as long as possible revealing their identity as a reporter. The question is a matter of ethics, and each newspaper must set its own policy.

When examining public records, how can I keep office personnel from suspecting what I am after? One device is to request many documents in which you really have no interest, along with those in which you do have an interest.

What about sources, tips, and evidence? How can I protect sources if they are not willing to be quoted and identified? These are often innocent parties who could be hurt in some way if identified. If you tell them you must identify them, you will probably get no information from them. Follow the tradition of the American press and refuse to make public identification of "protected" sources. Do not quote such sources if they are not essential to the story. If you must quote them to make the story clear, leave out the identity or any kind of recognition tags.

Should I follow up tips from persons who fail to reveal their identity? Follow up all tips. You never know when you have a "hot" one.

Can I burglarize an office to get evidence on the premise that the end justifies the means? No. No matter what the reason, a newspaper has no special right to break the law; as a matter of fact, the newspaper should set an example of good citizenship.

Do I wait until the entire story is "sewed up" before publishing what I have? This depends on the circumstances. Many times you should print what you have as you get information because one story may serve as a catalyst, bringing you new tips that move the story further along. Once a story unfolds, people become more willing to pass on what they know.

Ideas for Investigative Stories

Generally speaking, investigative news stories fall into two categories: master detective stories, that seek to bring out truths someone is trying to hide; and those that merely provide information to stimulate public action.

Here are some ideas concerning these types of stories:

Employee use of public property. Are employees using public automobiles and public gasoline for private business or pleasure? Have officials or workers diverted state property to their own use? Is public property being diverted by public office-holders who are profiting from the deal?

Prize-winning investigative reports include the following: (a) a television station spent several months recording incident after incident of city and county property (such as trucks and tractors) used by public officials for work on private property; (b) a daily newspaper revealed that a school official had taken a number of items, including a heater for a swimming pool, to his home for private use; (c) a weekly newspaper published a story telling all about a county commissioner who had built and furnished a hunting lodge with county materials.

Employee use of public travel funds. Were trips for which the employee was paid actually taken? Were expenses for the trip exorbitant? Is it possible that money claimed for legitimate expenses, such as taxis, tips, registration fees, and so on was actually used for personal entertainment, clothing, or gifts? Checking out items like these could involve many, many hours of close scrutiny of expense vouchers, travel requests, receipts, and other items submitted as evidence of an official's trip. Investigative reporters for the *St. Petersburg* (Fla.) *Times* and *Evening Independent* spent months researching the records of a turnpike authority before finding evidence of excessive and extravagant use of travel funds. The resulting stories brought the *Times* a Pulitzer Award for public service.

Fraudulent use of personnel. This includes use of public employees to do personal work for public officials. It includes requiring employees to kick back a portion of their pay to higher officials in order to keep their jobs or to help finance a political organization. It includes such management practices as allowing employees to take excessively long (unofficial) vacations, skip large parts of the working day, work overtime when no overtime is needed, or hiring unnecessary employees as a favor to a friend, relative, or important person.

Theft and mishandling of public funds. This could include theft or mishandling of pension and retirement funds, using false bookkeeping entries to cover up payroll padding, mishandling of petty cash funds, pocketing of cash receipts.

Use of a public job for personal benefit. This includes formation of "hidden businesses" to accept public contracts and failure to call for bids on a contract so the contract can be given to a "friendly" company that will reward the official for his efforts; manipulating specifications so a high bid will look honest and both the company and the public official can benefit; or the manipulation of licenses and other business privileges so that certain parties benefit and are willing to pay for the favor.

This area also includes a number of possible evils in law enforcement, such as sale for personal profit of confiscated items (drugs, liquor, gambling equipment), pocketing of fees by officials who are paid on a fee system, and acceptance by jailers of money for favors to prisoners.

Public building contract irregularities. Do buildings, roads, and other public projects meet official specifications? Is there a chance that shoddy building materials are being used and passed by inspectors who receive a kickback? Was the bidding for the projects proper? One newspaper unearthed a scheme in which one corporation had a number of "dummy" companies, each of which could send in bids, thus meeting the state law calling for at least three bids.

Abuse in the assessment of property. How is property assessed in your area: At fair market value? At seventy-five percent of value? Are certain persons favored in their assessments? Are high government officials favored in their assessments?

The election process. Are election procedures tamper-proof? Are registration lists kept properly so as not to favor one party over another? Do they meet all of the requirements of the law?

Irregularities in the purchase of property. This includes purchases by public officials of property known to be needed for public use, and then making a quick sale of the property to the government at an inflated price. It includes tips to friends or relatives to buy property already marked for public use.

Investigative stories that make certain information public, stimulate citizens to seek change, or help solve problems of one kind or another can be found throughout the community if the reporter is tuned to the needs of his time, listens to what people generally are thinking about, and is aware of trends taking place. Here are some general ideas for such stories.

Stories that show how people are affected by change. One example of this is a series of stories showing specifically how people will be affected by changes in federal, state, or local laws and regulations. Another is a story or series showing how social or economic changes will affect people.

Stories that reveal conditions or situations. This could be a story or series showing conditions in a city, county, or state prison, or in the prison system generally. It could be a series in depth on crime or juvenile delinquency in the community. The story could probe into health care in the community. It could deal with conditions in nursing homes or other places for the aged. It could reveal conditions in public schools.

Stories that deal with trends. An example of this might be a series on local population trends and how public services will be affected. It could be an investigation of local school enrollments and what the community must do to prepare for the future, or an analysis in depth of voting trends, a series on trends in economic growth of the area, or a series showing traffic trends and the need for better traffic management.

Stories that explode myths or dispel rumors. Many people today feel that public schools are "falling apart," that colleges are being "taken over by students," that all government is "inefficient and corrupt," that the motto of business is "let the buyer beware," that public morals have fallen to a "new low," that most young people are "hooked on drugs," or that the outlook for the future is "grim indeed." A series of stories could help explode popular misconceptions. Of course, it may be that certain rumors or popular myths prove true.

Stories that deal with human achievement. A reporter might write a story or series on an entire program or the efforts of an individual. It might be an analysis in depth of a local or state institution and the people who manage it.

These are just a few of the possibilities—all standard, all written before. But there are always new readers, and new actors in old situations.

Students in schools of journalism all over the nation are beginning to savor the excitement and satisfaction of doing investigative stories within their own states. The author of this book teaches a course in investigative reporting at the University of Florida. Over the years students have dug into such things as the condition of the Seminole Indians in Florida; the impact of the Cuban population on the city of Miami; the problems of beach erosion; problems and controversies that developed over the suggestion that the Suwannee River become a "wild river"; some mysteries that developed over the sale of land for a state park; the tidelands controversy; growth of private air transportation in the state; development of integration in the state university system; conditions that pointed toward the need for a local juvenile detention home; and conditions in the county jail.

How Not to Win Friends

Investigative reporting, no matter how professionally it is done and no matter how badly it is needed in every community, does not win many friends among the general public. People are likely to say, "Those prying newspapers are at it again, trying to give the town a bad name."

They are likely to reiterate one of the great myths: "Those newspapers are at it again—muckraking and trying to find something sensational to help sell their lousy fish wrapper!"

The fact is that few newspapers today depend much on street sales for circulation. The great bulk of their sales come through home delivery. Sensational headlines are not needed to push the product.

Ironically, if a newspaper fails to be aggressive and carry out its traditional watchdog role over government, the same readers are likely to say, "Our newspaper is no good, too tame, too lazy, never does anything, always takes the safe, middle-of-the-road approach to everything."

In fact, the newspaper and other news media do not get into investigative reporting to satisfy a public that is often fickle. They do so because of professional pride, as a way of making part payment for the privilege of doing business in a free society, and because their owners and writers have accepted the responsibility of watching over public affairs. Unfortunately, many people outside the news business refuse to believe this and refuse to credit the newsman with being a dedicated professional.

Take the case of the *Panama City* (Fla.) *News-Herald,* which won a Pulitzer Award for its investigations into crime and corruption in the city and county. After the award was won, the paper reported:

> So you'd like to win a Pulitzer Prize and a National Editorial Association award for meritorious public service. (Let's face it, any newspaper in the nation would.)
> Then be prepared for a tremendous amount of hard work, more hard work than you've ever known before, editorial department expenses running far above normal; hours and worries highly conducive to ulcers; moments of downright chilling fear—and unimaginable satisfaction in a job well done.

According to Woodrow Wilson, *News-Herald* publisher at that time, "Some of the overtime checks I had to sign made me wonder at times whether the paper could afford such a long, drawn-out campaign."

Said Edwin B. Callaway, executive editor, "If somebody told me that the papers would have to go through the same wringer, starting right now, I'd be tempted to join the Peace Corps or find some other quiet pastime."

Added Bob Brown, managing editor, "When the sheriff and police chief were removed from office, followed by their indictment by a federal grand jury, reaction set in. I realized how bone-weary I was—and my stock of ulcer-preventers depleted."

And W. U. (Duke) Newcome, reporter, said, "I admit I was plain scared lots of time during the campaign. I still draw the shades carefully at night, a habit I got into when things really got hot."

The wives of the men involved agreed almost unanimously that mass divorce would result from another drive any time soon.

There were long nights and many months of nagging doubts about whether any good was being accomplished, even doubts that everybody would escape with skin intact.

This is no exaggeration. Federal and state officers gave friendly, but deadly serious, warnings to the *News-Herald* staff: "Don't go into a bar, even for a beer; you'll be picked up on a drunk driving charge. Be careful crossing streets, particularly at night; an 'accident' can be so easily arranged. Drive home by different routes. Make sure your garage is well lighted. Don't walk by dark alleys." No wonder that editors and reporters considered sending their families away to stay with relatives.

Harder to face, perhaps, was the constant barrage of criticism from the public. Some criticism was discounted because it came from known friends and associates of suspects. But biting criticism also came from the average readers, largely because the investigation had not reached the point where many facts could be printed.

However, recognition does come to the investigative reporter and his newspaper or broadcast station. Once the evil has been uncovered, readers are likely to react favorably and speak with pride of the courage of their newspaper, radio or television station.

The number of organizations making annual awards for excellence in the general areas of investigative and depth reporting is on the increase. Topping these are the prestigious Pulitzer Awards for public service, followed by the Sigma Delta Chi Awards for public service, the Robert F. Kennedy Journalism Awards, and many specialized awards such as the Atomic Industrial Forum Award and those of the American Bar Association.

A Role for Research

There was a time when some newspapers considered interviews with ten people on Main Street adequate probing of some question. If the reporter was instructed to find out how college students felt about a new aspect of the Vietnam War, all he did was ask each of the first ten students he could stop long enough to pose the question. The result was a story that purported to tell readers how *all* college students felt about the question. Some newspapers still practice this kind of useless journalism. This is not to say that the "man on the street" approach does not have some merit, so long as it is used principally for entertainment and not passed off as any kind of scientific analysis.

In these days, however, technology has provided tools that can be of tremendous use to the newsroom in the analysis of great masses of data from reader surveys. Philip Meyer, of the Knight Newspapers Washington Bureau, is one of today's leading proponents of the importance of using computers and modern research methods to expand the horizons of the newsroom.

In the July—August, 1971, issue of the *Columbia Journalism Review* he wrote:

> Quantification is not the tedious work that it used to be. While the computer cannot think for us, it can remove the drudgery from counting and measuring. Moreover, computer time is no longer expensive, particularly when compared with the cost of hand-tabulating the same data. What remains expensive is the collection of the data. But there is precedent for newspapers to spend large amounts of money in research for news stories. If the story is important enough, a good newspaper will find a way to cover it.

Newspapers are quick to cover the news story that "happens." But what about those stories that are going on all the time, below the surface, in every community and in the nation as a whole? If we had been doing our research on attitudes and changing ideas among our youth in an earlier decade, we might have been able to develop stories that pointed to a future "drug scene." If we had been doing research on frustration and despair in our ghetto slums, we might have been able to report on conditions that would lead to the tragic riots of the 1960s. Events—the riots, drug addiction, campus disorders—are often only tips of news icebergs that have been around long before they burst into view to make screamer headlines. Meyer continues:

> Some stories are worth this heavy artillery. But for the new methods to gain currency in journalism, two things must happen. First, the editors must feel the need strongly enough to develop the in-house capacity for systematic research. Hiring an outside consultant or survey firm to prepare a report for a reporter to write about is not enough; the reporter's insight, fast reflexes, and ability to cope with deadline pressure are needed from the outset. The second need, of course, is for the editors to find the talent to fill this need. Many journalism schools are prepared to supply it.

Questions for Discussion

1. Do you think "the end justifies the means" in an investigative news story? Why, or why not?
2. Make a list of five investigative story ideas for your local area and explain how you would begin to gather material for one of the stories.
3. In what way is investigative reporting "detective work"?
4. Discuss one idea for a news story in your area that might be developed through research techniques.
5. As a newspaper publisher, what would be your philosophy concerning investigative reporting?

11 new horizons for the reporter

Most modern newspapers are still culling the same old beats as they search for news of today's world—beats such as the police run, city hall, the hospital, the fire department, and local government officials. But good newspapers have added new beats or changed their newsgathering methods entirely. Today we hear a lot about the television beat, reporting the environment, reporting public health, consumer journalism, and reporting of urban affairs.

The Television Beat

How has television affected newspapers and news presentation? How should the newspaper reporter view television news and documentaries? Will television news change newspapers even more in future years? Has television brought about a changing role for the newspaper reporters?

These are some of the questions discussed here. The answers come, for the most part, from managing editors of the nation's outstanding newspapers.

Changes in newspaper writing and editing. Some newspapers insist that all stories, including wire copy, be written in such a manner that they can be read in a hurry.

Leads must be held to a maximum of twenty-five words, paragraphs to thirty. They prefer simple sentences without complicated punctuation. These newspapers report that they are moving toward the use of more "human" news: accentuating women, writing stories on health or medicine, business, automobiles. They are doing more with fashions—both male and female—recordings, hi-fi, and the outdoors, especially stories on family camping.

Newspapers say people have more leisure time now. They have more time for hobbies: they go boating and fishing, take weekend trips to the mountains or the seashore, or build things. Television whets their appetites for these things, so newspapers must give them detailed advice and illustrations they can study.

Most editors believe that their newspapers must answer questions raised by television programs, including news programs. Suppose, for example, television shows an injured athlete being carried off the field on a stretcher. The newspaper reporter finds out exactly what happened to the athlete and how long he will be on the injured list. If there is some play in a game that requires interpretation, the newspaper makes a point of clarifying it.

Editors say they feel that television has increased public interest in many events and that a newspaper should take advantage of such interest by satisfying it.

Some editors report that television competition has forced them to think of more exclusive stories for their newspaper, stories that television or radio do not have, stories that other papers sold in their areas do not have. They feel this competition has forced them to produce more lively and interesting newspapers.

All seem to agree that people who have witnessed an event on television will demand something more than a routine newspaper account. They will want explanations and interpretations. George Beebe, associate publisher of the *Miami Herald,* tells this story:

"For years my wife and I watched the Wednesday night fights. We observed a distinguished looking couple always in the same front seats. He looked like a banker, always with a boutonniere; she a gray-haired matron, looking like a wealthy society woman.

"I asked AP who they were, and soon a picture story moved nationally.

"I was amazed to find the story a lively topic of discussion among many of my friends, who also had noticed the couple and wondered about them."

Television has forced newspapers to be more concerned about the "why" of a news event. Although television viewers have seen a professional golfer miss a thirty-inch putt, the incident gives the newspaper an opportunity to deliver the story on why the putt was missed and the golfer's reaction.

Editors agree that television competition has forced newspapers to be more painstaking and accurate than they ever have been before. As one editor put it, "We insist our stories be as accurate as humanly possible because readers who have watched an incident on TV know quickly now if a reporter makes a mistake."

Another editor says he feels that it is now necessary to explain to readers "what they *thought* they saw on the television screen." Therefore, someone on his staff monitors most television programs, especially local coverage of important gatherings such as political conventions and major sports events.

A third editor explains how his newspaper handles television competition:

"We have found that the best solution is to give our readers plenty of background on the news—a thing TV can't or doesn't do. We dress it up to be attractive to the eye and space the paper with human interest, which TV as yet has failed to use except, as one commentator says, we now have a closing story.

"The writing for newspapers must be briefer, brighter, but not 'purple-phrasish' and the editing must be sharp and critical.

"Cover all the news properly, with features geared to modern living, and I believe newspapers will survive and flourish.

"Campaign for civic betterment on a level that everyone understands, and a strong editorial policy helps considerably."

Another editor said, "In many stories we use a modified narrative style. In purely spot items we try to make them as sprightly as possible. We do not minimize detail, but feel that a story which has received a great deal of attention by TV and radio requires even more detail in the newspaper."

What to report about television. Newspaper editors all agree that television is here to stay. The next question is, then, what do you report *about* television?

First, the reporter must accept the fact that television itself is news to his readers. It is possibly the greatest entertainment medium of all time, judging by the millions of viewers who sit glued to a television set night after night. All of these viewers are also newspaper readers and they want to know:

1. All about new stations that are coming on the air in their communities.
2. All about policy changes, program changes, new television stars, problems, and even business news of the networks.
3. About feature stories on television personalities.
4. All about technical improvements in the industry that will affect their viewing.
5. The "how," the "why," and the "what" when these questions are not answered in depth during a television news program. They expect the newspaper to answer questions raised during television programs.
6. The same events covered in detail in the newspaper when television covers a major spectator sport or other national or local news events so that they can compare notes with reporters.
7. The reason why a television star leaves a favorite program. They want to know what the star plans to do and how the show will cover the vacancy.
8. That their newspaper is reviewing television shows, just as they review movies or other entertainment. They want

to know which programs were produced well or poorly so that they can compare their own opinions with those of the reviewers.

9. Television, like any other institution that solicits public approval, is controversial. Readers want to know what the "experts" say about television and television programming. They want to know what public officials and others say about it, too.

Readers want to know everything about television, reported as thoroughly and accurately as newspapers cover any other area in which there is high interest. That leaves the reporter a lot of room for reporting and writing.

The TV set can be your news source. Today many newspapers monitor television. Comments of editors indicate why they monitor this medium. One editor says, "We give careful coverage to the thoughtful news and information television programs, especially those on Sunday, and report whatever news emerges from them.

"We use television occasionally as a newsgathering mechanism for the coverage of the 'Sunday' programs mentioned above, for backstopping our sports department, even when we have a reporter at the sports event itself, and for backstopping the news department in the same circumstances when hearings and such events are being televised. Reporters who have written stories from advance texts of TV speeches by major government officials invariably watch the event over television to make sure that they can cover any additional remarks that are ad-libbed, for audience reaction, and so forth."

Another editor states: "In covering the national political conventions, we now insist that the editor in charge of the staff watch the proceedings on television rather than in the convention hall. We find that in this way the editor is able to sense what the public didn't understand in the telecast and to provide the proper background and interpretation."

A third editor explains: "Our executive sports editor monitors all major TV sports events and tries to determine what the reader will want to know next morning. Was it a raw decision, as the viewer believed before he shut off his set? Did the jockey throw a kiss to someone or was he just trying to regain his balance?

"We know that the most loyal readers of sports pages are the fans who attend the game or the fight. Viewing sports has exactly the same effect."

Still another editor says: "In general, television has not brought about any direct change in our coverage of the news and the writing and editing of it. However, I would be the last to deny, in fact I proclaim, it has had a substantial incidental effect. For instance, our coverage of large meetings like political conventions, inaugurations, and so on, has been altered considerably. This is evidenced by the fact we have reporters monitor television programs as an aid to the writer of the story in question. By covering TV this way, we not only feel we bring our stories more into focus in the public interest, but we also are able to pick up lively incidents which our reporters on the crowded scene could not possibly be aware of.

"We also feel our sports coverage has been affected considerably. This is especially true in that we have found new areas of sports interest, particularly among women. These interests include prize fights, baseball, golf, tennis, and other things which are televised in our community."

The reporter needs to remember that distant events become local news when they appear on the local television screen. One editor explains it this way: "Our sports pages are now compelled to cover a fight no matter how lousy the fighters, if it appears on a TV net in this area. The fight may originate clear across the country. The fighters may be wholly unknown, but if it's on the screen in the living room, hereabouts, we've got to get it into our paper."

This same editor continues: "Recently there was a fire just outside the windows of a TV station in Chicago. The fire didn't amount to a darn, but the Chicago station hooked it onto a net and it made a pretty spectacular show for a half hour or so on screens in New England. That is a story we had to get and cover, too, although ordinarily a minor fire in Chicago would mean nothing in this particular area.

"We have also, experimentally, used our music critic to cover brand new musicals on TV. The reason is obvious. They presumably had a very high viewer interest in this area."

Television has changed newspapers. An editor comments: "The most evident influence of television on the newspaper is, of course, as a news category. The modern newspaper has added a new department, television, to its news package, ranging from a column to four and five columns daily in extent, and blossoming into entire sections on Sunday. That has created a demand for newspaper workers who can evaluate television from a news viewpoint, and who are capable of acting as critics of the varied TV fare."

This editor describes how television has changed his newspaper:

1. The paper changed its press time to assure delivery by 5:30 P.M. in order to avoid conflict with TV programs.
2. The paper added a news and pictorial television department, one to four columns daily and two pages on Sunday.
3. The paper added more continuity features to the daily report (including a serialized fiction story, a daily food feature), and departmentalized the paper to a great extent.
4. The paper placed more emphasis on color, and layouts with art and special typographical effects.

Many newspapers believe that television's entry into the news field has brought about changes in newspaper photography. The managing editor of a metropolitan daily says, "On the picture side, a photographer must approach a news subject with the idea that TV may be covering too. Therefore, he must create a story idea that has reader appeal no matter whether it appears in print the next morning or the next afternoon. TV may have the flash picture, but the newspaper must have the photo the reader remembers and talks about. Such pictures will require an editorial concept as well as technical know-how on the part of the photographer."

Another editor cites what he thinks newspapers must do to meet TV competition:

1. Produce news stories that are shorter and better written and that contain more information.
2. Produce better, but not necessarily bigger, headlines.
3. Use more visual presentations, color pictures, charts, pictorial graphs, maps, and so forth.
4. Eliminate the "continued on page so-and-so" lines.
5. Use more "forum" formats, in which a real effort is made to present both sides of a story—the old "pro and con" done up in a sprightly, attractive layout.
6. Produce more enterprising stories—off the beat from the day's bulletin news—but nevertheless readable, informative, entertaining.
7. Come up with better printing, a more attractive product.

The daily newspaper is going to have to have more advanced planning, more thought, more competent people, more specialists on government, economics, gerontology, entertainment, public health, agriculture, industry, and so on.

No longer will it be possible to hire a hack who shows up for work without a thought in his head, who puts together material off the wires or from staff reporters. Instead, a telegraph or city editor must plan ahead for the next day's paper and put the results of that planning to work early.

Stories on television personalities. Personality sketches on television stars are much the same as personality sketches on politicians, movie stars, sports celebrities, and other well-known figures. The personality sketch may be a behind-the-scenes glimpse of a star's life; an explanation of recent news about the star; built around the star's views on certain subjects; or some combination of all of these.

Newspapers have no responsibility to promote television actors, but they must recognize the interest of their readers in the private and public lives of television personalities. A personality sketch can be short, and tied to a single idea, as in the following example:

NEW YORK—Alice Ghostley hates housework.
But, ironically, Miss Ghostley is doing just

that — housework — this season on "Mayberry R.F.D." which is seen Mondays at 9 P.M.on Channel 4. She has joined the Mayberry crew as Sam Jones' (Ken Berry) housekeeper.

The comedienne and her husband of eighteen years, actor Felice Orlandi, are newly ensconced in a house in the Hollywood Hills.

"It's the first home we've ever owned, after all those years of New York apartments," says Miss Ghostley, a Tony Award Winner from Broadway.

But as for the regular housework—forget it. "I have a cleaning woman," Miss Ghostley says. "Except for the week my husband's mother was visiting us from the East. She cooked those great Italian dishes and kept house so spotlessly that the cleaning lady just turned around and walked out."

Behind-the-scene story. Stories that take the television viewer behind the scenes come in many forms. These can be about the private lives of television stars; changes in program format; changes in the cast of characters of a particular show; or unusual problems in the production of a particular show or series.

These are by no means the only possibilities. The reporter is limited only by his imagination in writing about the world of television. The following story is a typical personality sketch justified by a change in the cast of a weekly television drama.

HOLLYWOOD—The closest anyone got to the big studio boss last season on NBC's "Bracken's World," the so-called glamorous exposé of motion picture life, was a phone call.

Never seen, and only heard from by telephone, Bracken was more elusive than Howard Hughes, because the show budget wasn't big enough to carry both secretary Eleanor Parker and her boss.

In midseason, star Parker quit, easing the budget. As the leading lady, she became tired of answering the darned phone. Relaying the studio head's orders was not Eleanor's idea of dominating the show.

With Miss Parker out of the way there would be enough scratch to pay for a Bracken, so the masterminds went out and hired an actor with authority for the executive role—Leslie Nielsen.

Nielsen, the former "Bold Ones" police chief, doesn't mind replacing a telephone. After years of hard-nosed cops, attorneys, and villains, Leslie, out of Saskatchewan, Canada, jumps at the chance to be a leading man in a romantic series, thus changing his image with fans and local film makers. His tough, strong-man parts literally pushed Leslie into the movie kingpin role—a leader with charm, who won't take any guff.

Since the show supposedly takes place today, in a Hollywood where the movie business has never been worse and empires are crumbling, Nielsen's Bracken is not Harry Cohn, L. B. Mayer or Darryl Zanuck. The celluloid tyrant of the past is obsolete, so Leslie's character must be streamlined, not flamboyant. He cracks out decisions with confidence while wearing blue jeans, a concession to the present, and is allowed to be slightly high in front of underlings, in another bow to reality. "I even play a little comedy," Nielsen disclosed. "People in the business don't know I can play it. Maybe we'll all find out."

The image switch for Nielsen means he will perform for a whole new television audience, and he may add his action following to the Friday night crowd. For some fifteen years, the Canadian accepted the image of the heavy or the tough cop, and he learned to "play the hell out of such parts." There was only one fallow season, 1961, after his "New Breed" series went off—then back to the heavies for Leslie.

The actor thinks this change to a romantic lead comes partly from an admiration for longevity. "Hey, he's still around," means the man must have something. "Just the idea you've lasted fifteen years is reason enough in Hollywood to take a second look," he believes. "It doesn't have anything to do with talent."

Nielsen is particularly satisfied with the Bracken part because it means he is no longer pigeonholed to action drama. He has popped out, and that will cause some anxiety to producers, since he can't be classified.

The man is also honest enough to evaluate "Bracken's World." "As an actor I found it professionally insulting last year," but he will swallow this in view of script changes.

"We are getting away from crisis drama and going back to people shows on television. A television explosion is beginning right now. In five years we will see major changes with the advent of cable TV and cassettes."

New programs make news. News of new TV offerings is eagerly awaited by viewers everywhere. In gathering and writing this kind of story, the reporter should consider the following:

1. What is the program about?
2. Is it designed for a particular audience—young people, old people, men, women?
3. When will it be on the air? How long, if it is a series?
4. Does the program have any special sponsors?
5. Can you obtain quotes from experts or members of the cast about the show?
6. Will the new show feature any well-known personalities?
7. Does the program deal with anything new or controversial for television?
8. Does the show seek a specialized audience?

The story below illustrates a new program announcement:

NEW YORK—Toning down the greedy urge is one of the first steps in civilizing a young child—and the churches are enlisting television to help do the job.

Four denominations have pooled funds to launch a new TV cartoon spot campaign aimed at replacing some of the selfish traits in youngsters with impulses of generosity.

"Sharing," is the theme of the four-part series, sponsored by the Episcopal Church, the United Methodist Church, the United Church of Christ, and the Christian Church Disciples of Christ.

We're not reaching kids today in the numbers we used to in Sunday School," says Hamilton Wright, Jr., a Phoenix, Ariz., layman and a film producer who turned out the series. "We've got to use the public channels of communications."

Several other religious groups also are producing children's material for television, including the Lutheran Church in America's widely shown cartoon series, "Davey and Goliath."

Others include: The American Bible Society's "Story Line," the Southern Baptist Convention's "Jot," the American Lutheran Church's "Great Bible Stories," and the program run by a United Presbyterian minister, Rev. Fred Rogers, called "Mr. Rogers."

"The fact that television can have a strong influence on the mind of a child is now beyond question," says Rev. Charles A. Hamilton, the Christian Disciples Church's broadcasting director, in explaining the trend.

In the new, jointly produced series, one episode shows a little cartoon-figure boy pointing to a buddy sharing his balloons with friends, "It's nice to share," the boy says, and the others sing, "Oh that's the way it is—truly, ooly, ooly is." But the boy himself is left out, with no balloon. "It's nice to share," he repeats plaintively. Then the others give him a balloon.

"When people share with me, I feel glad," he says, smiling. But there's another little fellow standing next to him, still without a balloon. "So what you gonna do today?" chants the chorus. He hesitates, then decides, "I think I'll share," and gives a balloon to the have-not boy, and it lifts him happily off his feet.

Rev. Robert M. G. Libby, the Episcopal radio-TV director, says tiny preschoolers "have the ability to grasp certain moral concepts," and such TV skits can help impart the basic Golden-rule concept of sharing.

Reporting the Environment

When you talk about environmental reporting you must understand words like "environment" and "ecology." The environment is the world we live in; ecology is the study of the relationship of living things with their environment.

David Hendin, news editor of Enterprise Science Service, says that environmental reporting means "reporting on the deterioration of ecological relationships, the upsetting of the ever-so-delicate balance of nature."

According to Ralph Otwell, managing editor of the *Chicago Sun-Times,* "the biggest challenge facing journalism in the 1970s is confronting the American people with the harsh reality of their self-destruction, and making them believe it."

Casey Bukro, environmental editor of the *Chicago Tribune*, believes "the basic theme of environmental reporting is the survival of mankind. That kind of assignment requires a new kind of reporting that crosses the artificial boundaries that traditionally have separated one reporter's beat from another. The world and everything in it is the environmental reporter's beat. A lot of people don't realize it yet, but that makes environmental reporting a new kind of journalism. It has no limits."

Environmental reporting often is depth reporting, and it often uses the investigative reporting techniques discussed in the previous chapter. Mike Albertson, environmental writer for the *Pensacola* (Fla.) *News-Journal,* says the major part of an environmental writer's task is to "scratch and dig for facts, many of which someone wants to hide."

Finding a subject. Is environmental reporting a fad? Will interest in ecology and the environment soon fade away and leave the specialist in this area little, if anything, to write about? The specialists already writing in this field say no. They admit that some of the frost has melted from the environmental pumpkin, but the pumpkin is still there. Where do you find subjects for stories?

You look for things that affect man's security, his way of life, his health, his happiness, his ability to enjoy nature. In local reporting, this means checking into such things as:

Changes in the zoning of an area. Will the changes eventually lead to urban blight? Will they lead to undue traffic congestion? Will they upset the natural drainage of the area and lead to flooding? Will they contribute to air or water pollution?

New industry located in the area. Is the location ecologically sound? Will the industry contribute to any kind of pollution? What about additional problems of waste disposal? Will the new industry cause a housing problem? New traffic problems? Will the new industry create a water shortage in the area? Will it affect wildlife in the area?

New roads, streets, and highways. How will these new constructions affect animal and human life in the area? Will the new highway cut through irreplaceable wildlife areas? Are there more desirable routes that could be followed? What will be the effects on streams, natural drainage, and lakes? Are fears expressed by conservationists supported by facts?

Oceanfront, river, or lakefront developments. How will these developments affect a citizen's access to waterfronts for recreational purposes? Will they add dangerously to water pollution in the area? What controls should be applied? What effects will the construction have on recreational and commercial fishing in the area? What about land erosion and destruction of forested areas? Does the development include land fill and dredging that will change the natural environment?

Need for parks and recreational areas. The environmental reporter should be aware of any need in his area for preservation of natural beauty and the addition of park land and other outdoor recreation areas. There are many stories in efforts by groups and individuals to bring new life to dead lakes, to remove pollutants from rivers and streams, and to develop new recreational areas.

The preceding suggestions are not intended to imply that an environmental reporter should resist all environmental change. But he does need to study changes to find out their effect on his fellow man.

Some dangers and problems. Environmental problems are often emotional. All too often the headlines go to the shrill voices predicting total disaster. Like any other good reporter, the environmental reporter must sift for the facts. His writing must always provide the balance that is often hard to achieve with a volatile issue. If he joins the doomsayers without documenting his argument, his writing may actually work against all those who work year in and year out to preserve the environment.

To this end, the environmental reporter must challenge all facts. He will attend many meetings where emotions run high and where speakers quote facts and figures that will not stand the hard light of truth.

Where do you find the facts? Go to the experts. Federal,

state, and county conservation and health agencies turn out an almost endless flow of reports on such topics as insect control, spread of diseases, use of insecticides, wildlife and fish populations, poaching on wildlife, aquatic weed control, pollution of water supplies, bacterial count in lakes and rivers, changes in the water table, annual flow of streams, and levels of air pollution.

University and government research centers are excellent sources. Such reports, however, must be interpreted with caution and with the help of the researchers. Conclusions are sometimes tentative, pointing to a need for further research.

The environmentalist and the environmental reporter must remember that there is much that man does not know and has not been able to discover about the balance of nature. What appears at one point to be an ecological disaster may simply be nature balancing itself, repeating a process existent long before man's arrival.

Consumer Journalism

What is consumer journalism? The name is somewhat misleading. We really mean *consumer affairs* journalism, and that means news of interest to anyone who buys goods and services—that is, everyone.

News stories and depth articles advising readers on goods and services are not new to magazine readers, but they are relatively new to newspaper readers and television viewers.

You may recall articles in *Reader's Digest* more than two decades ago reporting rackets in the auto repair business, and later, articles on fraud among TV repairmen.

Today, more and more newspapers are offering regular "Action Line" columns, designed to help consumers in their efforts to obtain fair treatment from businesses and government officials.

Some newspapers, like the *Rochester* (N.Y.) *Democrat and Chronicle,* have regular, full-page spreads on matters of concern to consumers. Here is one example, related by an editor of the *Democrat and Chronicle:*

Most states have laws, passed at the urging of pharmacy societies, that prohibit advertising of prescription drug prices. If a pharmacist wants to increase traffic into his store by running a special on commonly prescribed drugs, it is against the law for him to advertise that fact. Pharmacists call drug price advertising "unethical." Most consumer advocates call it avoiding competition.

The law works against the best interests of consumers because it prevents competition and because consumers are prevented from comparison shopping for drugs, unlike most all other consumer goods.

To illustrate the wide spread in prices of prescription drugs, "HELP! for the Consumer" took identical prescriptions to fourteen pharmacies and paid thirteen different prices, ranging from $1.79 to $6.00 to fill the same prescription. We printed the names of the pharmacies and how much each charged to fill the prescription.

A few months later we took another survey and this time found that nineteen pharmacies charged anywhere from $2.70 to $4.80 (77 percent difference) to fill prescriptions for identical tablets manufactured by a single company. We noted that the highest and lowest prices could be obtained at two stores in a downtown shopping plaza, located approximately one minute's walk away from each other. But because the law prevented the low-price pharmacist from advertising his prices, few consumers were aware of the bargain prices.

In addition to drug prices, "HELP! for the Consumer" has printed the names of fourteen local grocery stores and how they fared in a scientific testing of fat content of hamburger taken from each store. Three stores, including two branches of one of our largest advertisers, were in violation of state and federal laws which prohibit sale of ground beef containing fat in excess of 30 percent.

What are some of the things consumer-minded newspapers such as the *Rochester Democrat and Chronicle* do to serve the consumer interests of their area? They can:

1. Help employees collect overtime due from employers who violate the wage-hour law.

2. Help consumers obtain refunds on contract services when the contracts are violated by the seller.

3. Publish names of firms which fail to do anything about complaints registered with the Better Business Bureau.

The names of businesses and information on the
complaints are obtained from the Better Business
Bureau.

4. Publish names of firms which violate food laws.
5. Publish names of restaurants and other food es-
tablishments which violate city or county health codes.
6. Expose frauds involving door-to-door salesmen.
7. Publish names of food stores having on their shelves
canned goods or other food items banned by the
government.
8. Purchase cans of food to check contents by weight in
order to determine if the buyer is being cheated, for
example, by the addition of more water than vegetables.
All facts are then published.
9. Check weights of packaged meats to determine if actual
weight agrees with the weight stated on packages.
10. Check condition of boats rented at a lake resort to
determine if safety regulations are being followed.

These are only a few examples of public services being
provided through consumer affairs journalism. The scope of
this kind of reporting is limited only by the imagination and
courage of reporters and their newspapers.

Some hazards. Newspapers and consumer affairs
journalists should not enter this area of reporting if they are
not prepared to go all the way, publishing facts and names,
even at the risk of alienating advertisers. The consumer must
be made to feel that the newspaper is on *his* side. Consumer
affairs stories or "Action Line" columns concerned only with
trivialities, answering only questions that will not "rock the
boat," fail to serve their readers.

Consumer affairs journalism actually places the "power
of the press" in the hands of consumers. A mistake often
made by some newspapers is to assume that consumer
journalism is appropriate only on the "women's page." In
fact, men and women of all ages are consumers; consumer
news is of general interest and therefore should be treated as
such.

The Public Health Beat

This kind of journalism could be a specialized form of consumer affairs journalism, a branch of environmental reporting, or a field within urban affairs journalism.

The reporter on a public health beat should know all about city and county sanitation codes; state health regulations; regulations governing hospital care and nursing homes; sewage and garbage disposal regulations; disease control and epidemic prevention procedures; sources and kinds of water pollution; rodent and insect control measures; building and inspection laws pertaining to public health; federal and state regulations having to do with the health and welfare of the aged; and hospital care and sickness insurance programs.

This is a large order, calling for a trained specialist dedicated to public health journalism.

A special area within this field is mental health reporting; a few schools of journalism are beginning to train reporters who will confine their writing to the problems of the mentally ill, the need for public understanding of this area of public health, the progress being made in the field, the need for mental health care, and the prevention of mental illness.

The sources of news and feature stories in the field of health are unlimited. Public school health clinics, welfare agencies, city and county medical centers, county health officers, specialized health clinics, hospitals, health associations and foundations, and medical research agencies, are just a few.

The public wants to know all about:

The economics of health care—hospital costs, insurance programs; financial aid for indigent patients, and financial aid for persons unable to meet extended hospital care.

Progress being made in medical science—research on disease prevention and cure; inoculation programs, and new discoveries in medicine.

Dangerous health conditions—water pollution; spread of disease, or any unsanitary condition in the community.

General health precautions—health rules and

regulations; detection of danger signals; diet and weight problems; foods and how they affect health and what to do in emergencies until a doctor is available.

Community health problems—lack of adequate sanitary codes; abuse of health regulations; inadequate medical and nursing facilities; inadequate inspection procedures and insufficient personnel; poor health conditions in one part of the city and a need for more and better specialized clinics.

Health education—facilities available for health education, such as clinics and special classes; school health programs; short courses, workshops, and seminars available in the field of health and health care, and availability and value of health care literature.

Mental health—care and prevention, facilities, progress in mental health field as well as shortcomings, problems of mental health institutions, regulation of institutions.

Occupational health—health hazards in certain occupations, regulations that affect occupational health, problems that exist in a local area.

Urban Affairs Reporting

Concerning the "urban affairs" beat, Paul Gapp, a coordinator of the Urban Journalism Fellowship program (University of Chicago Center for Policy Study), says:

"The bounds of the urban affairs beat are irregular and stretchable (and, indeed, must be). By just about anybody's definition, however, this specialty embraces at minimum city and regional planning, architecture, housing, zoning, urban renewal, transportation, pollution, major inner city real estate developments, and conservation. Anything which imposes a major physical change in a city falls within the urban affairs reporter's domain."

If we accept Mr. Gapp's definition of this particular kind of reporting, clearly many aspects of urban affairs journalism have already been covered in this book: investigative reporting, depth reporting, environmental reporting, consumer journalism and the public health beat. However, there are a few special considerations which concern the reporter who writes on urban renewal, city planning and zoning, the architecture of the city, and the real estate speculations that are common in urban areas.

The urban affairs reporter should cover the *building* of cities more thoroughly in the planning stage, the building stage, and then take a critical look at the results. The reporter should consult the consumer, the person who must *use* the city. Too much reporting in the field of urban affairs today comes from interviews with public officials, planners, architects—the official decision makers.

The urban affairs reporter must develop a nose for news, one that senses early the future shape of the city he is covering. If he covers city development only by attending official "public hearings," he may often find that he has waited too long to make ideas and plans known for long term, full public debate. Decisions may have been made that cannot, or will not, be altered. A good urban affairs reporter must be *trained* to detect the moves planners make months, even years, ahead of public disclosure of their plans. Concerning this one point, Grady Clay, long-time real estate editor of the *Louisville Courier-Journal,* says:

> Invariably, there comes a point at which locations are decided and designs fixed. This may be months or years before the legal public hearing which newspapers routinely cover.
>
> Prior to that moment, you get the old dodge that "plans are not complete," and public discussion is "premature." Everything is "preliminary." To the good reporter, there is no such thing as "premature disclosure." Whenever you hear this, you can assume that one informal decision is being quietly stacked on top of another so that the course of events is determined, the pattern set. Then, at the public hearing, you will be assured that "so much engineering time has been invested in the plans (for highway, buildings, civic center, what-have-you) that it is too late for substantial change." Any change not already decided upon is a "substantial change."
>
> Public hearings, which we cover routinely, have often degenerated into legal formalities at which the reporter and public learn it's too late to change decisions already arrived at in private.
>
> To find the moment of decision is one of the toughest jobs

facing metropolitan newspapermen today. It is a little like trying to find the body before the murder takes place. It means plowing through a top layer of technical plans and documents, a secondary layer of consultants who are out of town just when you need to reach them, and several more layers of independent, autonomous agencies run by buck-passers.

In no other field is it quite so important to know the documents and background. We need to keep our own filing system and private reference libraries. Part of one's equipment should be copies of the comprehensive plan, zoning ordinances, consultants' reports, and special studies of your community—not in the newspaper morgue, but in your own desk. It requires one's own clipping files, and that mainstay of the city editor, the "six-month clip file" and calendar of stories to be looked into six months hence. Every candidate's platform should go into the file; so should all the fine programs, declarations of intent, and programs of construction which erupt every so often.

Each of us really ought to keep a file of promissory notes, those preliminary sketches we publish every so often. The how-the-new-Civic-Center-will-look kind of thing. Then six to twelve months later, we pull it out, and find out why nothing has happened; or why, you suddenly realize looking at the old clippings, the proposed jail has been moved a block away, and the fine arts library has disappeared from the plan, or a new architect's name shows up on the newest sketch.

The urban affairs reporter must learn to recognize what is at issue. George McCue, of the *St. Louis Post-Dispatch,* puts it this way:

In some cases the issue is a question of simple morality in preempting the land from some people to make room for other people. And in other cases, it's a matter of whether you're getting your money's worth from whatever new use is made of this land. The issues may take form in a combination of political, economic, moral, philosophical, mechanical engineering and all sorts of other circumstances, in various relationships to each other, and I think the whole thing illustrates how flatfooted the newspaper business has been caught by the overall issue of urban renewal. We're familiar with city hall problems because we are used to covering city hall. We know how to cover police stations, courts, and all the old, familiar well-tracked newspaper bulldozers. We take pictures of the demolition job, and later we show a new building. We think that in reporting these sequential steps, we are keeping up with the story, but we are not really sure what the story is. We don't know what the issues are, we confuse square feet with cubic feet, and we compare costs in different cities without making allowances for where the cities are, or for special circumstances that may throw irrelevancies into the comparison.

To be aware of the "shape of the future" in his city, the urban affairs reporter should be alert to requests for funds for feasibility studies and report to the public what is being proposed.

He must not neglect the type of interpretative story that evaluates a completed project. For example, the experts predict that a new expressway will relieve traffic problems in other parts of the city, that it will reduce auto accidents, that it will provide speedier access to the central city, that it will not harm business in the area through which it passes. After the highway is built, a series of follow-up stories should be written to examine these predictions. Were they merely wishful thinking or did they become reality? Or did the expressway create new problems not foreseen by the planners?

The urban affairs reporter must have an interest in the problems of people in the cities because he will continually investigate decisions that affect human values. He must therefore have a broad knowledge of government and its operation. He must know something of economics, of the problems of the architect, the city planner, and public works administrators. He must understand the sociology of the city, including its welfare structure and its population growth, and its inner tensions and frustrations.

The urban affairs reporter must always get at the reasons for a project or planning design—motives may *be* the story. By asking architects and planners *why* they are doing something a certain way, these decision-makers must, often for the first time, defend their judgment. Such cross-questioning may reveal self-interest or weaknesses in judgment. This must be written, of course, as good depth reporting and not as the writer's opinion; this means getting ample quotes from all those involved—politicians, bankers, architects, businessmen, and residents.

Questions for Discussion
1. Does television really compete with newspapers, or do newspapers compete with television? Is television itself news for the newspaper? Should the newspaper have a television beat?
2. Is the current interest in "environment" simply a fad? Will this interest fade, and if so, should it therefore be ignored by the news media?
3. Do you think consumer journalism ought to be a significant part of newspapers in the future? Why, or why not?
4. How many news or feature stories can you think of that might come from the public health beat in your community?
5. Compare the beat of an urban affairs reporter with that of a city hall reporter. Can the two be the same?

12 the meaning of responsibility

The intention of this study is not to lay down inflexible rules concerning good taste and ethics. The guidelines in this chapter have proven successful to me through experience, and so I recommend them to the student. No individual newsman or textbook writer can say to all reporters that they are "responsible" only if they adhere to a certain set of rules. It is hoped, however, that the advice in this chapter will help young reporters develop their own sense of responsibility.

What Makes a Good Newspaper?

"My own observation and experience tell me that the newspapers are less accurate than they were. I believe there has been a growing tendency among newspaper readers generally to distrust much that they read. Certain it is that today many persons in the United States, in print and by word of mouth, sometimes justly and sometimes otherwise, are harsh in their criticism of the newspapers with respect to their accuracy and fairness."

If the above quotation sounds familiar, if you are certain that you heard it just a few days ago, you are wrong. The statement was made in the mid-1920s by a staff member of the *New York World*.

Of course, he was not the first to question the accuracy of newspapers or to point to a credibility gap between newspapers and readers. Throughout history the press has had its critics, and doubtless will have them as long as it must report unpleasant news.

In response to criticism, however, publishers and editors in all periods of American history have attempted to make their newspapers as truthful and objective as possible. Since the beginnings of American journalism, as new newspapers were born, publishers set down in the first issue their objectives, their platforms of service to the community, the ideas and ideals by which they intended to govern the conduct of their new publication. Later, as newspapers banded together into associations, they developed codes of ethics attesting to their belief that the press was a public service, with tremendous power for doing good or evil in the nation as well as in communities.

The first such code, nationally, was born April 28, 1923, when the National Association of Newspaper Editors adopted the "Canons of Journalism."

Canons of Journalism

The primary function of newspapers is to communicate to the human race what its members do, feel, and think. Journalism, therefore, demands of its practitioners the widest range of intelligence, of knowledge, and of experience, as well as natural and trained powers of observation and reasoning. To its opportunities as a chronicle are indissolubly linked its obligations as teacher and interpreter.

To the end of finding some means of codifying sound practice and just aspirations of American Journalism these canons are set forth:

1. *Responsibility*

The right of a newspaper to attract and hold readers is restricted by nothing but consideration of public welfare. The use a newspaper makes of the share of public attention it gains serves to determine its sense of responsibility, which it shares with every member of its staff. A journalist who uses his power for any selfish or otherwise unworthy purpose is faithless to a high trust.

2. *Freedom of the Press*

Freedom of the press is to be guarded as a vital right of mankind. It is the unquestionable right to discuss whatever it is not explicitly forbidden by law, including the wisdom of any restrictive statute.

3. *Independence*

Freedom from all obligations except that of fidelity to the public interest is vital.

(a) Promotion of any private interest contrary to the general welfare, for whatever reason, is not compatible with journalism. So-called news communications from private sources should not be published without public notice of their source or else substantiation of their claims to value as news, both in form and substance.

(b) Partisanship in editorial comment which knowingly departs from the truth, does violence to the best spirit of American journalism; in the news columns it is subversive of a fundamental principle of the profession.

4. *Sincerity, Truthfulness, Accuracy*

Good faith with the reader is the foundation of all journalism worthy of the name.

(a) By every consideration of good faith, a newspaper is constrained to be truthful. It is not to be excused for lack of thoroughness or accuracy within its control or failure to obtain command of these essential qualities.

(b) Headlines should be fully warranted by the contents of the articles which they surmount.

5. *Impartiality*

Sound practice makes clear distinction between news reports and expressions of opinion. News reports should be free from opinion or bias of any kind.

This rule does not apply to so-called special articles unmistakably devoted to advocacy or characterized by a signature authorizing the writer's own conclusions and interpretations.

6. *Fair Play*

A newspaper should not publish unofficial charges, affecting reputation or moral character

without opportunity given to the accused to be heard;
right practice demands the giving of such opportunity in all cases of serious accusation outside judicial
proceedings.

(a) A newspaper should not invade private
rights or feelings without sure warrant of public right
as distinguished from public curiosity.

(b) It is the privilege, as it is the duty, of a
newspaper to make prompt and complete correction
of its own serious mistakes of fact or opinion,
whatever their origin.

7. *Decency*

A newspaper cannot escape conviction of insin-
cerity if while professing high moral purpose it
supplies incentives to base conduct, such as are to be
found in details of crime and vice, publication of
which is not demonstrably for the general good.
Lacking authority to enforce its canons, the journalism here represented can but express the hope that
deliberate pandering to vicious instincts will encounter effective public disapproval or yield to the
influence of a preponderant professional
condemnation.

Since the adoption of the "Canons of Journalism," many
state and regional newspaper associations have adopted
codes of ethics in an attempt to identify for both journalists
and readers alike the responsibilities and limitations of
newspapers. In 1947, the Commission on Freedom of the
Press, popularly known as the Hutchins Commission,
reported after lengthy study what it considered to be the
basic requirements of the press in a free society. These
requirements were that newspapers should:

1. Be forums for the exchange of comment and criticism;
2. Afford readers full access to the day's intelligence;
3. Present a truthful, comprehensive, and intelligent
   account of the day's events in a context which gives them
   meaning;
4. Be responsible for the presentation and clarification of
   the goals and values of society;
5. Project a representative picture of the constituent groups
   in the society.

Newsmen, generally, were critical of the Hutchins Committee report because there were no journalists involved in the study. Many of them asked for a similar study by a new panel which would include newspapermen. Because of the dissatisfaction, *Editor & Publisher* magazine helped establish in 1949 a new panel of both educators and newspapermen. The objective of the panel was to consider plans for a "joint appraisal of the self-improvement possibilities of American newspapers through studies of specific problems." As a result of some of the findings of this panel, a report was issued in 1950 by the American Society of Newspaper Editors, containing the following recommendation:

"The self-improvement of American newspapers depends chiefly upon the character of American newspapermen, their recognition and acceptance of the great responsibilities imposed by freedom of the press, their faithfulness to duty in giving the people of this country a truthful account of the day's news and fair comment thereon, and their willingness to profit by the intelligent criticisms of the newspaper-reading public."

This effort by newspapermen to reevaluate themselves and their product was renewed in 1960 when the Associated Press Managing Editors Association launched a new study that attempted to isolate and identify the criteria of a good newspaper. The first report of this committee was made public in 1962:

Criteria of a Good Newspaper

A good newspaper prints the important news and provides the information, comment, and guidance that is most useful to its readers.

It reports fully and explains the meaning of local, national, and international events which are of major significance in its own community. Its editorial comment provides an informed opinion on matters of vital concern to its readers.

By reflecting the total image of its own community in its news coverage and by providing wise counsel in its editorials, a good newspaper becomes a public conscience. It also must be lively, imaginative, and original; it must have a sense of humor, and the power to arouse keen interest.

To implement these principles of good editing requires a skilled staff, an attractive format, adequate space for news and comment, and a sound business foundation.

The staff must possess the professional pride and competence necessary to breathe life and meaning into the daily record of history. Good writing must be combined with an effective typographical display of copy and pictures to capture the full drama and excitement of the day's news. Good printing is essential.

News and comment of most immediate interest and importance to the local community shall have priority for the available space, which will depend on the size and resources of the newspaper.

To assure a financially strong and independent publication, and one that is competitive with other media, a good newspaper must maintain effective circulation, advertising, and promotion departments.

Finally, a good newspaper should be guided in the publication of all material by a concern for truth, the hallmark of freedom, by a concern for human decency and human betterment, and by a respect for the accepted standards of its own community.

A good newspaper may judge its own performance—and be judged by the criteria that follow:

1. *Integrity*

The newspaper shall:

(a) Maintain vigorous standards of honesty and fair play in the selection and editing of its content as well as in all relations with news sources and the public.

(b) Deal dispassionately with controversial subjects and treat disputed issues with impartiality.

(c) Practice humility and tolerance in the face of honest conflicting opinions or disagreement.

(d) Provide a forum for the exchange of pertinent comment and criticism, especially if it is in conflict with the newspaper's editorial point of view.

(e) Label its own editorial views or expressions of opinion.

2. *Accuracy*
    The newspaper shall:
    (a) Strive for completeness and objectivity.
    (b) Exert maximum effort to print the truth in all news situations.
    (c) Guard against carelessness, bias, or distortion by either emphasis or omission.
    (d) Correct promptly errors of fact for which the newspaper is responsible.

3. *Responsibility*
    The newspaper shall:
    (a) Use mature and considered judgment in the public interest at all times.
    (b) Select, edit, and display news on the basis of its significance and its genuine usefulness to the public.
    (c) Edit news affecting public morals with candor and good taste and avoid an imbalance of sensational, preponderantly negative, or merely trivial news.
    (d) Accent when possible a reasonable amount of news which illustrates the values of compassion, self-sacrifice, heroism, good citizenship, and patriotism.
    (e) Clearly define sources of news, and tell the reader when competent sources cannot be identified.
    (f) Respect rights of privacy.
    (g) Instruct its staff members to conduct themselves with dignity and decorum.

4. *Leadership*
    The newspaper shall:
    (a) Act with courage in serving the public.
    (b) Stimulate and vigorously support public officials, private groups, and individuals in crusades and campaigns to increase the good works and eliminate the bad in the community.
    (c) Help to protect all rights and privileges guaranteed by law.
    (d) Serve as a constructive critic of government at all levels, provide leadership for necessary reforms or innovations, and expose any misfeasance in office or any misuse of public power.
    (e) Oppose demagogues and other selfish and unwholesome interests regardless of their size or influence.

All of these codes, canons, statements of principles, and criteria for the guidance of the press and its public have a common weakness. Like the Constitution of the United States, they deal in general principles. The actual day-by-day conduct of a newspaper—how it interprets a code or set of guidelines—is determined by staff members. This is far tougher than might appear.

The Associated Press Managing Editors Association study says, "The newspaper shall maintain vigorous standards of honesty and fair play in the selection and editing of its content as well as in all relations with news sources and the public." What happens when the "interests of the public" and the self-interests of a news source conflict, as many newspapers believed was the case in the now famous publication of "The Pentagon Papers" by the *New York Times, Washington Post,* and *Boston Globe* in 1971?

Whether "secret" documents about the war in Vietnam, taken from the Pentagon, ought to have been published without permission from the U.S. government was widely debated by newspapermen. Typical of statements *against* publication of the documents were those of Franklin B. Smith, editorial page editor of the *Burlington* (Vt.) *Free Press:*

> We appear to be among a distinct minority of newspapermen who deeply regret the publication of the Pentagon Papers by the *New York Times* and other newspapers.
>
> Most newspapermen, in what is essentially a knee-jerk reaction, support the action of the *Times* because—in their view—this is a classic confrontation between governmental authority and press freedom. The fact remains that the published documents were stolen property. Also, there are laws against the publication of classified material.
>
> Who elected the *Times* to determine what government documents should and should not be published? This question has been asked repeatedly during the past couple of weeks, and the *Times'* answer has been this: the Constitution, specifically the first amendment. Such arrogance is to be deplored, especially by fellow newspapermen who are embarrassed and saddened by it.

Jack W. Germond, Washington bureau chief for the Gannett News Service, took the other viewpoint.

It is this independence of judgment that is at the *root* of the searing national controversy over the publication by the *New York Times* and several other newspapers of the Pentagon Papers.

The Nixon administration doesn't believe they should be published because they have been classified as top secret. The newspapers that have chosen to publish them have done so because they believe that classification is an overreaching by the government to protect itself that cannot be justified in the light of the contents. . . .

If a history that is, at its freshest, several years old can be suppressed on the grounds of national security, what's to prevent the indiscriminate use of classification stamps on records of current pertinence? Who's to say, for example, whether publication of studies of school integration might be forestalled on the theory they could contribute to unrest among blacks. That sounds far-fetched indeed, but the record of government is that openings are quickly converted to excesses.

What about the first part of the APME mandate—"The newspaper shall maintain vigorous standards of honesty and fair play in the selection and editing of its content . . ."? Suppose a man is arrested and charged with child molesting. As a reporter, you dig into the records and learn that this same fellow has been arrested, convicted, and imprisoned on this same charge nine times in the past fifteen years. If you publish his record of prior arrests and convictions, you may rob him of a completely fair judicial trial. He may be innocent this time. On the other hand, if you don't publish the record, society will not have one kind of information it requires to change its laws, in this case the handling of persons who habitually commit the same crimes. How does a newspaper in this situation "maintain vigorous standards of honesty and fair play"?

Let's take another of the APME principles. Under the general heading "responsibility" is the mandate: "Respect rights of privacy."

Suppose a young mother at the seashore momentarily takes her eyes away from her young son who is in the water, and at that moment the son drowns. As a lifeguard seeks in vain to revive the boy, a newspaper photographer happens by; he takes a picture of the scene, including the tear-stained face of the mother as she bends over her dead child. One might argue that the picture should not be used in the newspaper or on television because the private grief of the mother should be kept private. Someone else might argue that "public interest" overrides right of privacy in this case: the public needs to be dramatically reminded that young children at the seashore should be continuously watched so that drownings can be prevented.

The newspaper will probably use the picture, following another of the APME mandates: "The newspaper shall act with courage in serving the public."

The upshot of all this is that once ethics have been written, the newspaper must apply these to concrete situations. Newspapers often make spontaneous decisions at deadline time, when an ethical solution is far from clear. This does not mean, however, that newspapermen should cease to adopt codes or give up trying to follow them.

As a matter of fact, codes and voluntary agreements for handling touchy subjects are still in vogue. *Editor & Publisher* reported, on January 4, 1975, that, in a survey taken by the American Bar Association, a majority of newspaper editors, broadcast news directors, and bar association officials in twenty-three states of the United States favored voluntary agreements on fair trial-free press protection. Newspaper editors and broadcast news directors favored advance working agreements in crime news reporting by a margin of seventy-eight percent. Voluntary codes have been worked out and adopted in the twenty-three states for handling court news on a fair trial-free press basis. The survey results indicated that newspaper editors favored these voluntary agreements by a ratio of seven to one.

Objectivity—A Myth?

Is objectivity in a news story just a myth? Does "real" objectivity mean getting involved in the story yourself? Was Norman Mailer right when he said that "facts without their nuances are nothing?"

Here is what professionals in the news business are saying about this matter. George Bevan, editor of the

Corning (N.Y.) *Leader,* wrote in the May, 1971, *New York Press/Publisher:*

This month and in the months ahead the editor will be in a buyer's market. He can be more selective than in the past and he will be looking for a number of desirable traits when he interviews a prospective reporter. The most important trait is the ability and desire to do objective reporting. Some have called opinionated reporting "subjective," others hide behind the cloak of "interpretation," and still others pass it off as straight reporting—the cardinal sin of all.

Newspapers in the metropolitan areas have different criteria, demands, and responsibilities than do the dailies and weeklies of the smaller communities. Smaller newspapers such as the *Leader* are practically members of the families into whose homes they enter each night. If bias or opinion creeps into news stories, it can easily be spotted both by the subjects of the stories and by the readers. They too have their prejudices but they have a right to demand that the reporter's opinion be kept out of the news stories. They have been oriented to hope that the opinions stay on the editorial page or, if on the other pages, are clearly labeled as such.

The challenge to beginning reporters, to journalism schools and to the communications world is one of remembering that an informed public can sift facts from fiction, and fantasy—that an informed public insists on making up its own mind—that more and more the public is going to demand a labeling of news as news and opinion as opinion. If a young journalist can meet this challenge then he or she is a giant step closer to finding that first job.

Wes Gallagher, no slouch as a reporter before he became general manager of the Associated Press, last November told the Association of State Universities and Land-Grant Colleges: "What our profession does not require is the so-called 'activist' approach so much discussed by young people today. There are enough strident, partisan, intolerant voices without adding that of the journalist. His should be a clear voice of fact, not rhetoric, the voice of fairness, non-partisanship, the voice of reason."

Laurence S. Hale, editor of the *Binghamton* (N.Y.) *Press,* wrote in the 1971 issue of *Editorially Speaking:*

So we want our reporter to be objective in his motives, objective in his judgment and objective in his writing. We want him to give us facts, more facts, and more facts. But we must go farther than the formula guidelines of objective reporting. We must not only tell our readers what a politician says, we must tell them why or, if we have evidence that he does not mean what he says, we must tell our readers that, too.

Gilbert P. Smith, managing editor of the *Utica* (N.Y.) *Observer Dispatch,* wrote in the same issue of *Editorially Speaking* that a young activist reporter had said to him one day, "If I can't work for social change through journalism, I'll get out of journalism." The young man went on to explain he felt the theory of objectivity is moral cowardice on the part of reporter and newspaper. To this Mr. Smith replied:

> Objectivity is indeed difficult to achieve in every case. But, it can be done, and it must be the goal of reporter and editor. They must tell both sides of every story as well as they can be told within the framework of libel laws and good taste, two restrictive elements that our reader-critic sometimes tends to forget, or just does not understand.

In a 1971 speech to members of the Radio and Television News Directors Association, Jim Bormann, a broadcast news journalist for more than thirty-five years, said: "If we lose our credibility, we have lost everything. And that's exactly what is happening—both to the newspapers and to a lesser extent to the broadcast media. Why? Have we really changed so much? Have we strayed so far from the first principles of journalism: integrity, fairness, accuracy, objectivity? There are those who disbelieve we owe that kind of reporting to our listeners. David Brinkley is quoted as saying that complete objectivity is unattainable. And there are those—some of them in journalism schools—who use that quote to describe objectivity as a myth."

A year earlier, Nicholas von Hoffman wrote in the *Washington Post,* "In practice, printing the unvarnished facts can be highly deceptive. What editors and politicians call objective journalism is the present moment, the isolated incident without any secondary or qualifying information. This, with a few exceptions like John Chancellor, is what TV news provides and why it is so unsatisfactory."

In discussing the "old New Journalism" in the *Saturday Review* in 1971, John Tebbel said, "In all of this, there is an obsession with self, a kind of perpetual ego trip or literary paranoia. One is asked to believe, for example, that the state of Norman Mailer's psyche as he views a public event is far more interesting and important than whatever he is viewing. This leads quite easily to the conviction that the reaction of a reporter to the news is more important to the reader than the news, and to the even more prevalent absurdity that the critic is more important than the work he criticizes."

Those who believe that a journalist should become personally involved in a news story say that those who advocate objectivity believe only that both sides of a story should be told. They point out that both sides may be lies, that if one side is telling the truth and the other side is lying, the reporter is giving equal publicity to lies and truth. Editors and reporters who believe in objectivity point out that the reporter who believes in getting involved in his own story is likely to tell only one side of the story—his side. But, such a reporter would reply that he is more objective than his contemporaries who believe in giving the reader both sides, because he at least will tell his readers when someone is lying.

What this all adds up to is that true objectivity in news reporting is more than merely "telling both sides of a story."

To approach true objectivity the reporter needs some concrete, realistic guidelines. Instead of objectivity, perhaps he should think in terms of "fairness" or "balance" in a story. Instead of taking anyone's word at face value, he should look for material that can be documented. Instead of quoting secondhand sources, he should get information from primary sources. He should go more often to public and private documents for verification of facts. He should keep asking himself (and his news sources) "why" at every point. Why is he saying what he is saying? Why did he do what he did? Why did the event take place the *way* it did? What is the *meaning* of the event? Find someone who can tell you, or dig it out for yourself.

The People's Right to Know
What makes a newsman's job difficult is that there are

never neat answers. While this chapter offers guidelines to responsibility in the news business, when all is said and done, there are no guidelines that will address every real-life problem. We all agree "the people have a right to know," but *what* do they have a right to know and *when* do they have a right to know it?

Sometimes a newspaper and its reporters disagree on the answer to these questions. Anthony J. Lukas, Pulitzer Prize winning reporter for the *New York Times,* addressing members of the New England Society of Newspaper Editors, described some of his reporting problems in covering the 1968 "Chicago Seven" conspiracy trial:

> From the very start I was told that I could not describe Judge Hoffman's behavior on the bench. I could not characterize, for example, his tone of voice. I could not say, "He reprimanded a lawyer with a harsh tone of voice." Or a "sneer." I could not even say, "He snapped." I once got into an argument with my national editor after his desk excised three times the words, "Judge Hoffman snapped." I was then going down to cover a girls' basketball tournament in Iowa, and I said, "Just out of curiosity, suppose I'm at the side of the court and the referee turns to players and says, 'Get off the court, babe.' Can I say, 'The referee snapped'?"
>
> And he said, "Oh sure, you can say it there, but you can't say it in court. You know that's a stupid question, Tony. You can say things in sports writing that you can't say in a court story.
>
> "Courts aren't life. They're something separate. It's kind of sacred once it gets in those portals and you can't use the kind of language you can use when you're describing a basketball game."
>
> I'm not so sure about myself. Believe me, in the courtroom, that trial was more like a basketball game than it was like a trial.
>
> But I was told you can't use that kind of word in describing a trial. So one day, about the third week of the trial, Julius Hoffman was suddenly a different judge. He went through a transformation. We think he'd been talked to by somebody, maybe the chief of the district court, who said, "Look, Julie, cool it." So he came in and really, he was quite polite to Kunstler and to Weinglass and I called up the (editor's) desk in New York and I said, "Now what do I do?"
>
> I said, "There's a dramatic change in the atmosphere in this courtroom this morning. What do I say about it? Can I

say, 'Those things he was doing which we didn't tell you he was doing, he's not doing any more.'?"

And they said, "Hmmmm, that does pose a bit of a problem, doesn't it." So they had a big conference, and they finally called me back and said, "Well, we think we've found a way for you to do it." It was a very convoluted paragraph. . . . So I said, "The things that the lawyers charged he was doing, he didn't seem to be doing, the lawyers weren't charging he was doing them this week."

Anyway, I virtually took this paragraph by dictation from my national editor and sent it in with the copy and I picked up the paper the next day and guess which paragraph was excised? And I called my national editor and I said, "Look, now, it's one thing for you to edit me, but if you can't control your own copy editors when they start editing you, then we're really in trouble."

The point of view of the newspaper was expressed by Gene Roberts, national editor of the *New York Times,* when he discussed Lukas' reporting of the conspiracy trial with Loren Ghiglione, editor of the *Southbridge* (Mass.) *Evening News,* as follows:

There was a dispute going on at that time between Lukas and principally myself. But none of the dispute involved things like play or thoroughness or anything of that sort. In fact, just the reverse. Tony Lukas, in covering the trial, would like to have been highly freewheeling. He would like to have taken, and I'm not sure this is fair to Tony, a Menckenesque approach to the trial and covered it the way Mencken covered the Scopes trial . . . very freewheeling, part opinion, observation, this sort of thing.

I think I'm overstating my point; I'm not sure Tony wanted to go quite that far. But he did want to be freewheeling and flip and pithy and this is just not the way we cover trials on *The Times.* I'm not arguing that other papers might not want to cover them that way . . . . What they choose is up to them. But we feel trials, particularly major trials, are adversary proceedings and what we do is present the arguments of both sides to the best of our ability to present them. And we let the reader decide and the jury decide who they choose to believe. . . .

This is awkward for me because I'm not sure I want to say in print what I really think. What I think was the case was that Tony Lukas has been in the newspaper business for, I assume, about fifteen years. But he has never covered a trial until he covered that trial. And the longer he covered the trial, the less difficulty he had. . . . He's a bright reporter, and he's a damn good reporter. He really had very little difficulty all along. But I would say at the beginning that he was running into trouble on ten or fifteen percent of what he wrote. And at the end he was running into trouble on practically nothing. . . .

I objected in the first story, for example, to characterizing the trial as the trial of the century because how do we know before the trial has happened. And then I'm not sure I want *The Times* to get in the business of characterizing any trial as the best trial of the century, the second best trial of the century, the third—that's just not our job.

It seems that our essential job is to go into the courtroom and accurately convey what is going on in the courtroom. And I have no objections whatsoever to any reporter, anytime, any place, telling me about voice inflections or anything else. But what he ought to do is tell me about them head-on.

And I think to just blithely say that the judge sneered or snapped, crackled or popped is an easy way out. These are quick, flip, glib characterizations and there are other ways to do it. What you say is that, "One of the things that bothers the defense is the judge's voice inflections." And then you go and describe what the inflections are. And if it's becoming an issue in the trial, you simply say that, "The judge's voice inflections are an issue in the trial." But you don't snap, crackle and pop.

If you go back and look at Lukas's trial coverage, see if you don't get the message. If you can tell me, after reading this trial coverage, that, in the end, you don't get a picture of Judge Hoffman and the way he manipulated his voice then, in that case, I will owe the public an apology. But I think that you get it. The question was how was it going to be presented.

Lukas is a fine writer. He's a stylist and he fights over every word and I have no objection to him fighting over every word.

But flippancy is something I feel strongly about. The first argument that Tony and I got in on the trial was a sentence that he closed one of his stories with and I enjoyed the sentence. If I were editing a magazine I would have passed the sentence in a minute. He ended up the story with, "If the yippies don't burn down the courthouse tonight, the trial will resume at 10 o'clock tomorrow." I think that's a nice sentence and I got a little chuckle out of it but I wouldn't let it go in *The Times* because it's a kind of columnist approach and you run too many risks in our kind of mass newspaper of people thinking that you really think the yippies may really burn down the courthouse.

There are no major differences of opinion between Tony and I on this. It's over.

He wanted complete stylistic freedom. And I have reservations about complete stylistic freedom on a trial.

Use of Obscene Words

Whether you should quote four-letter words used by news characters, depends on the policy of your employer. Most news media today still do not use such words, unless their use is so vital to the meaning of a news story that not to use them would distort the news. Even in such cases, most media use them in some abbreviated form, for example, the first and last letters only.

During the past half century the news media have gradually relaxed their use of words that might offend the majority of readers. There was a time when such words as "rape," "syphilis" and even "cancer" were not used in newspapers. Some refused to use the word "snake," and in most newspapers women did not have legs, they had "limbs."

Times are changing, and today the mass media are seriously grappling with the problem of good taste. Norman E. Isaacs, former executive editor of the *Louisville Courier-Journal* and the *Louisville Times,* was quoted by the *Los Angeles Times* as saying, "And here we sit, trying to give an honest portrayal of what is going on in society right now. Very well, but what's going on right now in society is a veritable babel. And we struggle to achieve lucidity but still cling to the standard forms."

Newsmen, Mr. Isaacs said, should be honest and fair "so that the guy who reads the story gets a picture of what's going on in his town or his state, and can make up his own mind. Now if this gets into rough language, so be it! But how rough?"

Mr. Issacs' own newspaper quoted verbatim all of the obscenities included in summaries of the Walker Report on the violence at the 1968 Democratic National Convention in Chicago. In their use of four-letter words, newspapers and the other mass media will undoubtedly change as society changes. Meanwhile, most media will continue to use caution and try to tell all of the news without unduly shocking their audience.

Deception—Is it Necessary?

At a southern university a female reporter was assigned by her editor to pose as an unmarried coed seeking birth control pills from doctors at the university's infirmary. The purpose of the assignment was to prove that unmarried females could get birth control pills without any trouble. Said the newspaper editor: "The investigation was conducted because it was a legitimate news story of public interest. A newspaper has a right and responsibility to inform its readers of what is happening in the community and world around them, particularly of actions which may be in violation of legal and moral standards."

The reporter carried out her assignment without ever revealing that she was a newspaper writer on assignment. She obtained the pills and wrote a series of articles about her experience and the infirmary's practice in prescribing the pills.

On another occasion, two reporters hid in the university library until the library was closed for the night. They then made note of all the valuable items they could have stolen and left the building through an open window. The purpose of the stunt was to prove that security in the building was lax, especially in view of the fact that more than $2,000 worth of electronic equipment had been stolen from the building two weeks earlier.

In both cases deception was practiced, causing an official university investigation to determine if the campus newspaper had acted unethically or irresponsibly.

Newspapers and newspaper officials throughout the area failed to agree on the ethics of the situation. One newspaper stated in an editorial, "These were stories that any paper would jump at the chance to print—obtained by methods any editor would consider highly commendable reportorial enterprise."

A professor of law, a member of the Board of Student Publications assigned to investigate the ethics of the two cases, reported, "Some editors said it was in the public interest to identify oneself to a news source under any condition. Others were equally vehement in saying the reporter is under no obligation to reveal himself. There is a nebulousness here—everyone has his own opinion and no one agrees."

The Board of Student Publications committee, headed by the law professor, asked that no punitive action be taken against the campus newspaper. The committee argued that if professional journalists could not agree on a journalistic code of ethics similar to those ethics binding the legal and medical professions, then the student newspaper staff should not be expected to do so.

The ethical dilemma faced by the student journalists is not a new problem in the history of American journalism.

Newspaper reporters have managed to get themselves put in jail, into mental institutions, and in recent years have joined in riots in order to obtain stories. In the past years they have been known to steal photographs, bribe officials, and consort with criminals in order to get a news or feature story ahead of rival newspapers.

Today such practices are generally disapproved of. Most newspaper officials believe that their reporters have no right to break the law to obtain a story. Most believe that the alert, energetic reporter can obtain the story he wants through legal, legitimate methods, without being deceptive or even sneaky. They believe that in the long run the news media will be more respected and trusted if they are completely honest and fair in newsgathering practices.

On the other hand this kind of policy is merely a strong guideline that should be followed most of the time. There always will be an occasional exception in which the public interest is so strong that the newspaper editors will feel that the newspaper must take extreme measures in order to obtain the story. For example, investigative reporters believe, and their publishers believe, that if public officials ignore widespread gambling in their city, the newspaper has the obligation to obtain the facts, even if it means sending a reporter to pose as a gambler to get firsthand information.

Because newspaper reporters and editors feel that a newspaper should be free to judge each case on its own merits, it will always be difficult for lawyers and doctors, for example, to understand why the journalists cannot adopt a hard-and-fast rule as part of a code of ethics that says flatly, "No newspaper shall ever practice deception in order to obtain news for its columns."

Instant Analysis

News media should guard against "instant analysis" of the news, particularly when the news is about public policy. Facts are facts, of course, but in a breaking news story it is often extremely difficult to assess the facts. Many news items require perspective before they can be intelligently or fairly interpreted. A "crisis" is rarely born in a single news item.

During the 1971-72 U.S. price and wage freeze and "Phase Two" period that followed, when prices continued to rise despite government economic controls, the instant analysis by critics of the program was that these controls were a failure. Whether they were or were not a failure is not the question. The question is whether critics of the program could determine so quickly that the program was a failure. Should the mass media allow critics to use the news media to possibly create panic by their predictions? Such "manufactured" crises are often proven false in the long run. Then the news media are accused of crying wolf.

This kind of pandering by unthinking reporters to doomsday prophets and politicians who want to turn every event into a crisis has led some critics of the press to talk about the "bad news syndrome" which they think is typical of modern news media. They feel that the press goes out of its way to print only bad news. A standard reply of the press is: "We don't make the news. We just print it."

While this may be a sincere reply, even truthful, it is not enough. The news media have the additional responsibility of seeing that the news offering is fair and well balanced.

Actually, the "bad news" does not add up to more column inches than the "good news" or noncontroversial news in modern newspapers. Those who say that newspapers only run "bad news" often do so because news of violence, disaster, and unhappy events in general has a greater impact upon them and, insofar as they are concerned, the newspapers are filled with "bad news."

Questions for Discussion
1. What do you think are the qualities that make a good reporter? A good newspaper?
2. What is your opinion concerning objectivity in a news story? Can *you* write with objectivity?
3. What does the phrase, "the people's right to know," mean to you? Illustrate your answer with specific situations.
4. If you were the editor of a newspaper, would you use four-letter words of an obscene nature in the news? Why, or why not?
5. If you were the managing editor of a newspaper, how would you instruct your reporters concerning the use of deception to obtain news? Explain your answer.

13 the reporter and the law

News reporters, contrary to the belief of many persons, are as responsible to the laws of the land as any citizen. They may not break a law to obtain a news story; for example, they may not steal photographs or documents, and they may not trespass on private property or break into a home or business in pursuit of the news. They may not break traffic regulations in an effort to obtain a news story. They are not permitted to bribe public officials in order to obtain news, nor are they free to kidnap witnesses who have been called to testify at a trial. These would all seem to be self-evident examples — obvious violations of some law. Yet at one time or another, during the early days of American journalism, reporters did all of these things.

Obviously, if a reporter breaks into a home in order to get some names and dates from the family Bible for a news story, he has broken the law. But what about the reporter who describes a prominent citizen, wanted in two states for forgery, as a "jailbird," and attacks the man's character by quoting an "unidentified source" to the effect that he is the ringleader in a local gambling setup?

What about the reporter who clips an entire story from another newspaper or magazine and turns it in under his own by-line? What about the reporter who implies in a trial story that the judge hearing the case is not competent to serve? What about the reporter who reports a rape story and uses the name of the woman involved?

Did any or all of these reporters break the law, and if, so, why were they not protected by the first amendment to the Constitution of the United States?

In the following pages I will briefly answer these questions and, at the same time, consider some cases in which the newsman might come in conflict with state or federal statutes.

What the First Amendment Means

The first amendment to the U.S. Constitution says "Congress shall make no law . . . abridging the freedom of speech, or of the press." There are two points that need to be clearly understood:

1. Freedom of speech and the press is the right of all the people, not just the news media. Those who say that the press has "too much liberty," that the government should "make those news people stop their lying," are, in effect, saying that *the people* have too much liberty, that they themselves have too much liberty and should have that liberty curtailed. The citizen who demands the right of a free press and free speech for himself, but not for his neighbor, is calling into question the entire constitutional structure.

2. Freedom of the press and freedom of speech are not *absolute* rights. The first amendment bars anyone from preventing you from saying or publishing what you will. It does not bar someone from taking action against you *after* you have spoken or published.

The first amendment guarantees that there shall be no "prior restraint" on your speech or publishing. Why, then, are these rights not "absolute?" Freedom of speech and the press are rights "with strings attached," rights that must be used responsibly. They are not absolute in the sense that you can get away with anything you want to say or publish.

Libel

Reporters commit *libel* by defaming a person's character, by holding him up to public hatred, contempt, or ridicule or by injuring him in his calling, profession, trade, business, or occupation. When these same actions are committed orally, they are known as slander.

Libel can be both *civil* and *criminal.* Most actions, however, are brought as a civil case, in which one party sues another for monetary damages. A politician, for example, might sue a newspaper for $100,000 because he believes a newspaper has published something damaging to his reputation.

How can libel be criminal? What might a newspaper publish that would cause the state to issue a warrant for the arrest of an editor because of criminal libel? The newspaper must have published a statement so strong, so stirring that it actually did cause, or would tend to cause, a breach of peace in the community.

Suppose, for example, a newspaper editor wrote an editorial recommending that the men of the community enter the local jail in force to take a particular prisoner from custody and hang him. These words could constitute criminal libel even if no one acted on the editor's suggestion, because the words *tended* to cause a breach of peace in the community. Criminal libel charges are brought by the state as in any other criminal proceeding. Civil actions are sued by individuals.

You can commit *libel per se* by using words which are libelous *in and of themselves.* It is libelous, for example, to call a person a thief, a coward, a drunkard, or a murderer. It is libelous to use any words that in themselves will harm a person's reputation, make him appear ridiculous, or injure his business.

Libel per se is easy to determine because it is found directly in the language used. A second kind of libel, more difficult to determine, is one that results not from language itself but from the *circumstances* in which the language is used. Suppose, for example, a newspaper columnist wrote that John Doe was seen at the Green Lantern, a local night spot, dancing and "having himself a gay old time." There is nothing libelous in these words, but if Mr. Doe is an employee of a highly conservative bank whose president frowns on such activity and fires Mr. Doe, he might then sue the newspaper for libel on the grounds that the newspaper story caused damage to his reputation and consequently the loss of his job. A libel suit might also be brought if, through a mistake, a newspaper were to use a photograph of a local minister over a news story about a local person with the same name being arrested for gambling.

Responsibility. Who is responsible in a libel case? Who can be sued? State laws vary on this point. Some statutes include everyone who had anything at all to do with the publication of the libel — the newsboy who sells the newspaper on the street, the printer who sets the type, the reporter who wrote the copy, the editor who approved it, and the publisher who owns and operates the newspaper. In most states, however, responsibility is limited to the person who wrote the libelous material and the officials who approved it for publication as well as the publisher.

If the printer of the newspaper is someone other than the owner and publisher, he also would be liable in most states.

Publication. When is a libel published? Most states stipulate that a libel is legally published when it is seen by a third party. Thus, a person who sues for libel need only show that someone other than himself and the person writing the libel saw the material. In the case of a newspaper, publication is obviously far more extensive than the "third person" concept allows, and this leads to the concept "the greater the publication, the greater the libel," and therefore the damage. In the case of criminal libel, publication can legally occur without a "third person" because a breach of peace is possible as soon as a second person sees the libelous material.

Retraction. Suppose you libel a citizen in your community without prejudice? If he asks for a retraction — a correction and apology for the error — should you retract?

In some states the law says that if you retract in the same size type and in the same kind of display, the court will not add punitive damages if you are found guilty of libel. Punitive damages are those damages added to punish you for intentionally hurting someone's reputation. If you retract, you show good intentions, lack of malice. Often a retraction will prevent a libel suit because you have apologized and done what you could do to right the wrong, but retraction is no guarantee that the person libeled will not sue. As a matter of fact, since retraction is a kind of admission of guilt, the retraction may cause the damaged person to sue, but the damages assessed by the court will be less.

Defenses. There are three major defenses in a libel suit:

1. *Truth.* It is not enough for a newspaper to prove that a libelous statement was actually a quote. The paper must also prove that what was said was true. Let us say a newspaper reporter quotes one man as calling another man a communist. If the second man sues on the grounds that his reputation has been ruined, the *newspaper* would be required to prove that he is in fact a communist. In many states truth alone is not a complete defense. Such states require proof of honorable motives as well. A complete defense would thus be truth plus honorable motives.

2. *Privilege.* There are two institutions exempt from culpability for libel: courts of law and legislative bodies. It is necessary for witnesses in a court trial to be absolutely unfettered in what they say, and they cannot give full testimony under the shadow of a libel suit. Trial attorneys must also be free of libel. In the deliberation of public policy, it is necessary that legislators be free of concern for libel in legislative sessions. Such situations are said to be "privileged," *absolutely privileged.* This means that no matter how otherwise libelous the language used in a court of law or legislature, the principals have no fear of libel.

The reporter covering a court trial or session of the legislature is not, however, equally immune. He enjoys a "conditional privilege." This means that as long as he reports, without prejudice and without change in meaning, what was said in a legislature or court, he also can plead "privilege" in the event of a libel suit. This privilege does not operate, however, if it is proven that the report is inaccurate.

3. *Fair comment.* News media have a right to comment on and to criticize without prejudice the activities of public officials, sports celebrities, writers, actors, and anyone who sets himself up for public approval. Such comment, however, must be confined to the public activities of the individual and not to his private activities, unless it can be shown that these private activities have some important connection with the way in which a public official, for example, discharges his duties. Sometimes the line between public and private life is very thin.

A literary critic, for example, while reviewing a novel, might end up attacking the writer personally, calling him a "drunkard and a degenerate." The critic could be called upon in court to prove the truth of such a statement and would, in all likelihood, not be able to use fair comment or criticism as a defense.

Re-publication. What about the reporter who merely repeats in his news story what someone else has said? Neither the reporter nor the newspaper is protected from libel in such a case. The individual who repeats libel is as responsible as the one who originates it. If you quote a public official who makes a statement that harms, or tends to harm, the character of another person, you cannot claim immunity from libel by saying that you truthfully and correctly reported what the official said. It is true that damages are likely to be less in such circumstances, but the newspaper will not be exempt from culpability.

Identification. A person libeled need not be named in a news story in order for him to recover damages. If he can prove to the satisfaction of the court that people generally were somehow able to identify him, for example, through a description of his home, car, peculiarities, or appearance in the news story, he would have a case against the newspaper.

A feature story about a "town bum," unnamed in the story, could well be adjudged libelous if enough people testify that on reading the account they immediately thought of a certain individual, that is, the plaintiff.

Some safe practices. Here are a number of practices that will help keep you and your newspaper out of libel suits.

1. Don't copy libelous material from other newspapers, handbills, letters, or other printed or written sources. You will be held as responsible as the originator of the libelous material.

2. Never use a term such as "murderer," "forger," or "thief" until the person has been convicted and the sentence executed.

3. Do not make any allegations concerning a person's personal conduct or character unless you are prepared to prove the charges in a court of law.

4. Check out all names found on police arrest records. Check spelling of names, addresses, and other identification. It is not uncommon for persons arrested to give false names or names of prominent persons in the community.

5. Never *assume* something is true, especially if it involves someone's reputation or could be libelous in any way. Check it out. Believing or even "knowing" it is true, is not adequate. You may have to prove it in court.

6. Use caution with names. Check and recheck them. Be certain that you have the entire name spelled correctly. Use accurate identifications, including correct addresses and occupations with names. If you give George W. Jones, charged with a crime, the address of *another* George W. Jones, you could be in trouble.

7. If you have any doubt about the facts in a story, leave them out until they can be verified.

8. There is no privilege attached to preliminary investigations by police, public officials, or bureaus. This means that your plea of "privilege" in a libel suit would be weak if you should report police activities in connection with an investigation of gambling in the community and name persons suspected of participat-

ing, because the facts were in a preliminary police report. The court would probably say that the material was not privileged because no charges had been filed. It is safe to use facts and situations arising out of official investigations only after they have been made a matter of record and charges have been filed.

9. Conditional privilege does not preclude careful reporting or editorial discretion. Courts have held that a jury may decide whether a particular publication was a fair and true report, and jury actions are unpredictable.

10. If it is decided that a name should be withheld from a crime story, be certain that no damaging descriptive phrases are given. To write "an elderly janitor of a nearby apartment house" could lead to a suit from every elderly janitor in the neighborhood.

11. The fact that police question a man about a crime does not necessarily mean that he is a "suspect."

12. Don't identify a man in a crime story as a "veteran" or "former serviceman" unless it is pertinent to the story. The same applies to religious or racial designations. This is simply a matter of good taste.

13. Federal prisoners often are placed in county jails, but that does not mean that county officials, such as the sheriff or a deputy, can be quoted about such prisoners. Get information on federal prisoners and federal charges from federal officials.

14. A newspaper or a broadcast station is not competent authority for potentially dangerous material. Do not accept any unverified facts, regardless of the source. The first newspaper reporter may have erred. Check the facts out for yourself.

15. Give the exact names of institutions and prisons. Do not describe a Georgia prison camp as a "chain gang" or a hospital as an "asylum."

16. Picture captions must be as accurate and objective as a news story. You can commit libel in a caption as easily as in a story. The same is true of headlines.

17. Do not draw conclusions concerning a person's conduct or character. Let the facts tell the whole story.

18. Be careful about reporting business failures. Also, stories affecting the professional reputations of doctors, lawyers, preachers, teachers, and others who depend upon their reputation for their livelihood are dangerous.

19. Remember that the newspaper does not serve in the capacity of judge. It merely conveys to the public information which can be verified.

20. Do not use the telephone to cover controversial stories. If it is at all possible, talk personally with persons concerned.

21. Use the wording "pleaded innocent" instead of "pleaded not guilty." It is easy for the word "not" to be overlooked by a typesetter.

22. Language is privileged only if delivered in an open session of a legislature, in a court admitted to the record (but beware of testimony which the judge rules out), or if contained in papers officially filed for public view.

23. Beware of warrants for arrest which have been sworn out but not served. Many libel suits have resulted from unserved warrants.

24. Watch out for anything a lawyer says which has not been stated in open court or is not contained in a paper actually filed with the clerk of the court and thus become a part of the court record.

25. "Suspect" as a noun is a dangerous word. Having cautiously written that a man is being "held for questioning," don't slip up later by calling him a "suspect."

Right of Privacy

The various states recognize the right of a person to sue for damages resulting from an invasion of his right of privacy. Right of privacy, as defined by the Florida Supreme Court, is "the right to be let alone, the right to live in a community without being held up to the public gaze against one's will." How does invasion of privacy differ from libel?

1. In a libel case truth of the published material is a defense. Truth is not a defense in an invasion of privacy case.

2. In a libel case absence of malice on the part of the person

or newspaper publishing the libel can help in keeping damages at a minimum. Such is not the case in an action for invasion of privacy.

3. The plaintiff in a libel case often must prove specific damages, such as the loss of a specified sum of money. Such is not the case in an action for invasion of privacy.

One of the clearest examples of invasion of privacy is the use of a person's name or picture for advertising purposes. The use of a person's name or picture in a news story or feature article is protected under general agreement by the courts that such use is a matter of public interest.

Right of privacy is limited under the following conditions:

1. The person must be of "normal sensibilities." This means that an oversensitive person would have difficulty proving damage because the court might say that, while the oversensitive person *felt* he was damaged, the case did not meet the test of the "normal sensibilities."

2. If a person waives his right of privacy he cannot claim violation of the right. Such would be the case if he signed a statement giving consent to the use of his name or picture for advertising purposes. However, a conditional waiver of the right of privacy in one instance does not represent a blanket waiver of that right. Such waivers may also be revoked at any time.

3. Public figures give up at least part of their right of privacy. This means that a person who achieves fame or who, by his accomplishments, method of living, or adoption of a profession or calling which gives the public a legitimate interest in his character, becomes a "public personage," whether or not he wishes to do so, thereby gives up at least part of his right of privacy. Limitation in publishing material about such a person is decided by the courts, but the limitation is not great in practice.

4. Right of privacy is limited when information is considered to be in the public interest. This is a blurred area and, fortunately for the press, the courts have continued to rule in favor of the press in defining what "is in the public interest." As one court put it, "Right of

privacy is limited by the right of society and must be accommodated to freedom of speech and press and right of the general public to dissemination of information."
5. Right of privacy is a personal right and usually can be claimed only by the person who says his right to privacy has been invaded. This means that, generally speaking, a relative cannot claim invasion of right of privacy in behalf of a deceased person. Right of privacy, however, is a relatively new and developing concept and the courts do not always rule this way. There have been instances where states have permitted a recovery by parents for the unauthorized use of photographs of bodies of their children. Moreover, courts have ruled that "right of privacy" is *proprietary* in the case of persons of fame.

Limitations on Reporting Names

Every reporter should be familiar with the laws in his own state that affect his gathering and reporting of news. Many states have statutes that prevent the publication of the name of a woman victim in a rape case. A 1975 Supreme Court decision, however, has cast doubt on the legality of such laws. Some states do not allow publication of the name of a man charged with being the father of an illegitimate child. States have varying laws dealing with the publication of names of juvenile offenders. In some states names of juveniles are published at the discretion of the newspaper, but in others all court hearings and records are closed to the public and juvenile offender names may not be published unless the juvenile elects to be tried in an adult court. Sometimes traffic cases are exempt from these rules and names may be used.

Copyright and Plagiarism

Copyright law generally is designed to protect the proprietary rights of authors. A reporter cannot use copyrighted material to such an extent that it imitates the original work and thus deprives the writer of profits he might have made from the publication. Copyrighted material must include a notice that it has been copyrighted in a certain year by a certain person or company. Printed material that does not show such notice is said to be "in the public domain." Public domain material should be credited, however, to its original source. Such a policy is fair both to the reader and author.

Facts may not be copyrighted, but the way in which they are put together and used in an article or book may be copyrighted. A copyrighted news story is protected only to the extent that large parts of it cannot be used without the permission of the copyright owners. Facts in a story can be used; occasionally, you will see a news story that begins, "The *New York Times,* in a copyrighted story, said today. . . ."

Plagiarism, or literary theft, is a common law violation. Here, a writer takes the material of someone else and publishes it under his own name. Reporters have been known to turn in publicity releases, verbatim, to their newspaper as their own stories. The original writers are not likely to complain to the newspaper, since the purpose of a publicity release is to get it published, but such practices are marks of lazy and irresponsible newsgathering and should be avoided by the good reporter. Publicity releases should be rewritten, at the very least, or used as a tip for obtaining your own story.

Contempt of Court

Contempt of court can take one of two forms: direct or indirect contempt. *Direct contempt* results from actions within the courtroom that tend to impede justice or hamper the court in carrying out its obligations to the accused or parties involved in civil litigation. A person could be cited for contempt of court for causing a disturbance in the court room; a photographer could be cited for contempt for taking a picture inside the courtroom, contrary to a judge's order; a court official, a lawyer, or a witness could be cited for contempt for use of improper language.

Of more importance to the reporter and the newspaper, however, are citations for contempt of court for actions of the reporter and the newspaper *outside* the courtroom. Newspapers have been cited for *indirect contempt* of court for publishing arrest and conviction records of persons on trial for new crimes. The reasoning of the court is that a person is tried only on present charges, not for past crimes, and that he cannot get a fair trial if his past record is publicly displayed at the time of his arrest and trial.

Newspapers have been cited for indirect contempt of court for commenting editorially on a trial in progress, particularly when allegations are made concerning the fairness of the judge trying the case. Excessive "trial by newspaper" during the course of a judicial trial could lead to a contempt citation.

Contempt of court is a weapon that judges rarely use since they are keenly aware of the constitutional guarantee of freedom of the press. They are also restrained by a U.S. Supreme Court ruling which states that there must be a clear and present danger that the newspaper through its reporting has endangered the orderly process of justice.

In view of this ruling, reporters should remember that while they work under a constitutional guarantee of freedom of the press, the accused also has a constitutional right to a fair and impartial trial. A judge might rule there was "clear and present danger" if the newspaper were to publish a false and inaccurate account of a trial; material that discredits the court; material that tends to influence the outcome of the trial, and material showing some knowledge of facts in the case not known to the court and the newspaper refuses to reveal the source of such information on the grounds that it is against journalistic policy to reveal the identity of a news source. Even the so-called shield laws now in force in some states, giving a reporter legal grounds for refusing to reveal the identity of a news source, might not serve as adequate protection in such circumstances.

Contempt citations can be avoided by:

1. Reporting facts without any inferences as to the guilt or innocence of an accused.
2. Using extreme care in reporting confessions and statements of accused persons.
3. Using care in reporting any history or criminal records of persons on trial.

4. Avoiding criticism of court officials during a trial, unless public interest and justice to the accused are in extreme jeopardy.
5. Knowing where you stand legally in refusing to reveal the identity of a news source.
6. Obeying grand jury subpoenas. The United States Supreme Court in a 5-4 decision in 1972 ruled that newsmen, like all citizens, have an obligation to answer grand jury subpoenas and supply information in criminal investigations. The decision rejected the contention that the First Amendment grants reporters special immunity, protecting them from disclosing material obtained from confidential sources. This decision may invalidate state laws that now protect the right of a reporter to keep secret the name of a news source.

Questions for Discussion

1. What is meant by "law of the press?" Is there a special body of law that is applied specifically to the press?
2. Explain what you think the framers of the Bill of Rights meant when they drafted the first amendment to the U.S. Constitution. Are radio and television stations protected under this same amendment? Explain your answer.
3. Some people, including several members of the U.S. Supreme Court, believe that the first amendment to the Constitution gives the press unlimited freedom to print what it pleases. Do you agree? Explain your answer.
4. What is the nature of the power of a judge to cite a newspaper for contempt of court and what do you think of the contention that this power has the potential to destroy freedom of the press? Explain your answer.
5. Generally, which better serves the public interest: a person's right to privacy or the public's right to know? Why?

14 getting into the news profession

This chapter will deal with two topics: (a) the education and background necessary for success as a newsperson, and (b) how the beginner breaks into the news profession.

Background and Training

The young person who desires a career in the news profession should understand that he or she will need to get at least a four-year degree from a college or university. More and more newsrooms are being staffed with persons who have master's degrees and an occasional doctorate is beginning to show up.

You will find challengers to the above statement, persons who can point to successful newsmen and women who do not possess college degrees. This is true. There have always been successful professional people who learned their professions in the so-called school of hard knocks. If you talk to any of those people, however, they will tell you to get all the education you can get. They will agree that they "did it the hard way."

In the news profession, men and women without college degrees are in the minority, and all will tell you that the profession is more demanding now than it ever has been.

Among other qualities, it calls for wide-ranging knowledge; skill in dealing with people; sound judgment; tact and understanding; a sense of responsibility and fairness; an understanding of laws governing libel and right of privacy; thorough insight into governmental organization and practices; a toughness that resists attempts to deceive; enough skepticism to keep the newsperson prying and digging for the truth, but not so much that he or she becomes a chronic cynic without trust or belief in anything or anybody; a questioning mind that is forever seeking answers; a strong belief in, and dedication to, the role of the press in America; pride in the profession of journalism; a sense of being important to the democratic process in this country; and last, but not least, consummate skill in the art and craft of writing.

How does one get to be this kind of person? Must one be a natural-born journalist, or can he acquire these characteristics through some kind of educational process?

Sooner or later around a newspaper you will hear an editor say disgustedly, "There's no substitute for brains," as he observes a piece of copy with an obvious error. What he means is that somewhere along the line, in this instance, the educational process failed, an educational process, incidentally, that must continue throughout the life of the newsperson.

Thus, the answer is that newspeople *can be educated* for their jobs. They do not have to be born wearing green eyeshades.

The question, however, that puzzles young people who want to become newsmen (or newswomen) is, "What kind of education do I need? Some editors tell me to go to a school of journalism and others say that I should get a liberal education in college and let them teach me how to gather and write the news after I arrive on the job."

Occasionally a student tells me that some managing editor has told him to major in political science or history, get a general education in a college of liberal arts and sciences and then look for a newspaper job. This kind of advice is often given by a managing editor who has not been on a college campus for more than twenty years. The editor does not know that his kind of advice seldom produces a staffer for his newspaper for the following reasons: (a) many of the social science departments in colleges of liberal arts and sciences, such as political science, history, and sociology, are staffed by teachers who are strongly critical of the newspaper profession and tend to turn would-be journalists in other directions; (b) many liberal arts and sciences programs have such heavy concentrations in the major field that a student is unable to acquire the overall, liberal education his editor friend envisaged; and (c) there is always the possibility that the student will lose interest in the profession of journalism by the time he has spent four years in the pursuit of a general education.

None of the above is intended to slight the importance of general education in the life of the journalist. In fact, just the opposite is true. The ideal education for a journalist, now standardized by the American Council on Education for Journalism, is a degree from a good school of journalism that mandates 75 percent of its degree requirements in general education and only 25 percent in professional journalism courses devoted to writing, editing, law of the press, history of journalism, ethics, journalistic problems and policies, and internships and on-the-job practice.

Schools of Journalism. Where do you find information about schools of journalism? First of all, the names vary greatly from state to state. Some colleges and universities have departments of journalism; others have schools of journalism, and still others have organized their journalism program in a college. The name "journalism" may not be apparent in some programs that carry names like "department of mass communication," or "school of public communications," or "college of journalism and communications." More and more the word "communication" is being used to mean a program in journalism, advertising, public relations, radio and television, and film.

A general directory of all journalism and communication educational programs in the United States can be found in each year's January issue of the *Journalism Educator.* A list of the nationally accredited programs in journalism and communications can be obtained by writing the American Council on Education for Journalism, School of Journalism, University of Missouri, Columbia, Mo. 65201. The *Editor & Publisher International Yearbook* also carries a listing of schools and departments of journalism each year.

What should you look for in a school of journalism? The following standards set by the American Council for Education in Journalism should provide you with some excellent guidelines:

1. Objectives
   (a) A school should state its objectives in as concrete form as possible, including specific objectives for sequences offered, and these objectives should be published in its catalogue and descriptive literature.
   (b) A school should claim to educate students only for those areas of this broad field for which it has competent faculty, adequate library facilities, and appropriate equipment.
   (c) A school should be evaluated in terms of its stated objectives. A small school that claims to prepare students for reporting assignments should be judged on the basis of its claims. A school that claims to offer programs in several of the various phases of journalism and mass communication should be judged on the basis of its claims. If the objectives prove to be either too limited or too diffuse, the Council may consider the school's program beyond its purview.
   (d) No school will include sex, race, color, or religion in standards for enrollment, grading, hiring, and promotion.
2. Background Education
   (a) All programs in journalism and mass communication should be based on a wide and varied background of competent instruction in the liberal arts and sciences.
   (b) The program should be located in an institution with a four-year accredited program in liberal arts and sciences.
   (c) The liberal arts and sciences background of the student should include wide study in such fields as economics, English, history, languages, literature, philosophy, political science, psychology, sociology, and the sciences, as well as depth in one such field.

(d) Any school designated by ACEJ as an institution in which a student may obtain a professional degree should provide sufficient instruction in the discipline and area of concentration to give the student in his first employment a distinct advantage as to reliability and general productivity. ACEJ expects an accredited program to provide the student with basic skills, and also to encourage the motivations of a working professional. The number of credit hours required to provide this vital part of the student's professional education may vary from school to school, but the essence of its fulfillment is considered a requirement of all accredited divisions of journalism and mass communication. As a guide in evaluating the emphasis in fulfilling the foregoing, ACEJ suggests about one-fourth/three-fourths as an equitable ratio between courses in journalism and mass communication, and courses in the arts and sciences. In applying this general ratio, the council recognizes that certain courses labeled "journalism" and "mass communication" may be of a distinctly liberal nature and that "arts" courses at times carry vocational emphasis.

3. Professional Courses
(a) The required professional courses for a program should vary with the objectives of the program or sequence, but all students should be instructed in the basic elements of factual writing, communications law, and the theory, history, and responsibility of mass communication.
(b) A school should concentrate its professional courses in the last two years of a four-year program, and should not offer more than two full-year professional courses (or equivalent) below the junior year. The purpose of this standard is to permit the student to acquire a basic background in the liberal arts and sciences.

4. Faculty
(a) The number of full-time faculty members shall depend upon the scope of sequence offerings. Any sequence offering, however, should embrace a faculty of sufficient size, academic attainment, and professional experience to provide realistic instruction, research, and service in the area of concentration. Some person must be designated in charge of any sequence for which accreditation is sought.

(b) A faculty should bring appropriate professional experience and advanced academic preparation to its students in the areas in which instruction is offered. It is recognized that certain courses are enriched more by professional experience on the part of instructors than are others. It is further recognized, however, that there are points of little return in long periods of professional service, just as there is little to commend part- and short-time periods of service in the profession as grist for enlightening professional experience. ACEJ's increasing emphasis on the student's need for a broad general education should not be interpreted as an abdication of interest in the need to bring the experience and insight of the practitioner into the classroom.

(c) To insure reasonable class sizes in laboratory performance courses, ACEJ recommends that the student-teacher ratio in such courses not exceed 15-1.

5. Facilities
(a) A school should have facilities adequate for the objectives that it has established.
(b) A school should have available an adequate collection of library materials in professional journalism, in the social sciences, and other areas related to journalism and mass communications.
(c) Special facilities should be available if the school proposes to prepare personnel for special fields.

6. Graduates
(a) The professional performance of graduates should be considered as a major item in the accrediting evaluation.
(b) To offer an acceptable program, a school should produce at least five graduates per year. Accreditation of a specialized sequence should not be sought unless an average of five graduates a year over a three-year period and at least five in the year preceding inspection have availed themselves of the opportunity to specialization.

7. Relationship with the Media and with Professional Organizations
A qualified school assumes an obligation to maintain a working relationship with the various media in those areas in which it offers educational programs and should cooperate with professional organizations for the maintenance and improvement of standards.

These standards are long and rather complex; therefore, it is not expected that every prospective journalism school student will have the time or the opportunity to explore all of these points with college authorities, but the list of standards should provide the basis for some intelligent questions about the school's various programs.

What about the high school student who wants to begin preparing for a career in the news profession? Such a student should concentrate on perfecting his or her spelling, grammar, and general writing ability, and cultivate reading habits that include at least a major daily newspaper, news magazines, and periodicals of known value. These students should be encouraged to read widely in the best literature of the ages and to take a strong interest in the affairs of their school, community, state, and nation.

Prospective journalism students of high school age should seize every opportunity to write for print, including working for any high school publication and offering their services to the local newspaper or other news media.

In addition to classroom work, the same kinds of extracurricular activity should follow the high school student on into his or her college years. Such publication activities will aid the student in getting a news job after graduation from college.

Is there scholarship help available if you want to attend a school of journalism?

Scholarship help varies from university to university. For a general listing of scholarships available in the journalism and communications fields, write The National Newspaper Fund, P.O. Box 300, Princeton, N. J. 08540, for the booklet, "Journalism Scholarship Guide and Directory of College Journalism Programs."

Write the director of the school you wish to attend to learn about scholarships that may have been set up after the Newspaper Fund booklet was published. Write the state offices of the various newspaper associations, advertising groups, and broadcasting associations. Officers or directors of these groups will be able to tell you about scholarships offered by the groups themselves or by their members. Local media people can give you these state office addresses.

If you are interested in scholarships and loan funds of a general nature offered in the university of your choice, write the office of student loans and scholarships. Even if the office has a name like "student financial affairs," or some other designation, your letter will be sent along to the appropriate officer for reply.

Many journalism students work their way through school by working for various on-campus offices that hire student writers or by working as student assistants in the journalism department or school itself. They work as reporters in the university news bureau, the athletic public information office, the editorial offices in the agricultural extension service, the various information offices of the medical and health areas, and the information offices in industrial engineering. They work as "stringers" for various daily newspapers whose editors are interested in campus news. They work as newspersons for local radio and television stations and do part-time public information work for local businesses and charitable organizations.

There usually are numerous jobs on campus and in the community for journalism students. Such jobs help finance the student's education, but the student must be energetic in pursuing such employment.

Breaking into the News Profession

Getting a job in the news profession today is a lot harder than it was ten years ago. From World War II through the 1960s, journalism students found a student's market when they went job hunting. The media were short of help and the journalism graduate was able to select the job he or she wanted in almost any city or town in the nation. In many respects, those years were abnormal. Now the job situation is back to normal; that is to say, graduates must work hard at getting a job and must be willing to take almost anything they can find and be willing to work hard to keep their jobs.

Those hiring in the news profession are looking for some experience, fresh writing ability, a willingness to work and to learn, humility, sound judgment, good work habits, a liking for people, and a strong desire to be a good newspaper man or woman. How do you get experience? If you were to make a simple poll of a number of successful news people, you would probably find that most of them began writing in high school for their school newspapers and continued that interest on through college. The student who really wants to break into the news profession is not usually a student who decides on a news career at the last moment before graduation from college. The successful ones are those who have planned and worked at a career in journalism for many years and have accumulated a considerable amount of experience and a scrapbook of published material.

There are exceptions to this rule, of course, but even students who decide on a journalism career after they have tried one or two other vocations must use every opportunity to get some experience at news work before they try to enter the work force in journalism. Today's editor wants to know what you have done besides college. He wants to know what you read and why. He is likely to ask your opinion about some current news situation to learn if you keep up with the news. He may ask to see samples of your writing. If you go through high school and college without producing a piece of publishable copy, your editor prospect is likely to be cold to your request for a job. He may well wonder if you really want to be a journalist, since you have never tried to get a story published.

How do you get into print so you will have something to show?

1. In a good school of journalism, you will be required to write for publication. This may mean writing for the college newspaper, for a laboratory newspaper, or for some other publication, or you may be asked to submit magazine articles and feature stories to Sunday newspapers and various magazines that use free-lance material.

2. Get yourself involved in your local community to the extent that you can write a good letter to the editor about some current problem.

3. Weekly newspapers usually are not able to afford a paid correspondent at a state university, but they will be glad to use your copy if you send them stories about their hometown students at the university. You may not get paid for this copy, at least not at first, but you can gain a lot of experience.

4. Visit a local newspaper, radio, or television station and make known to a news official your desire to be a journalist. Ask for advice and don't let the official forget that you are eager to break into the news profession.

5. Many newspapers and other news media have internship programs under which they will hire you during the summer. The purpose of the internship is two-fold. It gives you a chance to find out if you like news work and it gives the news media an opportunity to observe your writing ability and general work habits. Write the media direct to find out about their internship programs and how they work.

In the future, persons who present themselves to the media for news jobs will have to be brighter and have better journalistic aptitudes than the average graduate of the past few years, because (a) as new technology takes hold throughout the industry there may be need for fewer, better trained employees rather than great numbers of employees; (b) there will be fewer vacancies, due to depressed economic conditions, which may or may not continue.

In this book I have written about new horizons for news and have discussed reporting specialties. Won't these areas offer new opportunities for breaking into the news profession? The answer is yes, but the student must be careful to structure his college program so that he obtains real depth in some specialized area, such as environmental journalism, public health journalism, or one of the other fields mentioned earlier in this book. The graduate who goes to his news job with more background in law enforcement, or our legal structure, or advancements in science will find that he has a great advantage over those who have no such specialties.

glossary

Every writer, especially newswriters, should develop a passion for words and proper word usage. How can you expect to relate to other persons the truth of a situation if the words you use do not convey the intended meaning? One person might say to another, "Come see me tomorrow after I move into my new *home.*"

The second person would be correct in replying, "You mean your new *house.* It is not yet a *home.*"

This glossary is a short dictionary of problem words, words that are troublesome to most writers at one time or another.

accept and **except.** To *accept* means to receive something or agree to. *Except* means excluded or left out. "I accept your proposition." "Everyone passed the examination *except* Tom."

according to. Do not use this expression except in cases of controversy where it is necessary to quote authority. Do not use it merely to drag a person's name into the news. Most of the time authority for news can be indicated without the use of *according to.*

acted. Do not write, "Mr. Smith *acted* as chairman." He *was* or *served* as chairman.

added and **continued.** *Added* should be used when a

speaker adds to a previous statement a closely connected comment. *Added* should not be used to indicate that the speaker merely continued his speech.

administer and **deal.** Medicine, laws, and oaths are *administered.* Blows are *dealt.*

admittance and **admission.** It is correct to use *admission* when you mean "granting rights and privileges, as for example, *admission* to a theater, *admission* to the United States, *admission* to the club. *Admittance* is used in the sense of allowing a person to enter a building or locality. "*Admittance* to the field house was denied."

advise. Do not write, "The police *advised* the mayor of the arrest of the thief," when you mean the police informed the mayor. Use *advise* in its primary sense, "to give advice to."

affect and **effect.** To *affect* is synonymous with "to influence," "to cause change," as "the weather *affects* your health." To *effect* means "to produce," "to bring to pass," "to accomplish." "He *effected* changes in management policy."

afterward, toward, upward. Write *afterward, toward,* and *upward* without a final *s.*

aggravate. This word should not be used as a synonym for "irritate," "annoy," "vex," "provoke," or "exasperate," as in the sentence, "Stop *aggravating* your brother." The word properly means "to make something worse," "to add to someone's woe," as in the sentence, "His words seemed only to *aggravate* the situation."

all and its compounds.

All ready — "They were *all ready* to begin," meaning everyone present was ready to begin.

Already — This is an adverb of time. "The football game had already begun when we arrived."

All right — Always as two words. "The plan is *all right* with me." Do not use "alright."

All together — This expression is used to mean *united.* "The Boy Scouts were *all together* around the campfire."

Altogether — Means "entirely." "He is *altogether* wrong about the matter."

All-round — Sometimes used as "all-around." "He is an *all-round* athlete," meaning "versatile."

Although — Never "all though." "Though" is acceptable and means the same as *although.*

almost. Do not use "most" as a shortened form of *almost,* as in the sentence, "Most everyone was present." Write, *"Almost* everyone was present." There is no word "allmost."

also. Usually modifies the word it follows. Watch where you put it in the sentence. These statements do not mean the same: "The children *also* went swimming." "The children went swimming *also."*

alternative. Do not write, "He had three *alternatives."* The word means one of *two* choices. "Two *alternatives"* is redundant.

alumni. Graduates of a school or college. The Latin declension is maintained in English. Examine the following changes carefully:

"Mr. Brown is an *alumnus* of the state university." (Male, singular.)

"Mrs. Brown is an *alumna* of the state university." (Female, singular.)

"The women are all *alumnae* of the same college." (Female, plural.)

"The man are all *alumni* of the same university." (Male, plural.)

"The men and women who belong to the University Club are all *alumni* of the state university." (Plural, both sexes together.)

among and **between.** *Between* should be used when there is a selection of two persons or things. "He must choose *between* two colors." Use *among* when there are more than two persons or things. "He must choose from *among* the several candidates.

ante and **anti.** *Ante* is a prefix meaning "prior to," "before." *Anti* is a prefix meaning "against," "opposed to."

anticipate and **expect.** *Expect* a record crowd, don't *anticipate* it. You might say, however, "Manager

Green *anticipated* a record crowd by providing extra accommodations."

any and its compounds.

Anybody — Should be used as a single word. *"Anybody* may attend the lecture."

Anyhow — Should be used as a single word. "What you have said does not matter *anyhow."*

Anything — Used as a single word. *"Anything* you say will be used against you."

Anywhere — Used as a single word. "I would not take you *anywhere."*

Any rate — Used as two words. "At *any rate,* I will be going to the fair."

Anyone — When used as one word, the emphasis is on *any.* *"Anyone* may attend the lecture," meaning "everyone who desires."

Any one — Used as two words, meaning "one of many possibilities." *"Any one* of these coats will do."

anywhere. Do not use *anywheres.*

argument and **quarrel.** These words should not be used interchangeably. No one was ever killed in an *argument.*

as. Do not use *as* in the same sense of "because." Do not write, "I went downtown *as* I had to do the shopping."

audience and **spectators.** An *audience* hears a musical program; *spectators* see a football game. An *audience* both sees and hears a television program.

authentic and **genuine.** *Authentic* implies "corresponding to facts"; *genuine* means "real, unadulterated, derived from the original stock." "The testimony of the witness was *authentic."* "The article was made of *genuine* leather."

avocation and **vocation.** *Avocations* are activities we do for the love of doing them; *vocations* are careers by which we make a living, or profit.

avoid. Do not use *avoid* in the sense of "prevent" or "hinder." The word means to shun something or someone.

awful and **awfully.** Do not use *awful* in the sense of "very," as in this sentence: "She was *awful* (or *awfully)* nice to the doctor." *Awful* means appalling. "After the hurricane passed, we saw the damage and the bodies in the street. It was *awful.*"

bad and **badly.** *Bad* is an adjective, *badly* is an adverb. "He was *badly* bitten by the dog." "The meeting went *badly* for him." "He is a *bad* boy." "The food tastes *bad.*" "The fish rotting in the bay smelled *bad.*"

balance and **remainder.** Do not use interchangeably. "I will spend the *remainder* (rest) of the evening at home," not "the *balance* of the evening."

banquet and **dinner.** Do not use *banquet* unless the affair is in fact an elaborate meal, say a state occasion. The difference between *banquet* and *dinner* is a matter of degree. Most official meals held by government and various organizations are *dinners* and do not become *banquets* unless they are extremely elaborate.

belong and **member of.** You do not *"belong* to a lodge," you are "a *member of* the lodge."

beside and **besides.** *Beside* means "near." "I stood *beside* him." *Besides* means "in addition to." *"Besides* the mother, there were three children to feed."

blame. Do not write, "We can *blame* it on Jones." "We can blame Jones," is correct. "On" is unnecessary with the verb.

blond and **brunet.** *Blond* and *brunet* are masculine; blond*e* and brunet*te* are feminine.

body. *Body* is preferred to "corpse" or "remains." "Dead body" is redundant.

bridegroom and **groom.** Do not use *groom* when you mean *bridegroom.* A *groom* takes care of a stable.

bring. The prisoner was not *"brought* to the station," he was taken. A policeman might say, "The prisoner was *brought* in at 10 p.m." *Bring* indicates motion toward the speaker or writer.

burglar. A *burglar* is one who breaks into and enters premises. A "thief" steals by stealth; a "robber" steals from your person by force.

can't help but. Avoid this phrase: "I *can't help but* admire his courage." Write "I *can't help* admiring his courage."

capitol and **capital.** The *capitol* is a building; a *capital* is a town, or something principal, as a *"capital* letter."

cause and **reason.** In many instances it is not necessary to use the phrases "the *cause* of" or "the *reason* for." For example, in the sentence, *"The cause of* the high price of home-grown tomatoes *is due to* a hailstorm that destroyed 50 percent of the crop," the italicized phrases are redundant.

censored and **censured.** To *censor* means to edit out material that is objectionable by some standards. "In some countries newspapers are *censored* by government officials." To *censure* means "to find fault with," "to condemn." "The chairman of the committee was *censured* by the membership for his handling of the hearing."

claim. Do not use the verb *claim* in the sense of "declare," "assert," or "say." A person may "stake a *claim"* — "He *claimed* the property" would be correct. It is correct to say that "something *claims* his attention."

clench and **clinch.** *Clench* means to "close tightly" the hands or teeth. *Clinch* means to "settle" and argument or "secure" a nail.

climatic and **climactic.** *"Climatic* conditions in the South favor the mint julep." "The war has reached a *climactic* stage." The adjectival form of "climate" is *climatic.* The adjectival form of "climax" is *climactic.*

collide. This word means "to come together." When one of two objects is stationary, it is incorrect to speak of a - *"collision."*

compared with and **compared to.** Things of the same class are *compared with* each other, while one thing is *compared to* another of a different class. "He *compared* New York *with* Chicago," but, "He *compared* the train *to* a blacksnake."

complement and **compliment.** Do not confuse *complement,* "that which fills up or completes," and *compliment,* "a flattering comment."

complexioned and **complected.** "The man arrested was dark *complexioned,*" not dark *complected. Complected* means "complicated."

compose and **comprise.** These two words are not interchangeable. "The committee is *composed* of seven members and a chairman," not *"comprised."* "The poem was *composed* by Mr. Greene. It *comprised* six stanzas."

confess. A man *confesses* a crime to the police, he does not *confess* to the crime.

consensus. "It was the *consensus* of the membership that the vote should be allowed." *Consensus of opinion* is redundant; *consensus* means "opinion."

considerable and **considerably.** *Considerable* is an adjective, *considerably* is an adverb. "The new man is of *considerable* help in the store." "When the night shift arrived, it helped *considerably.*"

consist of and **consist in.** Write, "The overcoat *consists of* wool and cotton," or "Water *consists of* hydrogen and oxygen," when you are using the words in the sense of something being made up of something else. Write, "A good vacation *consists in* your getting a lot of rest and relaxation" when you are using the words in the sense of something being inherent in something else.

contemptible and **contemptuous.** *Contemptible* describes a person or thing worthy of one's contempt, while *contemptuous* describes one's attitude toward that which may be considered *contemptible.* "I am *contemptuous* of the loose morals of that contemptible person."

continual and **continuous.** A *continual* action is one that recurs, although it may be interrupted frequently. A *continuous* action is uninterrupted. "If I am exposed to *continual* interruptions, I cannot pursue a *continuous* train of thought." "I am *continually* trying to improve my knowledge of the German language."

convene and **convoke.** The legislature *convenes* but the legislature is *convoked* by someone. Do not write, "The legislature is *convened.*"

correspondent and **corespondent.** There is no similarity in meaning between these two words. A *corespondent* is one who answers jointly with another; a *correspondent,* one who communicates in writing.

council, counsel, and **consul.** "The city *council* will meet to discuss a new parking ordinance." "On advice of *counsel* I refuse to testify." "The American *consul* in Tokyo was robbed."

credible and **creditable, credulous.** *Credible* means that which is "possible to believe." "The story he told was entirely *credible.*" *Creditable* means that which is "praiseworthy." "He gave a *creditable* performance." A *credulous* person is one easily imposed on, one who accepts without question what is told him.

dampened and **damped.** Do not write, "His enthusiasm was dampened." A person may be *dampened* by a shower, but a person's spirits are *damped.*

dangerously and **critically.** One is not *dangerously* ill, but "critically" or "seriously" ill.

depot and **station.** *Depot* is a military supply center or warehouse. A *station* is a transportation departure and arrival point.

deprecate and **depreciate.** *Deprecate* means "to express disapproval." *Depreciate* means to "disparage," "belittle," or "undervalue." "The automobile will *depreciate* in value."

destroy. Do not write, "A building was completely *destroyed.*" It was or was not *destroyed.*

differ from and **differ with.** *Differ from* means "to be dissimilar in quality." "Artificial silk cloth *differs from* pure silk cloth in many ways." *Differ with* means "to hold an opposing opinion." "I *differ with* your point of view."

different from. Do not write *different to* or *different than.*

discharged and **dismissed.** Prisoners and hospital patients are *discharged;* court cases are *dismissed.*

distinctly and **distinctively.** *Distinctly* means "plainly"; *distinctively* means "distinguishingly," "characteristically." "The custom is *distinctively* American."

drowned. Always write, "The man drowned," not "he *was drowned.*" The second form (was drowned) implies murder.

due to and **because of.** The adjective "due" can properly be used only with a noun: "His death was *due to* old age." You should not write, "He died *due to* old age."

during and **in.** These two words should not be used interchangeably. If you write, "He was ill *during* January," you mean all of the month. But if you write, "He was ill *in* January, you mean he was ill at some time (unspecified) of the month.

each other and **one another.** *Each other* is used when only two persons are involved: "They are fond of *each other.*" Use *one another* when three or more persons are involved. "The sisters are all fond of *one another.*"

eager and **anxious.** A person is *eager* to go on vacation; he is *anxious* over (or about) an impending operation.

emigrant and **immigrant.** An *emigrant* is moving *out* of a country; an *immigrant* is moving *into* a country.

entertain. Do not write, "The group was (or will be) *entertained.*" An audience is not necessarily *entertained* by a performance.

envelop and **envelope.** *Envelop* is a verb meaning to surround. "The forest *enveloped* the town." *Envelope* is a noun: "He went to the post office to buy a stamped - *envelope.*"

exceptional and **exceptionable.** *Exceptional* means "unusual." "She is an *exceptional* person." *Exceptionable* means "objectionable." "At dinner last night, her manners were *exceptionable.*"

execute (execution). You witness the *execution* of the prisoner, not the *execution* of the sentence.

expire. *Expire* means "to exhale." Do not used *expired* to mean "died."

eyewitness. Newspapers prefer that you do not use "eye" with witness, even though the word is in most dictionaries. You assume that the witness has eyes. This is a matter of brevity and saving space. One may write of an *eyewitness* account of an event.

farther and **further.** *Farther* usually refers to distance. *Further* refers to time, quality, or degree in general. "I live *farther* down the road than you do." "He is *further* along with his studies than you are." *Further* also suggests continuation. "He will consider the matter *further.*"

feel and **believe.** Do not use *feel* to mean "believe," "said," or "thought." Do not write, "I *feel* he will get well" when you mean it is your opinion that he will get well.

fiance and **fiancee.** *Fiance* is masculine; *fiancee* is feminine.

field of. This term is usually superfluous: "I am majoring in *the field of* communications." Less wordy is: "I am majoring in communications."

filed. Lawsuits are "started" or "begun," not *filed.* Affidavits, complaints, and other legal papers are *filed.*

flout and **flaunt.** *Flout* means to disregard, *flaunt* means to "wave conspicuously," or "display ostentatiously."

following and **after.** Do not use *following* for *after.* "*After* the meeting the group toured the campus." Do not write, "*Following* the meeting the group toured the campus." It is correct to write, "The rain, *following* months of dryness, brought relief to a broad area."

good and **well.** *Good* is an adjective; it should not be used as an adverb ("He talks *good*"). *Well* can be either an adjective ("healthy," "pleasing") or an adverb. "He is a *good* speaker," but "he speaks *well.*"

grant and **award.** Medals are "won" and then *awarded.* Medals may be *presented* to someone besides the person who *won* them. Divorces are not "won" or "awarded." They are *granted* or "obtained." It is incorrect to write, "Mrs. John S. Brown was *granted* a divorce today." Write, "A divorce was *granted* today to Mrs. John S. Brown."

happen, occur, and **take place.** Things *take place* by design; they *happen* or *occur* unexpectedly. "The wedding will *take place* on Monday," not "The wedding will *occur* on Monday."

healthful and **healthy.** *Healthy* means "possessing health," *healthful* means "causing health." "I had a *healthful* vacation and now I feel *healthy.*"

heart failure. Everyone dies of *heart failure.* Write "heart disease," or specify the heart ailment.

human. If you are writing about a person, use *human being.*

hung and **hanged.** A man is *hanged,* not *hung.* Pictures are *hung,* but criminals are *hanged.* (Both forms are the past tense of "hang," but the different forms are used as noted here.)

if and **whether.** "You should learn *whether* or not he likes the movies before you go." "Ask *whether* or not the light is bright enough." But, "You should go *if* you are told."

illusion and **allusion.** *Illusion* means "a deceptive appearance," as an optical *illusion.* An *allusion* is a casual reference or mention, such as "an *allusion* to his wealth."

imply and **infer.** *Imply* means "to suggest" or "hint"; *infer* means "to deduce" or "conclude." "The policeman *implied* we knew more than we would admit." "We *inferred* that someone had been talking." "We do not wish to *imply* that you are dishonest." "Am I to *infer* that you do not approve of the committee's action?" A speaker *implies;* a listener *infers.*

in and **at.** "The convention will be held *in* New York." But, "The various committees will meet *at* the Union Hotel."

in front of and **behind.** You may write, "He parked *in front of* the house," but "He parked *behind* the house," not "in back of the house."

inaugurate. Use *inaugurate* only when describing the installation of high public officers, or the opening of large enterprises or institutions. Do not write, "We plan to *inaugurate* a new sales policy next month."

incredible and **incredulous.** That which is too improbable to be believed is *incredible.* The person who does not believe it is *incredulous.*

incur and **suffer.** A person does not *incur* injuries. He may *incur* (become liable to) a debt, but he *suffers* injuries.

inflammable and **inflammatory.** That which is capable of being set on fire or which is combustible is *inflammable.* That which tends to inflame, kindle, irritate, to incite to anger or sedition, is considered *inflammatory.*

ingenious and **ingenuous.** A talented, clever person is said to be *ingenious.* A trustful person is said to be *ingenuous.*

injure and **damage.** Inanimate objects are *damaged,* not *injured.*

inside and **inside of.** "The bodies were still *inside* the wrecked plane." "The bus will arrive within the hour," not *"inside of* an hour."

insure and **ensure.** Either is correct.

interested, uninterested, disinterested. *Interested* has two opposites: *uninterested,* which is its negative, and *disinterested,* which means "not motivated by personal interest, impartial." "The student was *uninterested* (not interested) in American history." "A *disinterested* (impartial) person was chosen to break the tie vote."

interment and **burial.** *Burial* is preferred. A typographical error might easily change *interment* to "internment." *Burial* is shorter, more easily understood.

introduce and **present.** Persons unknown to each other are *introduced.* A person is *presented* at court, to the governor, or other officials.

irregardless. The prefix "ir" is incorrectly added. Use "regardless."

judgment and **judgement.** *Judgment* is the standard spelling. *(Judgement* is British.)

kind. Use "this kind," "that kind," "these kinds," and "those kinds." Do not write, "I do not like *these kind* of apples."

kind of and **sort of.** Should not be followed by *a* or *an,* e.g., *"kind of* a good movie." Write *"kind of* ship" and *"kinds of* ships." Do not use this *sort of* ship."

lady and **woman.** Use *lady* when the woman referred to has the official title *Lady:* "Lord and Lady Baltimore."

latest and **last.** Do not write, "His *last* book concerns the life of the ant." Use, "His *latest* book." He may write another.

laudable and **laudatory**. *Laudable* means "worthy of being lauded," "praiseworthy." *Laudatory* means "pertaining to (or expressing) praise." "He spoke in the most *laudatory* terms about the man." "His action is *laudable.*"

lead and **led**. *Lead* (verb) is present tense. *Led* is the past tense and past participle. "He *leads* the parade." "He *led* the parade yesterday."

leave and **let**. It is incorrect to say, *"Leave* go of the rope." It should be, *"Let* go of the rope." It is proper to say, *"Leave* him alone," if you are asking someone to go away from another person. If one person is harassing another person, you say, *"Let* him alone."

leave and **survive**. Write, "He *leaves* an estate valued at $50,000." Do not say "He *leaves* a wife and sixteen children." He is *survived* by a wife and children.

less and **fewer**. *Less* is used with quantity; *fewer* is used with numbers. *Less* corn, but *fewer* ears of corn.

liable and **likely**. Do not say, "I am *liable* to do that" when you mean that you are *likely* to do something. Use *liable* to mean "exposed to damage, penalty, expenses, burden, etc." "The newspaper is *liable* for damages." *Likely* indicates possibility.

lie and **lay**. I *lie* down on the floor, but I *lay* the book on the table. To *lay* means to cause something to *lie*. "I *lie* down now." I *lay* down earlier." "I have *lain* down several times today." "I am *lying* down now." "I have been *lying* down all morning." "I *lay* the book on the table." "I *laid* the book on the table yesterday." "I have *laid* the book on the table yesterday." "I have *laid* the book there many times." "The book has *lain* there for many months."

line. It is unclear to say, "My *line* is auto sales." Better: "I work in auto sales." It is wordy to use the expression "along the *line* of" when speaking of a type of work.

lives and **resides**. Write, "He *lives* on Sycamore Drive," not "He *resides* on Sycamore Drive." *Resides* is more formal and stilted. *Home is preferred to residence* except when an official residence is meant. "The White House is the President's official *residence.*"

locate. Do not write, "I have been trying to *locate* him." *Locate* means "to place something." I will *locate* my business here (on this location)."

lose out and **win out.** *Win* and *lose* are sufficient.

majority and **plurality.** If Senator Jones gets twelve votes, Frank Greene five, and Ted Avery three, the Senator has a *majority* because his total exceeds the combined votes of his opponents. If the Senator polled only six votes, however, he would have a *plurality* measured by his one-vote advantage over his nearest rival, Frank Greene.

mantel and **mantle.** Grandpa sits before the fire with his feet on the *mantel.* Grandma wears a *mantle* (cloak) when she goes out.

matter and **subject.** Do not use the word *matter* when meaning *subject* or "question." Do not write, "The *matter* before the council today concerns every citizen."

may and **can.** *May* entails permission or opportunity; *can* means "to have physical, moral, or intellectual ability to do something."

more than and **over.** Do not write, "I have *over* $4." Do not use *over* to mean "in excess of." Use *more than.* "I have *more than* $4." (Do not say, "I have better than $4.")

obtain and **secure.** You *obtain* permission. When you *secure* something, you make it fast. "The boat was *secured* to the dock."

of and **with.** You are ill *of* the measles, but not *with* them. You can suffer from the measles.

off. Do not write *off from* or *off of.* "The man fell *off* the porch," not "*off of* the porch."

oftentimes. *Often* is better.

on and **upon.** *On* is preferred to *upon* except where rhythm is involved.

on account of. "I rode a horse to town because (not *on account of)* the car was out of gasoline."

only and **also.** Put each of these words next to the word it modifies. The following sentences have different meanings: "I went *only* to see the movie." "*Only* I went to see the movie." "I went to see the *only movie.*"

ordinance and **ordnance.** An *ordinance* is a law or regulation; *ordnance* means "military weapons."

part and **portion.** Do not use *portion* to mean *part.* Do not write, "During the first *portion* of the program."

part from and **part with.** You *part from* a friend, but you *part with* your possessions.

partly and **partially.** *Partly* is used in the sense "as regards a part and not the whole," and *partially* in the sense "to a limited degree." "The floor was *partly* brick." "He was *partially* to blame."

past and **last.** If the week, month, or some other period just *past* is meant, use *last.* "I have spent the *last* five weeks in jail."

people and **persons.** People is not the plural of *person.* Two *persons* were killed in the explosion, not two *people.* Use *people* to refer to a body of persons united by race, government, or common characteristics: "the American people."

percent. Use *percent* with a number, as in "50 percent." Do not write, "The biggest *percent* were unemployed." Write, "The largest *percentage* of the townsmen came to the meeting."

pleads. A defendant *pleads* guilty *of* a crime, but he *pleads* guilty *to* a charge.

policeman and **officer.** Use *policeman* or "patrolman," not *officer,* unless the person holds rank. Do not say, "Police *officers* are searching for the escaped convict."

practicable and **practical.** Use *practicable* to mean "possible of being accomplished." Use *practical* to refer to something that is "adapted to actual conditions." "The plan of attack was *practical* but it turned out to be *impracticable.*"

preventive and **preventative.** *Preventive* is preferred to *preventative.* "*Preventive* measures are being taken to check an epidemic."

principle and **principal.** *Principle* means "a settled rule or law of action or conduct; a truth which is general and plain." "He is a man of strange *principles.*" "I am studying economic *principles.*" *Principal* refers to the first or highest in rank, value, degree, or importance; it also means "a sum of money drawing interest." "I talked to the *principal* of the school."

prone and **supine.** *Prone* means lying face downward. *Supine* means lying face upward. A man can not lie *prone* on his back.

propose and **purpose.** *Propose* means "to suggest"; *purpose* (verb) expresses intent or determination. Write, "He has *proposed* a new plan for the committee." "I *purpose* to change the rules now being followed."

provided and **provide.** *Provided* means "conditional." *Provide* is a verb form. "I am *providing* the money for his education." "The sidewalks will be built *provided* the citizens pay their taxes." *Provided* is, of course, also the past tense verb: "the money provided by the legislature."

quite and **quite a.** Do not use *quite a* while to mean "a long while." Also do not use *quite* to mean entirely.

recollect and **remember.** *Recollect* means to "recall to memory." *Remember* means to "retain in memory." "I have been trying to *recollect* what happened a year ago today." "He *remembers* many stories from his childhood days." *Recollect* connotes effort to recall to mind.

regretful and **regrettable.** *Regretful* means "feeling (or manifesting) regret". *regrettable* means causing regret. "He was *regretful* for the damage he had done." "The bombing of the city was *regrettable.*"

reputation and **character.** These two words should not be used interchangeably. "His *character* is above reproach." "He has a *reputation* as a fighter." *Reputation* means "the estimation in which a person or thing is held by others."

resolutions, bills, and **laws.** *Resolutions* are adopted, not passed. *Bills* are passed and *laws* are enacted.

sanitorium and **sanatorium.** *Sanitorium* is a hospital specializing in rest cures. A *sanatorium* is a hospital specializing in treatment of tuberculosis.

sculptor and **sculpture.** The *sculptor* is the artist who works in stone or other substance. The *sculpture* is the art work itself.

set and **sit.** *Set* means "to place or put." "I *set* the flower pot on the window sill." *Sit* means "to occupy a place." "The robin *sits* on the eggs in her nest." Incorrect: "The house *set* on a hill." Correct: "The house *sits* on a hill."

sewage and **sewerage.** *Sewage* is the matter carried off by *sewerage* systems.

shipped and **sent.** Do not write, "The body was *shipped.*" Say, "The body was *sent.*"

shape and **condition.** Do not write, "He was in bad *shape*" when you mean "he was in bad *condition.*"

since and **because.** *Since* should be used to denote passage of time and *because* the reason for an act. *"Since* you ate the last apple we have picked a bushel of apples." The meaning here is that in the interval of time after the eating of the apple, we have picked more apples. If we mean the apples were picked *because* you ate the last one, then the sentence should read, *"Because* you ate the last apple, we have picked a bushel of apples."

site, sight, and **cite.** "They have decided on a building *site."* "He has regained his *sight." "*He *cited* a verse from the Bible."

speak to and **speak with.** "I shall *speak to* him" implies that one person will do the talking. "I shall *speak with* him" implies there will be a conversation.

specie and **species.** *Specie* means "coined money." *Species* means a subdivision of a genus. "He has discovered a new *species* of fungi."

stay and **stop.** To *stay* means "to remain for a while." To *stop* means "to cease from motion."

stated. Reserve *stated* for reference to formal announcements. Poor: "Mrs. Jones *stated* to police that her purse was stolen." Better: "Mrs. Jones *told* police her purse was stolen." "In his message to the legislature, the governor *stated* that he would veto the labor bill."

suspected. The police *suspected* (not *suspicioned)* the man was guilty.

trustee and **trusty.** A *trustee* (plural: *trustees)* is a person or corporation to whom property is legally committed in trust. Colleges often have boards of *trustees.* A *trusty* (plural: *trusties)* is a convict to whom special privileges are granted.

unconscious and **oblivious.** Do not use these two words interchangeably. *Oblivious* means "forgetful" or "not mindful." *Unconscious* means "without sensation or cognition, not conscious."

unknown and **unidentified.** "An *unidentified* (not known) man was found today." Do not write, "a fire of *unknown* origin." Write, "a fire of *undetermined* origin."

upon and **over.** A man is struck *upon* the head, not *over* the head.

verbal and **oral.** *Verbal* means "expressed in words," either spoken or written. *Oral* means spoken.

where. Do not use *where* to mean "that." It is incorrect to write, "I read in a magazine *where* smoking cigarettes is bad for you."

index